THE
ENTREPRENEUR'S
HANDBOOK

Standard Book Number: 0-89006-041-X

Library of Congress Catalog Card Number: 74-82601

THE
ENTREPRENEUR'S
HANDBOOK
2

Joseph Mancuso

Head, Management Engineering Department
Worcester Polytechnic Institute

ARTECH HOUSE

Table of Contents

CHAPTER 5
THE GROWTH CRISIS

When the man and his idea have made it through the start-up and venture financing stages, they face a growth crisis. The entrepreneur must now concentrate on the application of business fundamentals to take the firm through the growth stage. The unusual talents that were required to start the business will not necessarily ensure its survival through the growth stage. Sources of new capital must be located for growth and expansion; delegation instead of doing-it-alone must become the rule; administrative procedures must be developed; product life cycles must be monitored, and new products evaluated; long range planning suddenly becomes an issue; and the consumer must be re-examined to determine product acceptance. As the business grows, methods and procedures to manage the business must grow, too. New practices must be integrated to cope with the changing business environment. A complete understanding of basic management principles is vital if the growth is to be effectively managed and not managed by a putting-out-fires-process. It is now time for the venture to be placed in perspective as an on-going enterprise.

An entrepreneur has a life cycle, as does the company. It is during this stage in the company's development that the entrepreneurial skills which enabled him to start a business begin conflicting with the skills needed to manage the business. He soon senses that organizational charts, planning, meetings and personnel supervision are not satisfying his motivational needs. The characteristics that made him a successful entrepreneur, able to create a new business from nothing, are not the same characteristics that will enable him to become an effective executive. If the entrepreneur is concerned about the future growth of the business, he will often choose a professional management team to manage the firm's operations, while he continues to optimize the unique entrepreneurial skills.

Laurence Lamont describes in considerable detail the knowledge and experience gained from mastering the process of starting, financing, and managing a technical firm for the first time. He claims many who do it for the first time eventually choose to do it again. And, in his opinion, each time they get a little better.

Mr. Louis Allen, who also authored an excellent book "How to Start and Succeed in Your Own Small Business" offers an insight into the issue of executive self selection in small business. Mr. Allen is an authority on venture capital and in his position at the Chase Manhattan Bank he has worked with and supported many entrepreneurs. His article highlights the problems and long hours needed to be a successful small business executive.

The other articles in this section by John Doutt and Arnold Cooper reveal pitfalls resulting from traditional thinking on the product innovation process, and they identify the factors for successfully approaching the competitive marketplace with new products within a small company. Hiring a creative individual with sufficient curiosity and drive to successfully implement new product ideas may be a wasted effort if top management is not aware of and concerned about these other factors.

The need for an innovative climate is just as important in the small business as in the large corporation according to Doutt. Although, admittedly, the large, generously capitalized firm can usually absorb more blunders and false starts than the small business. But usually, the scenario of the corporate based new business venture is in many ways similar to an externally based small company venture activity. Product champions working in a stimulating and supportive environment are still the key to successful product developments and marketing. This, Doutt claims, is the same in both large and small companies.

In the other article, Arnold Cooper evaluates the seriousness of these perceived barriers by presenting his observations from a study of five small companies engaged in technically advanced product development projects. Having at least one creative and committed individual, an enthusiastic attitude for involvement on the part of top management, and a propensity for taking risks, a small business possesses the basic ingredients for overcoming these potential constraints on expanding their product line through the use of internal resources. Undertaking this advanced technology development can provide the small firm with more

1

opportunities to improve its place in the market. This can provide one more means to achieve increased company growth by repeating a process which the firm has already done well during its inception.

Included as the last article in this section, is a second paper written by Professor Arnold Cooper entitled "The Founding of Technologically-based Firms" and published by the Center for Venture Management in Milwaukee, Wisconsin. By special permission from the Center, we have included the entire study. Following is the synopsis of this paper, as written by the Center for Venture Management.

THE FOUNDING OF TECHNOLOGICALLY-BASED FIRMS

The emergence of clusters of high-technology companies near San Francisco, Los Angeles and Boston, has been the envy of industrial development planners everywhere. In large part, these new entrepreneurs, former employees of small and larger companies, responded to the needs of the U.S. space program and the many defense weapons systems projects. These programs required new research and rapid exploitation of new technologies. Much of the mystery surrounding this explosion of entrepreneurs has now been explained in a study, "The Founding of Technologically-Based Firms". The study was supported and published by The Center for Venture Management. It is the work of Dr. Arnold C. Cooper of the Krannert Graduate School of Industrial Administration of Purdue University, but started when he was Visiting Professor at Stanford University in 1968-69. The cluster of enterprises studied are those in the San Francisco Peninsula area near Palo Alto. The three-pronged investigation consisted of intensive interviews with thirty technological entrepreneurs, assembling information on two hundred twenty additional firms, and consulting with managers of established industries from which new businesses tend to "spin-off".

Analysis of the resulting data indicated that the typical firm is started by two founders, both in their mid thirties, well-educated, more competent and energetic than average, and who were at odds with the programs of the company for which they worked. Founders usually remain in the same general productive and geographical areas as their "parent" industries.

Incubator firms with high entrepreneurial "spin-off" rates are the smaller organizations, or departments within larger firms, with policies which foster a broad professional outlook, and encourage interdepartmental communication. In this milieu, complimentary partnerships emerged.

Industries with high rates of growth spurred by rapidly changing technology are the best incubators. Those requiring heavy capital investment or large-scale organizational effort discourage the competition of budding enterprisers. Regional factors are also influential: successful enterprises in an area create an environment favorable to similar undertakings, with a feedback of every increasing new ventures and ready capital.

Dr. Cooper's study will be of special interest to industrial development planners, potential entrepreneurs, investors, directors of established industries and everyone concerned about the innovative health of American enterprise.

As a recap, one must keep in mind that during the growth stage the firm may be in danger from the entrepreneur who, having started the firm with an idea and dream, continues his romance with his product. Maximizing profits and managing an organization are seldom the chief strength of the entrepreneur. It is during this stage that the firm's management team must become more deeply involved with the human beings in and around the firm and the application of basic business planning procedures. To continue a successful business development, management must be able to realistically reflect back on themselves and determine where changes in their plans and products are required. It becomes an organizational crisis when the entrepreneur cannot recognize that he no longer has the proper blend of talents for running his creation. The first symptoms of this phenomenon emerge during the growth crisis.

I might note, a handful of entrepreneurs perform well during this growth stage and show a unique ability to adapt to the newly emerging needs of the firm. These rare individuals manage to stay around to build large companies. Mr. Ken Olson of Digital Equipment Corporation, Mr. Ed Land of Polaroid and Mr. Bill Hewlett and Dave Packard of Hewlett-Packard are a few that come to mind. However, they are the exception, not the rule.

PROBLEMS IN REVIEW

REPRINTED FROM
HARVARD BUSINESS REVIEW
SEPTEMBER–OCTOBER 1966

Small Companies Can Pioneer New Products

While the development of technically advanced new products entails elements of risk which some small manufacturers may well decide to leave to others, many of these barriers can be overcome. This analysis, based on a survey of five small companies and supplemented by interviews with executives of 18 other organizations, provides (1) a basis for judging the extent to which major problems might be barriers to all small companies, and (2) considers ways in which these can be overcome or minimized. The author is Arnold C. Cooper, Associate Professor, Herman C. Krannert Graduate School of Industrial Administration, Purdue University.

• THE EDITORS

Small Companies Can Pioneer New Products

By ARNOLD C. COOPER

"Since World War II, the most profitable industries and companies, and the ones with the best growth records, have been those that had an outstanding performance in research and innovation." [1]

Leonard Silk has thus summarized the tremendous importance of R & D to U.S. manufacturers today.

My concern is with small companies and how they can participate profitably in this "Research Revolution," despite certain problems which may arise because of their size. This article is based on a detailed investigation of the decisions made and the problems faced by managers of five small companies which developed new products involving significant technical advance. (Significant technical advance was deemed to exist if, at the time a project was undertaken, there was substantial uncertainty as to whether the desired product was technically feasible or as to the development time necessary to achieve certain essential product goals.)

In all instances, the companies were already established and had existing product lines. The new products were developed at the companies' own expense; there were no externally financed development contracts. The data from these five case studies were supplemented by interviews with executives of 18 other companies that had experience in this area.

Most development conducted in U.S. companies probably involves little significant technical advance and, of that which does, much is usually government financed. Nevertheless, the kinds of projects studied here should be of unusual interest. Obviously, the character-

istic of being technically advanced does not ensure that a new product can be produced and sold profitably. However, if such products are carefully designed to meet market needs, they may give the innovator significant competitive advantages. Because of the technical advance involved, they are more likely to be different from existing products; because of the development effort needed to create them, they are less likely to be copied by rival manufacturers immediately. Company-sponsored projects — as distinguished from those financed by outsiders, such as government agencies — are more likely to result in products which can carry large profit margins, and products to which the developer has proprietary rights.

Most small companies have done very little development work of this kind. Lacking creative personnel, or being hesitant about taking risks, or lacking experience in dealing with the particular problems and decisions which may arise, they have left to others the chance to seize opportunities through the development of technically advanced new products. Possibly, many managers of small companies are unaware of what their compatriots in other small organizations have been able to achieve. I have talked to men who have felt that pioneering must be left to the large companies — those with engineering manpower and the financial resources to exploit success and to absorb failure. Certainly, there is much in the literature to reinforce any timidity which the executives of small companies may have. There is frequent mention of the problems facing small organizations but, un-

fortunately, very little reporting as to how these problems can be overcome.

Many people are quite pessimistic about the ability of established small companies to develop significantly advanced new products at their own expense. I can recall, at the time I began my study, predictions that it would be impossible to find instances of this kind of activity. Although the cases studied do serve as evidence that this can be done, my primary purpose in this article is more specific. I have two aims:

1. To discuss certain major problems which may constitute barriers to small companies seeking to do self-financed advanced development.

2. To consider — in the light of the experience of the organizations studied — the seriousness of these problems as well as the ways in which they can be overcome.

THE COMPANIES STUDIED

The actual identities of the five organizations studied have been disguised, although the names used are descriptive of their traditional fields of activity. The order of the following list indicates my judgment of the apparent degree of technical advance involved in the projects undertaken:

Company	Number of personnel
Electric Controls	200
Electronic Engineering, Inc.	105
Plasma Research	45
Transistors, Inc.	30
Forest Products Equipment	24

Here is a brief description of each company and its advanced development project:

Electric Controls sought to develop a new type of home thermostat. This

[1] Leonard S. Silk, *The Research Revolution* (New York, McGraw-Hill Book Company, Inc., 1960), p. 175.

undertaking probably involved the least technical advance, in that while management believed the proposed product was technically feasible, it was very uncertain as to how much effort would be required.

Electronic Engineering, Inc. attempted to develop an accurate control which could be installed on certain kinds of textile equipment. There was uncertainty as to whether such a control could be developed which would meet both accuracy and cost requirements.

Plasma Research tried to develop an industrial cutting torch utilizing plasma. Because so little was known about plasma technology, there was uncertainty as to the feasibility of the technical approach thought necessary in order to give the cutter the required operating characteristics.

Transistors, Inc. sought to develop a new type of silicon transistor whose technical feasibility seemed highly problematical.

Forest Products Equipment undertook the development of a process which would separate chips of bark from chips of wood. Such a process, although previously attempted by others, had never before been achieved, and there was great uncertainty as to whether a process with the required operating characteristics could ever be achieved.

FIVE MAJOR PROBLEMS

I shall consider five major problem areas often said to face small companies when they attempt to develop technically advanced new products. In my opinion, there is no doubt that these problems exist and are serious. However, I believe their seriousness is often exaggerated. In the discussion, the problems will be stated from the viewpoint of someone arguing that small organizations cannot — or should not — engage in this activity. The evidence from the companies studied will then be analyzed (a) to provide a basis for judging the extent to which these problems might be barriers for all small companies, and (b) to consider ways in which these problems can be overcome or minimized.

I. *Creative development requires people of considerable education and unusual abilities. Small companies have tremendous difficulty in recruiting and keeping such people.*

If an organization is to attempt advanced development, it is tre-

mendously important that it have the services of skilled technical people. Management should not assume that all or even the majority of its engineers have the ability to create new products. These skills are not widely found. Some of the companies studied employed several engineers, and yet, as they reported, most of their really creative development was performed by only one or two of them.

There is no question that small companies have some disadvantages with regard to recruiting and keeping such people. They often have a less certain future, fewer fringe benefits, little in the way of training programs, and less opulent surroundings; and they can offer fewer professionally trained colleagues. In addition, small companies rarely are organized to recruit men as they emerge from college.

Yet small organizations can and do attract competent technical people. Each of the five companies studied had at least one highly creative engineer; none had difficulty in keeping the engineers it had hired; and one had a waiting list of engineers who were working for other, larger companies but who wished to join this small organization whenever the staff might be expanded.

It is quite significant, I think, that these small companies bypassed the young, inexperienced engineer just emerging from college who might have a strong predilection to go with a well-known company, and who certainly would not be in a position to make a major contribution until he had acquired some experience. Instead, all of the engineers in the projects studied were older men who had some measure of previous experience with other companies.

How, then, did these small companies attract and keep creative technical people? Three of the companies studied were founded by technically trained people; and the creative development work in two of these three was undertaken by a man who had helped to found the company. The incentive for such men to ally themselves with

these companies was considerable. They owned stock and could share in the rewards; they were officers and could gain satisfaction through influencing the major policies of their companies. Even the project engineers who were not founders enjoyed many of the benefits accruing to the founders. In two of these organizations, the engineers also owned stock.

In all five situations studied, the engineers could see a relationship between their own efforts and the success of the companies. An environment existed so that a technical man, rather than considering himself as having been "hired by management to work for them," thought of himself as having "joined the management team." In this respect, it is perhaps significant that each of these creative technical men participated in the decisions to undertake advanced development projects.

Although many small companies may have difficulty in adding good technical people, those studied were highly successful in their recruiting activities. Their characteristics and approaches suggest how other small organizations can attract highly creative people for themselves.

II. *Even if a small company attracts a good engineer to its staff, it is unlikely to have much success in developing advanced new products. Such an engineer will lack the benefits of "team research," and will often have to interrupt his long-range development plans in order to solve short-range problems. Unless a company is large enough to support a development effort of, say, $100,000 per year, it is unlikely to be very successful in advanced product development.*

It is quite true that the small companies studied could ill afford the luxury of assigning a number of men to long-range projects. The kinds of talent needed to create advanced new products were also valuable elsewhere, notably in modifying existing products to meet the needs of particular customers. Initially, the project was usually a part-time assignment, one of many things bidding for the engineer's time. And there was always the danger that "fire-fighting" would take so much of the engineer's time that he would never quite get around to long-range development.

How was this manpower problem overcome? In three companies the low priorities of the projects clearly caused the development time to be greater than it would otherwise have been. However, in each of these companies time still was found to develop the new products. In part, this was due to the personal commitment of the engineers, who made room in their schedules for projects which interested them — often by working in the evenings and on weekends. In part, too, it was due to the great sensitivity of the other members of the management team to these problems. As a consequence, thoughtful attention was devoted to decisions about priorities and, in the later stages of product development, to duties being assumed by other executives so that the project engineer might be free to devote more time to the specific task.

In the projects studied, there were no "research teams" — that is, in the sense of a number of men devoting their full time to a single project. However, every member of the management group knew about the advanced development project, and many of them made suggestions as to how particular technical problems might be overcome. Furthermore, suggestions for problem solving in some cases were offered by people outside the technically trained group. For instance, at Forest Products Equipment, the general manager made a suggestion which overcame an especially difficult technical problem. Possibly such contributions were forthcoming because the departmental lines were less than sharply drawn; every member of the management group was familiar with the problems of the others and was in the habit of discussing a wide range of problems.

Unlike their counterparts in large companies, who can restrict their efforts to a particular aspect of development effort (e.g., encap-sulation in the design of transistors), the engineers connected with the projects studied had to be generalists. This might seem to be a considerable disadvantage, and it undoubtedly is one of the reasons why some writers extol the virtues of team research. However, there are also advantages to having one engineer work on all aspects of a project. Coordination is much easier; specifications can be relaxed or tightened on a particular part of a system without fear that some colleague will resent the action because he was not consulted or because the change made his task unduly difficult.

Even though these technical men were generalists in the sense that they worked on all aspects of a particular project, they rarely approached problems *de novo*. Their companies had traditionally concentrated on relatively narrow areas of technology, which meant that they had acquired considerable background in regard to the kinds of technical problems they were most likely to encounter. Thus the personnel of Forest Products Equipment thought they knew more about the removal of bark from wood than any competitor, regardless of the number of technical specialists who might be employed by that competitor.

There have been many statements about the amount of capital a company should allocate annually in order to mount a reasonable development effort, with the phrase "critical mass" sometimes being used in this context. One author has suggested that the minimum amount a company should spend is $100,000 per year.[2] Underlying such statements are probably a number of concepts, such as the presumed advantages of team research, the need for specialized equipment, and the advantages which arise from being able to finish a project more quickly through applying a higher level of effort to it. These factors may be important under certain conditions, particularly when very large projects are undertaken. Nevertheless, evidence based on the experience of the five companies studied suggests that effective de-velopment can be conducted on a relatively small scale.

While the companies studied kept no records of their annual expenditures for product development, an analysis of the number of personnel devoted to this activity provides a basis for judging the magnitude of their efforts. Transistors had only 1 engineer devoting most of his time to product development. Forest Products had 2 men devoting varying amounts of their time — but not all of it — to product development. The three larger companies mounted more extensive efforts, with Electronic Engineering's 21 engineers being by far the largest technical group. However, each of these three companies had done significant development work when their technical groups were much smaller. For instance, Electric Controls had only 1 engineer when it began to build a competitive position based primarily on its ability to design new products to meet particular needs which were not being met by mass-produced controls.

III. *Even if a small organization is able to develop a significantly advanced new product, it is unlikely to have the resources needed to exploit it.*

Studies of invention and innovation have often shown that developing something which will "work," although a major step, is much less costly than perfecting and exploiting that product. Since development essentially is a knowledge-producing activity, it is important that the company producing that knowledge have enough resources to exploit it.

In all of the projects studied, more money and more manpower were required to perfect and exploit the new products than were needed to develop them to a workable state. The fact that these projects did involve considerable technical advance undoubtedly increased the difficulty of exploitation. The products were more radical, raised more questions in customers' minds, and departed

[2] P. R. Marvin, *Top Management and Research* (Dayton, Ohio, Research Press, Inc., 1953), p. 88.

more from traditional manufacturing methods.

Nevertheless, three of the companies studied had enough resources to perfect and exploit the new products which they developed. In particular, they were helped by working closely with prospective customers and by asking suppliers to provide certain components needed. Of course, such practices are common for any company, regardless of its size, but the point is that *some* small organizations do have sufficient resources both to develop and to exploit certain advanced new products.

The other two companies studied, Forest Products and Electronic Engineering, did find that the final stages of perfecting and exploiting their new products required more funds than their managements thought they could spend. In the former case a full-scale pilot operation, estimated to cost $30,000 to $70,000, was needed. In the latter case determination of the accuracy of the control which had been developed required the investment of about $5,900 in production tooling and possibly another $12,000 in manufacturing costs for an initial production lot. In both instances there would also have been other costs involved in final technical and market development. Had this development work been conducted in large companies, the capital needed could probably have easily been supplied. In these small organizations investment of such amounts might have involved risking the very survival of the enterprises themselves.

Even so, the approaches taken by these two companies illustrate ways in which advanced product development can be profitable despite the fact that the resources to perfect and exploit the new product are not available. Consider:

◖ Electronic Engineering probably could have afforded to make the necessary investments. However, the company lacked both the manufacturing and marketing know-how which would have permitted management to assess the probabilities of success and the potential returns with greater confidence. Accordingly, management sought to find a company which would (a) make the investments needed to produce production lots of the new control, (b) work with potential customers, and (c) give Electronic Engineering royalties on sales.

This was not quickly done, but after negotiations with several firms over a period of ten months, a contract was signed with one company which had the requisite manufacturing and marketing know-how and a willingness to make the further investments needed. A short time later, promising results from initial market tests made it appear that the arrangement might be a highly profitable one for Electronic Engineering.

◖ Forest Products, in its development of a process to separate bark chips from wood chips, achieved considerable success with some materials on a small prototype machine. Before the process could be marketed, it seemed desirable to construct a large installation so that (a) costs and flow rates might be determined more accurately, (b) techniques and equipment might be perfected to meet the needs of a particular customer, and (c) a demonstration model would exist which could be shown to prospective customers. The cost was more than management thought could be invested.

Therefore, a search was begun for a large potential customer who would cooperate with Forest Products, underwrite the expense of an installation, and possibly underwrite further development. After discussions with a number of companies, an agreement was reached with a large paper mill: Forest Products retained its proprietary rights to the new product, and the investor agreed to provide technical and financial assistance and material to be used for tests.

Both of these companies were successful in obtaining outside assistance. However, in each instance, a great deal of time and effort was required to find those investor companies which had the necessary financial and technical capabilities, as well as the top executives who had the vision and willingness to take the risks required. Considering the problems encountered, it would have been easy to visualize the two projects grinding to a halt, with the products never being perfected or introduced to the market.

With an advanced development project, it often is difficult to predict the amount of resources needed to complete development and to exploit the new product. Thus requirements may exceed expectations; and when this occurs, the small organization may find itself needing outside assistance. Although, as indicated above, there are ways by which this outside assistance may be obtained, management should recognize that this may greatly delay a project and substantially increase the uncertainty associated with it.

IV. *A small company may be lucky in that some of its early efforts to develop advanced new products may be fruitful. However, it can seldom afford to support very many such projects, and it almost always lacks the resources to support a "run of bad luck." The risks in this kind of activity are enormous for the small company.*

It is indeed true that the chances of success of an advanced technical project are quite small — regardless of whether it is undertaken by a large or a small company. Initially, there is uncertainty not only about technical feasibility, but also about the product attributes which can be achieved, the eventual manufacturing cost, ultimate consumer demand for the proposed product, and so forth. The risks involved are suggested by the results of a survey of practices in a number of large companies: "About seven out of every eight hours devoted by scientists and engineers to technical development of new products are spent on projects that do not reach commercial success." [3]

The managements of the five small companies studied recognized the risks, and undertook their projects with the realization that failure might result. The uncertainty was greatest during the early stages of development. As the projects proceeded, uncertainty about factors such as technical feasibility, probable manufacturing costs, probable performance attributes, and so on decreased.

A significant factor bearing on the ability of these companies to

[3] See *Management of New Products* (New York, Booz, Allen & Hamilton, 1960), Foreword, p. 3.

invest in such projects was that the initial expenditures to investigate feasibility were typically quite low. It was only in later stages — when a host of minor technical problems remained to be solved, when the construction of more elaborate prototypes was undertaken, and when production planning and market development began — that the rate of expenditures devoted to a single project became substantial.

The managements of these organizations were concerned that the initial investments in projects, when uncertainty was greatest, should be kept low. There were particular efforts made to keep costs low until technical feasibility could be established. During the initial stage, usually only one engineer worked on a project, and he often devoted only part-time to it. Even then, much of that effort was "after hours." Prototypes incorporated, insofar as possible, existing components which might be used in the company's current product line when the model was dismantled.

The typical approach is illustrated by the experimental model built by Forest Products. Nothing was more elaborate than it had to be. For instance:

The motors and certain other components were of the type used on the company's major product line, and old oil cans were used as receptacles in certain stages of the process. Later, a visiting engineer from a large company commented that had the same model been built in his laboratories, it would have used heavy conduit for the wiring and other fancy components, and probably would have involved an expenditure of $15,000. The out-of-pocket cost to Forest Products was only about $3,700.

A company such as Forest Products could in all probability support a number of unsuccessful advanced development projects *if the unsuccessful projects were discontinued at a relatively early stage* — before the commitment of large amounts of capital. Each company studied utilized a sequential decision-making process in which there were "decision points" to reexamine the future of the project.

A typical occasion for such a reexamination occurred when an increase in the level of resources applied to a project was being considered.

For example, this kind of change took place when funds were needed for prototypes or when consideration was being given to having another technician join the original engineer on the project.

It should be recognized, however, that concern with keeping initial development costs low and with stopping unpromising projects at an early stage might result in some potentially attractive projects being killed before they ever had a real chance.

As contrasted with managers in larger companies, managers in the organizations studied were intimately involved in the technical failures and successes and initial market inquiries. This detailed knowledge probably placed them in a better position to judge the prospects for success of their new products. Counterbalancing this, however, close involvement with the projects undoubtedly made it more difficult for them to judge their new products objectively. In all five of the small organizations studied, there was only one company-financed advanced development project being pursued at a given time. Thus there was a management tendency to want to believe that each project would be successful.

When conditions such as these exist, there is a danger that a project may drift toward completion without receiving hard reexaminations in light of information that becomes available as technical problems are solved and as more is learned about the market for the developing product. Accordingly, in my opinion, it is particularly important for a company to plan on having explicit reexamination points, which serve as occasions to evaluate with increasing precision the steadily mounting mass of information bearing on the probable profitability of the new product.

As contrasted with large companies, the organizations studied probably did have better chances of succeeding in developing new products because their definitions of "success" were more modest. Their managements tended to appraise market potential by first estimating how many units, or what dollar volume, of the new product would have to be sold or achieved to make the project a success. Then they judged whether there seemed to be a good probability that sales volume could be achieved. Because these organizations were so small, the "successful" volume was often quite modest — in one case, only $50,000 in sales per year. These radically new products involved education of prospective customers, and in many instances the initial market for a new product would be quite small. However, this initial market might still be large enough to be very attractive to a small company.

V. *Even if a small organization is successful in developing and exploiting a new product, it is likely to face formidable competition from large companies which enter the field.*

A company's willingness to assume the risk of developing a new product offers no assurance of future success or freedom from competition. The study of the new products described here ended before the passage of sufficient time to determine the reaction of competitors. However, discussions of the problem with the executives of these companies, and consideration of their experience with other new products developed previously, suggest that the danger of competitive reaction may be overestimated in many instances.

Several of the companies studied applied for patents covering certain aspects of the design of their new products. Thus, while it would take time to determine the strength of their respective patent positions, it can be said that this factor might make it more difficult for competitors to enter the field.

In addition, there are barriers of technological know-how which competitors need time to overcome. Admittedly, in some instances, competitors can acquire valuable technical knowledge from examining samples of the new products. However, this is not true in all instances. For example, the management of Transistors believed that very little could be learned about how its new transistor worked simply by examining and testing it.

In other instances there may be a lack of incentive for potential competitors to make the investments and take the risks involved in trying to develop a product similar to one which a small company has developed. Two of the companies studied, Electric Controls and Transistors, had policies of trying explicitly to develop products for small markets. They believed there would be little incentive for competitors to try to challenge their established positions in such markets.

One difficulty in implementing this strategy is the uncertainty about both the kinds of product attributes which can be achieved and the eventual demand for a proposed product. For instance, when Transistors achieved a breakthrough in the design of its new transistor, the immediate annual market appeared to be at least $10 million. However, instead of being overjoyed, Transistors' management viewed this departure from the company's traditional strategy with considerable apprehension, since this was a great incentive for competitors to try to develop their own versions of the new product.

It is interesting to note that in four of the company situations studied management was concerned lest the market for its new product develop too quickly. This would mean that the small company would be hard put to meet the demand, and that considerable incentive would exist for competitors to move in. Except in the case of Transistors, such fear was probably exaggerated. Yet it demonstrates the concern of these managers for minimizing the incentive for competitive action.

The incentive for well-established companies to attempt to develop their own versions of new products may be somewhat lessened because of their commitment to established products against which any new products might compete. For example:

❡ Plasma Research, at the time it undertook considerable risks in trying to develop an industrial cutting torch, had no investment in conventional cutting methods. The management of Plasma Research knew that while a division of a large corporation had the technological background which might permit it to develop a competitive version of the plasma cutter, the larger organization was also a leading supplier of conventional cutting equipment.

Management understood that the large company had already utilized its technology to develop a type of plasma cutter. However, the operating characteristics of this cutter were such that it was applicable only to a rather narrow market; it had been developed, and was promoted, only for those cutting applications which could not be satisfied by conventional methods.

Possibly this large firm will someday join with Plasma Research in trying to revolutionize the industrial cutting field. However, for the time being at least, its heavy investment in conventional methods undoubtedly removes some of the incentive for such an undertaking.

Finally, it should be recognized that even the largest companies have some areas in which their interests and know-how are concentrated. Advanced new products somewhat out of these areas of primary interest may be difficult to copy. Thus Transistors has particular competence in making silicon transistors by the alloying process. Many potential competitors have concentrated their efforts primarily in making silicon transistors by the diffusion process; others have experimented primarily with germanium transistors. It would be possible, of course, but awkward, time-consuming, and expensive for these competitors to try to copy Transistors' new alloy product too closely.

CONCLUSION

I do not wish to suggest that the development of advanced new products is an activity which every small manufacturer could and should undertake. The companies studied had three attributes which are probably essential for this strategy:

1. The presence of at least one highly creative technical person in the organization.

2. An attitude — primarily, an enthusiasm for emphasizing product development as a major element of strategy — among the chief decision makers in the company.

3. A willingness to take risks.

Clearly, there are many small companies which lack these kinds of creative people and these managerial attitudes. They may have unusual capabilities in other areas, such as being able to produce standard products at low cost. Strategies that involve advanced product development are probably best left to others.

Advanced product development is no easy matter. The projects studied here were selected because they had met with technical success, and had thus demonstrated the full gamut of issues from project inception to market introduction. These same companies may have more or less success with other projects; assuredly, they hardly expect to be completely successful with every project they undertake. At the same time, there are also risks in other kinds of business activity, just as there are elements of risk in doing nothing or in hoping that a competitor will miss an opportunity to make your major products obsolete.

The development of advanced new products is within the reach of many small companies. The experiences of the five companies studied demonstrate that the difficulties involved can be overcome.

— Arnold C. Cooper

A reprint from
CALIFORNIA MANAGEMENT REVIEW
© 1966 by The Regents of the University of California

FRANK F. GILMORE

Strategic Planning's Threat to Small Business

What effect will the accelerating adoption of long-range planning in large corporations have on the traditional management approach in small businesses? What can small businesses do to insure their survival and growth?

⚜ ONE OF THE MOST EXCITING ASPECTS of the current phase of the managerial revolution is the widespread adoption of strategic planning. The accelerating rate of change-over to this new approach is every bit as dramatic as developments in quantitative analysis and electronic data processing. While change has first occurred in very large organizations as a movement toward long-range planning at both headquarters and division levels, this movement will have its strongest impact on small businesses.

For our purposes, strategic planning can be defined as the determination of the basic long-term goals and objectives of an enterprise, the adoption of courses of action, and the allocation of resources necessary for realizing the goals.[1] Viewed in this light, such phrases as "long-range planning" and "formal business planning," which I will use later, are synonymous with strategic planning, and it will serve no useful purpose to attempt greater precision of definition.

Frank F. Gilmore, S.M., Professor of Business Administration, Cornell University, was at Harvard Graduate School of Business Administration from 1946 to 1951 and at Washington University from 1952 to 1955.

The primary concern of this article is to determine the potential effect of the accelerating adoption of strategic planning in large organizations on small business management. Sufficient evidence is now in hand to make it important to weigh the implications of strategic planning. Chief among these are such questions as:

■ How does the new strategic planning approach differ from the traditional concept of the chief executive's job?

■ Can the traditional small business management approach succeed in light of the change-over in large organizations?

■ What can small business management do to meet the threat posed by this new top management approach?

The evidence which makes a meaningful exploration of these questions possible is to be found in the experience of numerous large business and public organizations which have undertaken strategic planning in recent years. Companies such as E. I. du Pont de Nemours & Co., Standard Oil (New Jersey), and Sears, Roebuck and Company have been engaged in such activities for a long time.[2] Others like Lockheed Aircraft Corporation, North American Aviation, Inc., and the Ford Motor Company adopted strategic planning ten to fifteen years ago. However, the most exciting evidence is the rush to embrace strategic planning which has been occurring during the past few years. I have been privileged to observe these developments in several large companies and have been closely identified with the evolution of long-range planning in a major oil company since 1962.

The job of the chief executive is shifting from "adaptation to change conditions" to "management in accordance with a strategic plan." This shift represents a fundamental change in approach which will have a far-reaching impact on many companies and possibly on the economy as a whole.

The Swing to Planning

Development of strategic planning. The evidence indicates that there has been a significant swing to strategic planning in large organizations during the past few years. In 1963, roughly two-thirds of the United States firms with sales of $250 million to $1 billion engaged in some formal business planning.[3] Approximately half of these firms had undertaken such planning only during the previous four years. Among very large firms with sales of over $1 billion, 80 per cent engaged in formal business planning, but, even for these firms, where we would expect a

high incidence of planning, about 45 per cent had undertaken formal planning only during the previous four years. Of the 500 largest industrial companies, 60 per cent were carrying out long-range planning in 1963, and 24 per cent stated that they intended to establish planning programs soon. More broadly, about 720 of the 3,600 largest United States manufacturing companies had formal planning programs in 1963.

More specific evidence of the swing to strategic planning in large organizations during recent years was reported at a seminar on long-range planning conducted at the University of California, Los Angeles, in 1962.[4] Table I indicates that, of the seventeen organizations which took part in the University of California, Los Angeles, seminar, ten initiated long-range planning during the five years ending in 1962 and thirteen in the period from 1957 to 1962.

Only four of the seventeen organizations included in the tabulation initiated long-range planning before 1957. One of these, Lockheed Aircraft Corporation, began its long-range planning in 1953 and, in 1954, formulated what was referred to as its second master plan—in fact, an important strategic plan.

A significant feature of this trend is the keen interest which chief executives have taken in strategic

TABLE I.—INITIATION OF FORMAL LONG-RANGE PLANNING IN ORGANIZATIONS PARTICIPATING IN 1962 UCLA SEMINAR

	1954 or earlier	1955	1956	1957	1958	1959	1960	1961	1962
Aeroject-General Corporation						x			
Allstate Group			x						
American Airlines, Inc.									x
Atomic Energy Commission									x
Autonetics Division (North American Aviation, Inc.)	x								
Bendix Corporation							x		
Continental Copper and Steel Industries, Inc.							x		
Continental Oil Company						x			
Department of Defense								x	
Federal Aviation Agency						x			
Ford Motor Company	x								
Glendale Federal Savings				x					
International Business Machines Corporation				x					
Lockheed Aircraft Corporation	x								
National Aeronatuics and Space Administration						x			
Southern California Edison Co.	x								
Standard Oil Company (Indiana)								x	

planning. For example, during the 1950's, Robert Gross, then chief executive officer of Lockheed, required the adoption of long-range planning as a key element of the chief executive's job. In subsequent years, this became a dominant feature of Lockheed's planning efforts. This action was paralleled by L. F. McCollum, President of the Continental Oil Company. In the early 1950's, he stimulated interest in formal long-range planning; by 1959, his efforts culminated in the establishment of a long-range planning committee.

Most of the companies which have undertaken strategic planning have assembled expert staffs. In each instance, it is apparent that the purpose of the staffs is to assist in making special studies, define assumptions and planning premises, coordinate planning efforts of others in the organization, and integrate plans for top management—but **not to do the planning for management.**

The policies originated and adopted by Gross and McCollum have pervaded planning activities in other companies. The line organizations and, ultimately, the chief executives are responsible for the strategic plan of the enterprise. But the planning staffs are critically important elements. Nearly all companies have exerted great efforts to acquire the best and most highly qualified scientists, engineers, economists, and specialists in marketing and finance for their planning staffs. These staffs have been established at two levels. Headquarters planning staffs assist the chief executive in developing the strategic plan for the enterprise. Less comprehensive planning staffs have been located in the product divisions of some decentralized companies to assist the general manager in developing the plans for his division.

Planning Goals

Above all, the most significant distinguishing characteristic of this new approach has been that executives are beginning to manage in accordance with a constantly up-dated strategic plan. In many of these large companies, there are three clearly discernible elements which, together, comprise these strategic plans:

• The "mission" of the company—the kinds of business in which the firm is planning to operate, together with the quantitative goals that will be sought, particularly with respect to return on investment. Significantly,

although the primary emphasis is on economic objectives in present planning efforts, other types of objectives are being considered, such as those which derive from management's preferences as to the kind of company they want to run and management's sense of obligation to groups other than the stockholders.[5]

• The course of action by which this firm's mission will be accomplished. This has to do with plans for products, markets, and sales approaches, together with the functional goals that will need to be realized to implement the mission.

• The program through which courses of action and the mission are to be carried out, beginning with near-term moves and extending five or more years into the future.[6]

Another characteristic found in most of these efforts is recognition of the importance of identifying clearly the assumptions and premises that must be agreed upon and established by top management as a planning basis for all parts of the company. Frequently, extensive special studies are undertaken to establish such premises. In addition, uniform planning procedures have been established by many companies to insure that plans developed in various parts of the organization are comparable and can be integrated into a common plan.

Finally, it is generally recognized that constant surveillance is required to detect changing conditions, rendering assumptions and premises invalid, so that the strategic plan itself may be reappraised and possibly revised.

The Old Approach

Adaptation to changing conditions. Prior to this current shift to management in accordance with a strategic plan, the major job of the chief executive was viewed as adaptation to changing conditions. This approach developed during the period between World Wars I and II when unpredictable and violent economic fluctuations meant adaptation or failure.

Several milestones marked the refinement of this technique. The French industrialist, Henri Fayol, first defined this concept in the early 1920's when he attributed much of his success as an industrialist to his making what he called a general survey as the basis for every important decision.[7] Management consultants employed a similar method in a service to clients, popularly known during the 1920's and 1930's as the "General Survey." This consisted of an estimate of the situation facing the company in terms of outlook for the economy and the industry; the competitive situation; the financial and operating picture of the company; and analyses of sales, production, costs, product development, and the executive organization. This estimate was followed by recommendations for action, possibly involving the further services of the management consultant. Such general surveys were usually requested only when the management of a company had lost its bearings and faced deepening problems.

In the early 1930's, James O. McKinsey, one of the pioneers among management consultants and later Chairman of the Board of Marshall Field and Company, described the top management approach, which had grown out of his experience, as "adaptation to changing conditions."[8] Melvin T. Copeland refined and enlarged upon this concept in his definition of "the job of the executive."[9] From the 1920's through the 1950's, case studies gathered by various universities indicated that the characteristic top management practice, particularly among small businesses, but by no means limited to them, was to decide on a course of action in light of an estimate of the situation facing the company at a particular time.

Under this scheme, concern was mainly with **immediate profits and adaptability to meet changes in current conditions.** There was seldom a clear concept of objectives or long-range plans to which management was committed. Objectives which may have been in mind at the launching of a new enterprise were frequently lost sight of as the business grew and became more complex. Plans, determined at some point in the existence of a company, often became obsolete and forgotten as the organization drifted with events. Changes in the direction in which a company was heading sometimes went unrecognized by management. Indeed, the planning cycle was initiated only when management sensed that a major executive problem existed, such as a threat to the company's competitive position or an increase in the number of problems plaguing the business. But there was no sensitive mechanism for alerting the chief executive that such an executive problem was present. The fact of the matter was, that as long as present business was satisfactory, top management was not particularly concerned about the future.

The New Approach

Job of chief executive changes. The change from "adaptation to changing conditions" to "management in accordance with a strategic plan" constitutes a fundamental change in the job of the chief executive. Emphasis is shifting from concern with near-term problems to plans for capitalizing on long-term opportunities. Traditional management is shifting from sizing up the situation as a basis for a new course of action to reappraising an existing strategic plan in light of the changed environment. Sporadic diagnosis has changed to constant surveillance.

The concern for immediate profits and adaptability to meet changes in current conditions has given

way to a focus on long-range return on investment, growth, flexibility, and stability. Occasional preoccupation with such questions as "Where are we?" and "Where are we going?" (appropriate when on the bridge of a sailing vessel) has been replaced with constant attention to such questions as "Are we making satisfactory progress with respect to plan?" and "Are our plans still valid?" (more appropriate when on the flight deck of a jet airliner). The aim of simply maintaining health has been replaced with encouraging dynamic growth. With these changes, a much higher proportion of the chief executive's effort is being devoted to the long-range future of the enterprise.

The introduction of strategic planning at the corporate level is providing top management with powerful new approaches for directing the profitable progress of large, multidivisional organizations. Acquisitions, mergers, and the creation of new divisions can be handled more effectively in the light of existing strategic plans. Moreover, divisional progress can be more effectively measured in relation to strategic plans, both divisional and corporate.

Threat to Small Business

The swing to strategic planning in large organizations constitutes a serious threat to small business management. It challenges one of the important competitive advantages which the small company has enjoyed—being faster on its feet than the larger company in adapting to changing conditions. It is perfectly clear that mere adaptation in the short run will no longer suffice. Trends must henceforth be **made, not simply coped with.** The threat takes several forms.

Technological obsolescence. The first threat to small business management is technological obsolescence. Not only does the rapid expansion in the research capabilities of large organizations in itself threaten the small business, but these organizations have far better guidance for their research activity as a result of developing strategic plans for a long period into the future. In addition to the sharper focus such guidance makes possible, their planning necessitates a more comprehensive and timely surveillance of technical developments outside the company, thus reducing the possibility of major mistakes in strategic planning that could conceivably mean failure for the company as a business en-

terprise. Increasingly, strategic planning staffs include highly competent scientists and engineers who devote their talents to detecting technological trends and developments which may hold promises or threats for their companies.

Economic obsolescence. The second threat to small business growing out of the trend toward strategic planning is economic obsolescence. Under strategic planning, the significance of economic trends both in this country and abroad is being more carefully evaluated. To do this, many large companies are adding expert economists to their planning staffs. While business economists have been established for many years in consumer goods industries, their appearance on the staffs of producer-goods and defense-oriented industries dates from the change-over to strategic planning.

One of the important functions of economists is to assist in the development of assumptions and premises which can provide the basis for planning over the long term. Not infrequently, their work discloses opportunities for new product-market developments earlier than would otherwise be true. In addition, their more effective surveillance of competitors' activities points to possible new problems and opportunities long before they would have shown up in the normal course of events. The new capabilities which economists bring to the strategic planning staff, coupled with the greatly increased surveillance, constitute an increased threat of economic obsolescence for small business.

Benefits from combination. The third area where small business is being threatened by the movement toward strategic planning lies in the increased opportunity available to large business for realizing the benefits of joint endeavor through mergers, acquisitions, and combinations of two or more divisions. Benefits from combination—the favorable impact on costs and profits which can result from unions where the "fit" is right—are being actively sought in the diversification efforts of many planning staffs. To the extent that such combinations are more feasible for large companies because of their greater resources, small business stands to feel the pressure of a further squeeze on profits.

Planned defense procurement. A final threat to small business stems from the new approach to planning in the Department of Defense introduced by Secretary Robert F. McNamara which will make it difficult for a small company interested in securing defense orders to continue with traditional planning.[10] The Department of Defense is giving greater attention to systematic planning and programming over longer time periods. The increased demands for contractor studies and longer-range projections from both the military departments and the Office of the Secretary of Defense require the development of new capabilities and skills in strategic planning. This will affect many small, as well as large, companies, either as prime contractors or subcontractors. It will become increasingly important for companies to weigh the long-range desirability of defense business during the study stage.

A major challenge to the small company which wishes to be a prime contractor is that it must do long-range planning to determine where it will place its limited resources and where it will put its research dollars so as to be in a position to make the strongest technical proposals. The traditional planning process does not develop the capabilities and skills required for these recurrent planning tasks to anything like the degree to which the new approach does. Consequently, the trend toward planned defense procurement constitutes an additional threat to the small, traditionally managed business.

Dangerous Drifting

Traditional management is in jeopardy. The dangers of continuing with the traditional concept of the chief executive's job in light of the above threats are obvious. From now on, drift into less profitable areas can be more expensive; opportunity costs will be immeasurably higher; the danger of complacency will be greater; and loss of momentum can have more serious consequences, because competitors will be more watchful for opportunities to capitalize on weakness. Without strategic planning, functional emphasis may become unbalanced, thus generating unnecessary cost. But, above all, the traditional approach does not provide the sensitivity to the need for change that strategic planning does. Clearly, to persist in the traditional method in the face of the movement toward strategic planning would be folly for small business.

Small business management can meet the threats posed by the movement toward strategic planning in large organizations if the chief executive will adopt a different approach to his job. It is understandable for the small business manager to take the

attitude that there is little that he can do about the situation. Overloaded with current problems as he characteristically is, he may throw up his hands at the prospect of the additional task of strategic planning. He may be prone to view planning as a luxury that can be afforded only by the large organization. He is likely to decide that his salvation is to work harder to reduce costs, to develop specialized products and services, and to cling to the hope that he will intuitively sense when the time has come for an estimate of the situation and possible change in course.

But this approach will not be sufficient from now on and, indeed, does not have to be adhered to. Small business management can plan, too, if the chief executive will recognize that:

- Strategic planning is feasible for small business.
- Costly, expert planning staffs are not essential.
- A new executive approach is needed.

Planning is Possible

Strategic planning is feasible. The experience of numerous large decentralized companies points to the feasibility of strategic planning for small business units. In addition to strategic planning at headquarters, these large companies have encouraged their product divisions to undertake similar activity.

The problems of managing a product division and a small business are similar. In each case, the chief executive is responsible for the profit outcome of his enterprise. In many instances, size will be comparable. Both organizations are usually concerned with a homogeneous product line and are usually organized on a similar functional basis. Both organizations are limited as to the amount of staff help that can be afforded. Thus, if long-range planning is feasible for the product division of a large decentralized enterprise, it should be feasible for a small business.

Use of Consultants

Expensive staffs not essential. As noted earlier, one of the distinguishing characteristics of the swing to strategic planning has been the appointment of highly competent planning staffs at the corporate level. However, as would be expected, it has not proved necessary to duplicate this talent at product division levels. Rather, expert assistance is

rendered to the product division planners by the corporate planning staff, in such areas as technology and economics, on a consulting basis.

In like manner, a small business does not need to set up an expensive staff. As in the case of the product division, competent assistance to provide surveillance of technical developments outside the company and special studies in areas of possible interest can be acquired from qualified consultants at a fraction of the cost of a permanent staff. New products developed elsewhere can be appraised with the help of outside consultants when a potential opportunity needs to be evaluated.

Thus, just as the product division of a large corporation needs to call on headquarters staffs for expert help for which it pays, so too can the small company find the necessary help by turning to outside consultants. The important point is that the small business can get the necessary technical assistance without expensive staffs, if the chief executive knows what questions to ask.

Staff Planning

The need for constant surveillance of economic trends and developments presents a similar problem. Again, the needs of the small business can be met through the part-time use of consultants rather than by employing permanent staff members. Various services provide excellent statistical informa-

tion at reasonable cost, and special studies can be carried out on occasion by a consultant. Again, the key is determination on the part of the chief executive to keep informed and to keep trying to find economic factors that will spell either threat or opportunity for his business.

As to the formulation of a revision in the strategic plan, it is far better that the chief executive and his functional department heads do the planning themselves than to delegate this critical task to any staff, no matter how expert. It is generally felt that strategic plans for the future must represent the decision of the chief executive, but active participation by the entire top management group is also considered critically important. To the extent that small business does not have a planning staff, such healthy participation is likely to be encouraged.

It should not be inferred that small business can afford no planning staff help at all. Depending on its size, a small business might be able to have at least one staff man who could devote a significant portion of his time to strategic planning. An interesting possible combination of activities, with which there should be some experimentation, would be the assignment of staff responsibility for strategic planning, organization planning, and manpower planning and development to an assistant to the president. Training in economics and organization theory would be helpful for such a staff man, but he should also have operating experience.

Executive Role

New executive approach needed. If small business management is going to be successful in meeting the threat growing out of the movement to strategic planning, a new approach to the chief executive's job is essential. A useful way of getting started is for the chief executive to seek answers to the following questions. Arranged under five major phases of the strategic planning process, these questions can provide a practical framework for the planning cycle in a small business.

1 / **Identification of present strategy:** What business is the firm in? What objectives are being pursued? What program of action is being followed?

2 / **Reappraisal of present strategy:** What environmental trends and developments appear probable? What will be the company's prospects and problems if the present strategy is continued? What is the firm's strategic problem?

3 / **Formulation of alternative strategies:** What are the most attractive opportunities in the company's environment? What are the firm's distinctive capabilities? What kind of business does management want to operate? What kind of business does management feel it ought to operate? What alternative combinations (strategies) of these considerations appear worthy of evaluation?

4 / **Evaluation of alternative strategies:** How do alternatives compare with respect to quality of opportunity? How do alternatives compare with respect to required capabilities? How do alternatives compare with respect to management's preferences? How do alternatives compare with respect to management's obligations?

5 / **Selection of new strategy:** What business should the firm be in? What objectives should it seek to attain? What program of action should be pursued?

After regular long-range planning has been launched, the first step is no longer necessary. Like the booster rocket, it can be jettisoned once the company has gotten into the strategic planning orbit.

Conclusion. The rapid upsurge of strategic planning in large business and government organizations must be matched by a similar development in small business. No longer will profitable survival be assured under a management which engages in planning only when problems cry out to be solved. Rather, it will be necessary for small business management to adopt the same type of strategic planning approach which the large companies are evolving. Small business management can meet the threat of the swing to strategic planning in large organizations if the chief executive decides that he is going to make management, according to strategic plan, the dominant element of his job.

REFERENCES

1. Alfred D. Chandler, Jr., *Strategy and Structure* (Cambridge, Mass.: The MIT Press, 1962), p. 13.
2. *Ibid.*
3. "Planning in Business" (Menlo Park, Calif.: Stanford Research Institute, 1963).
4. George A. Steiner, ed., *Managerial Long-Range Planning* (New York: McGraw-Hill Book Company, 1963).
5. Learned, Christensen, Andrews, and Guth, *Business Policy* (Homewood, Ill.: Richard D. Irwin, Inc., 1965).
6. Frank F. Gilmore and Richard G. Brandenburg, "Anatomy of Corporate Planning," *Harvard Business Review*, Nov.-Dec., 1962, pp. 61–69. For a more comprehensive analysis of the planning process, see H. Igor Ansoff, *Corporate Strategy* (New York: McGraw-Hill Book Company, 1965).
7. Henri Fayol, "Administrative Theory in the State," *Papers on the Science of Administration*, eds. Luther Gulick and L. Urwick (New York: Institute of Public Administration, Columbia University, 1937).
8. James O. McKinsey, "Adjusting Policies to Meet Changing Conditions," American Management Association, General Management Series No. 116, 1932.
9. Melvin T. Copeland, "The Job of an Executive," *Harvard Business Review*, Mar.-April, 1940, pp. 148–160.
10. George A. Steiner, *op. cit.*, chap. 11.

A reprint from
CALIFORNIA MANAGEMENT REVIEW
© 1967 by The Regents of the University of California

GEORGE A. STEINER

Approaches to Long-Range Planning for Small Business

The author presents some new thoughts on long-range planning specifically designed to assist the small businessman.

❧ THERE IS LITTLE DOUBT that the great majority of small businesses do little, if any, long-range planning. While the virtues of long-range planning have been rather well "sold" to most of the large corporations, the job still remains to be done among the small business community.

Expansion of long-range planning among smaller enterprises can best proceed upon two platforms.

1 / The small businessman must be convinced that long-range planning is worthwhile, and he must develop a genuine desire for it.

2 / He must adopt methods and principles suitable to his situation.

The essence of long-range planning is thinking systematically about the future and making current decisions on that basis. Implicit in this concept is the idea of examining future consequences of present decisions, as well as choosing bases for making current decisions from among future alternative courses of action. Long-range planning, therefore, is not without current impact.[1]

Every businessman thinks ahead. But what is new in long-range planning today is looking ahead in a methodical, organized, and conscious fashion. Managers have found that the formalization of the long-range planning process produces better results.

This new concept of long-range planning does not imply an exhaustive inquiry into the future. The process actually used in a company should merely be adapted to the particular circumstances existing in the company.

The typical small businessman is likely to give one or more of the following responses when asked why he does so little (or no) long-range planning:

That's for big companies, not me.

Why should I? I'm doing O.K.

You can't forecast the future, so how can you do long-range planning?

I am in a cash squeeze, and that's all I can think about now.

It's too complicated.

My business is simple, and I know what the problems are.

I can do all the planning I need in my head. Anyway, I don't want to discuss my plans with anyone. Why give someone a chance to find out and lose my competitive advantage?

The average small businessman is faced with

Among recent books by UCLA's Dr. Steiner are Government's Role in Economic Life, Managerial Long-Range Planning, Multinational Corporate Planning, *and* Industrial Project Management (*in press*).

many barriers to long-range planning. He is pressed for time. He has most of the problems of an executive in a medium-size company, but must solve them without helpers. He is constantly fighting "brush fires," and, as anyone who has followed business planning knows, these pressures drive out long-range planning. He is a man of action and has a habit of doing things by himself. Typically, the small businessman keeps his ideas, plans, and intentions secret. He is reluctant to discuss plans which may not materialize because he does not want to be thought foolish or inept.[2]

Finally, although the literature on long-range planning is increasing, most of it is not very helpful to the small businessman. He needs detailed guides to tell him how to go about long-range planning, which are not easy to find.

Yet none of these obstacles can justify a businessman's avoiding systematic long-range planning.

The matter of forecasting the future seems to bother many businessmen. Of course, no one can foresee the future. Forecasting, however, is making a judgment about the future on the basis of present knowledge. The more accurate the forecast, the better a plan will be, but planning can be effective even if a forecast is not too accurate at first. Whether they realize it or not, all businessmen forecast. The only difference is in how well they do it. If a manager, for example, decides not to purchase a new machine, he is in effect forecasting that his profits will not be increased in the future by the purchase.

The meanings of forecasting and planning are confused in the minds of some businessmen. Forecasting is not planning, but only a part of it. Planning is determining what a manager wants in the future and developing methods to achieve it. Forecasting may tell which type of environment can be expected; planning will determine how to take advantage of it or, if it is inhospitable, how to prevent it from taking advantage of the firm.

Answers to some of the other reasons given for failure to plan ahead are obvious. If long-range planning is important, a businessman simply must and can find the time to do it. Actually, long-range planning is simpler than many businessmen imagine. The businessman who rejects planning for the future because he is doing so well today could not be more misguided. Products as well as production methods are growing obsolete faster, and customers

are becoming more fickle. Prosperity today is no assurance of tomorrow's profits.

Long-range planning is essential for a small as well as a large business for no other reason than that it permits them to take better advantage of the opportunities which lie in the future and to forestall the threats which it contains. This is the essence of entrepreneurship. Long-range planning should stimulate this function. Only a few small businesses have the financial reserves to cover the unexpected loss that occurs when they must shift from dependence on a single obsolete product or a few major customers. Yet this sort of crisis may be avoided by recognizing that it can happen and taking early action to avoid it. And there are other advantages to long-range planning for a small businessman. For example, he will find banks and other sources of cash much more willing to finance his needs if he has a well-designed long-range plan. He may be able to "go public" much more easily and without fear of losing his business. And he can be sure of perpetuating his business beyond his retirement.

Before discussing a variety of possible approaches to long-range planning, it is useful to set forth a simple conceptual frame of reference for types of business plans and steps in their development. Figure 1 is a simplified sketch of different types of plans needed in a business. It also shows the general flow of action in the process of planning.

Two important facts should be mentioned before discussing Figure 1:

• A very large number of companies doing long-range planning have systems that fit this model.

• The structure is exceedingly flexible and can be adapted to just about any size of business, style of management, type of business, or stage in the development of organized planning.

So long as a manager is really interested in long-range planning, this conceptual model can be used with any magnitude of resources, and it can be applied equally well to a very small and a very large enterprise.

To the left of the chart are the fundamental premises that go into any planning effort. First are the basic purposes of the firm, usually expressed in broad terms. Many companies have only recently written out their basic purposes, but it is not necessary to put them on paper so long as businessmen think about them, for they are the starting

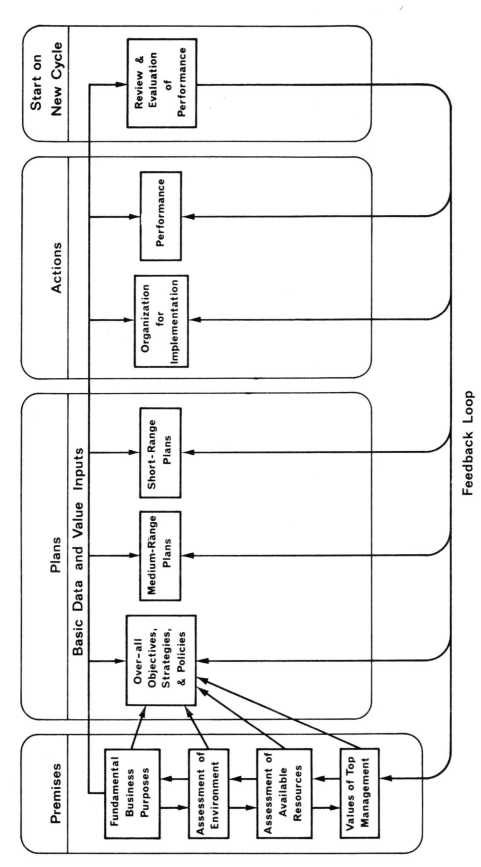

FIG. 1.—The Structure and Process of Planning For a Business.

point in long-range planning. Of major significance, too, are the values, ideas, and philosophies which a businessman holds. These, of course, permeate all he does and are major determinants of all the decisions he makes. For example, a businessman who is working to enlarge a small business will go about his long-range planning in a far different manner from one who wishes to work alone to invent new products in his own small laboratory.

Planning also must be based on an assessment of the future environment, both within and outside the firm. The possible number of elements to be examined is very great, and the art of long-range planning involves an ability to choose those which are of major importance to the firm.

Upon these bases the over-all objectives, strategies, and policies of the firm can be set forth. They can be few in number or many. They can concern any element of the business. The more concrete they are, however, the better the plans are likely to be. The time dimensions of objectives, strategies, and policies extend from the immediate future to the infinite. For example, a firm may set as its objective to be the top quality producer of microelectronic products in the industry. This has no time limit. On the other hand, the objective to hire a chief engineer by next month has a short time dimension.

Medium-range plans cover a fixed time dimension set by a manager. A large number of smaller companies consider two years to be a suitable period for medium-range plans. Four- and five-year plans are more frequent among larger companies. In this kind of plan one finds more expectations placed on such parts of the business as sales, profits, finance, production, research, and facilities.

The short-range plans usually apply to quarterly or monthly cash budgets, raw material purchase schedules, production schedules, and shipment schedules.

To the right of the diagram are actions needed to complete the process, assuring that arrangements are made to operate on the basis of plans and then reviewing and assessing performance during and after operations.

Operational versus analytical steps in planning. Analytical steps have been set up as the preferred procedures in all problem solving. They take the following basic form for business planning:

- Establish objectives.
- Prepare basic premises.
- Determine alternative courses of action to achieve objectives.
- Examine different alternative courses of action.
- Choose alternatives to be followed.
- Put the plan into action.
- Review plans periodically.

These steps are implicit in **Figure 1** and are fundamental in all effective planning. But a businessman may not follow this sequence at all. The sequence of operational steps in planning may be much different from the analytical steps. For example, it is rare to find a planning program proceeding from one step to the next without retracing or overlapping. A tentative goal found too high or too low may be changed after examining various alternative courses of action to achieve it.

In the following sections a number of operational steps for planning are presented. While they differ markedly, they will be more easily performed if both the conceptual model of planning structures and the analytical steps are kept in mind. But precisely what sequence is followed and what depth of analysis is employed will depend on many considerations: type and size of business, nature of top management, available help, nature of problems facing the business, and whether long-range planning is just beginning or has been in operation for some time.

The following suggestions begin with simple and conclude with complex methods—which need not be mutually exclusive. All of them can be incorporated into advanced, sophisticated systems, and all have actually been used with success by small businessmen.

Asking questions. Columella is as correct today as he was centuries ago when he said, "The important part of every business is to know what ought to be done." But this is not as easy as it sounds. Consider the case of the small businessman whose sales grew rapidly but whose receivables did not turn over quickly enough to finance his current needs. He had to borrow, but, because he was not well established he had to pay high interest rates for his loan, and this wiped out his profit. This man was not asking the right questions.

A survey of over one hundred small manufacturers concluded that "the hardest part of planning seems to be getting started."[3] A simple way to get started in long-range planning is by asking some basic questions. A good place to begin is with objectives. It is most naive to say, "Our objective is to make a profit—period." Of course it is, but maximizing profits involves answering questions such as:

What business am I in?

What is my place in the industry?

What customers am I serving? Where is my market?

What is my company image to my major customers?

What business do I want to be in five years from now?

What are my specific goals for profit improvement?

Need I have plans for product improvement? If so, what?

What is my greatest strength? Am I using it well?

What is my greatest problem? How am I to solve it?

What share of the market do I want? Next month? Next year?

Are my personnel policies acceptable to employees?

How can I finance growth?

For those small businessmen who are preparing such lists and are answering the questions, this is one excellent way to get started down the path of systematic and useful long-range planning.

It is readily apparent how a decision about any one of these questions can have an important impact on most of the others. What is most useful is to get at the major issues, think about them continuously, and set up specific plans of action.

Key to success. Every business, both large and small, will succeed or fail depending on a limited and variable number of strategic factors. The best way to get started in long-range planning is to try to discover those few strategic factors which will be responsible for future success. Since finance is such a critical factor to most small businessmen, this area is traditionally the prime subject of analysis for them as well as for scholars who are interested in small business problems.

But other factors may be just as important strategically. Imagination may be the strategic factor responsible for the success of a toy company or an advertising firm. Quality may be the strategic factor responsible for the success of a company making components for a complicated aerospace product. Cost control and cost reduction may be the strategic factors responsible for success of a company producing standard metal stampings for an automobile manufacturer.

TABLE I.—A New Product Check-Off List

Relationship to present operations

♦ Does the product fall within the manufacturing and processing know-how of the company?
♦ Will the product benefit by the present research and engineering activities of the company?
♦ Does the product fit into the lines now handled by our sales organization? Will it permit more efficient utilization of our present sales organization?

Character of the Product

♦ Will the product capitalize on the engineering strength of the company?
♦ Is there a reasonable volume potential?
♦ Can the product maintain a high degree of distinctiveness in comparison with competing products?
♦ Will the product contribute to the company's reputation?

Commercial Considerations

♦ Is the product necessary or desirable in maintaining completeness of line?
♦ Does the inclusion of this product in the line have any effect on the other lines?
♦ Will it strengthen our position with distributors?
♦ Will the company name be of aid in marketing the product?

Strategic factors like these should come to light in a comprehensive long-range planning program. But if no such program exists, a small businessman may start his long-range planning simply by drawing up a list of possible strategic factors which may be responsible for his future success. Once the pertinent ones are identified, they should, of course, be the subject of deep thought and appropriate action.

Check-off lists. Some firms use so-called check-off lists to guide their planning. These lists cover important elements of planning such as sales and marketing, research and development, products, land and property, personnel, organization, finance, and competition. The list of questions in Table I concerning the addition of new products illustrates this approach. For many of the questions absolute measurement is difficult, if not impossible; simple ratings, therefore, are usually given for each question, such as: "excellent," "good," "average," "poor," "unsatisfactory."

Simplified master planning. Questions like those in Table I are helpful, but more systematization is desirable. Roger A. Golde, a small business consultant, has devised a form to help the small businessman organize his planning (Tables II and III).[4]

TABLE II.—MASTER PLANNING FORM

Item	Change		Comment
	Next Year	Year After Next	
Research & Development			
Products			
Product Mix			
Service			
Supplies			
Suppliers			
Inventory			
Subcontracts			
Storage & Handling			
Quality Control			
Space			
Leasehold Improvements			
Equipment			
Employees			
Fringe Benefits			
Customers			
Sales Outlets			
Terms of Sale			
Pricing			
Transportation			
Advertising			
Promotion			
Packaging			
Market Research			
Financing			
Insurance			
Investments			
Management Reports			
Management Procedures			
Management Organization			
Governmental Environment			
Economic Environment			
Industrial Environment			
Competition			
Community Environment			

INSTRUCTIONS: All changes are estimated in relation to the preceding year.

If a quantitative change is anticipated—i.e., change in size or amount—use the following symbols: L=large, M=medium, and S=small. Quantitative changes are assumed to be increases unless preceded by a minus sign.

If a qualitative change is anticipated, use the following symbols: l=large, m=medium, s=small.

Note that the notions of small, medium, and large changes are obviously subjective and will vary with the person using the form.

In general, a small change denotes some sort of minimum level of change which is thought important enough to make note of. Most of the expected changes will probably fall in the medium category, indicating significant change of some magnitude. The large category will usually be reserved for unusual changes of striking impact.

A manager-owner can work with Golde's form at odd moments, informally, with or without help. This form has the great virtue of getting at the major elements of success or failure of a firm. Working with it will raise questions and encourage decisions. For many small businessmen, starting with comparatively abstract goals and strategies is difficult. The practical approach of Golde, however, should eventually lead them to a better understanding of objectives and strategies.

Selecting concrete key objectives. Not all objective setting need be abstract. An approach developed by Dr. Gunther Klaus, a small business management consultant, is concrete, pragmatic, and leads directly into systematic planning. He begins with a framework for decision which is illustrated in Table IV. This particular exhibit concerns sales objectives, but it could also be used for profit. The assumption here is that, if sales are considered first, the profit objectives will follow in logical fashion.

Klaus begins with an objective for sales as far in the future as it is practicable for the small businessman to contemplate, in this case five years. The question is, What dollar volume of sales do I want five years from now? When that question is answered, it naturally raises a great many more. One immediate question is whether the present product line will permit the achievement of that objective. If not, a number of other questions arise: Can the target be met by product modifications? If so, which ones? If not, what new products can be produced? If this will not permit target achievement, should a joint venture be considered? Penetration of new markets? Acquisitions? Dealing with these questions opens up a "decision-tree" with many other branches. What manpower will be needed? What financing will be required? What will my costs be? Must some employees be sent to an executive training program to get prepared to assume larger responsibilities?

This approach, like the preceding ones, is quite adaptable to different conditions and sizes of businesses.

The notion of qualitative changes may need some clarification. This category of change would cover such items as a change in customer mix (which might or might not result in an increased number of customers). Using a new source of supply for raw materials and changing the media allocation of the advertising budget would also be examples of qualitative changes.

SOURCE: Roger A. Golde, *Harvard Business Review*, XXIV: 5 (Sept.-Oct. 1964), 151 f.

TABLE III.—Hypothetical Completed Master Planning Form

Item	Change Next Year	Change Year After Next	Comment
Research & Development	Mm	−S	Start development of new altimeter for executive planes.
Products		Ss	First sales of new altimeter.
Product Mix			
Service		s	Slightly different for private planes.
Supplies		s	Needed for new altimeter.
Suppliers			
Inventory			
Subcontracts		S	Most of subassemblies will be subcontracted.
Storage & Handling			
Quality Control			
Space		S	Little bit of production space for new altimeter.
Leasehold Improvements	M		Need for dust-free area.
Equipment	S		New test equipment.
Employees	S		Couple of technicians for development work.
Fringe Benefits			
Customers		sS	Plan to hit owners of executive planes.
Sales Outlets		Mm	Will need more sales representatives rather than own sales force.
Terms of Sale			
Pricing			
Transportation			
Advertising		−M	Not so effective to private owners.
Promotion		m	Will switch to more demonstrations and trade shows.
Packaging			
Market Research	S		Informal poll of private owners known by company.
Financing	S		Additional working capital for production.
Insurance			
Investments			
Management Reports		1	Need for simple product costing system.
Etc.			Etc.

Source: Roger A. Golde, *Harvard Business Review*, XXIV: 5 (Sept.-Oct. 1964), 151 f.

The planning gap. A modification of this approach is to identify the so-called planning gap.[5] This calls for the establishment of tentative sales goals and the forecasting of current momentum, or what present and anticipated lines of business will produce in the future. The difference, as shown in Figure 2, is the planning gap. The issue is, How will the gap be filled? (Similar charts can be drawn for profits, costs, personnel, floor space, etc.) Asking and answering this question leads to the same sort of analysis as that discussed above.

Return on investment. Another approach is to concentrate on the return on investment calculation

TABLE IV.—Sales Objectives

Area	First Year	Second Year	Third Year	Fourth Year	Fifth Year
Product modification					
New products					
Joint ventures					
New markets					
Acquisition					
Totals					BEGIN HERE

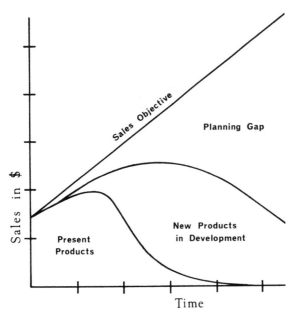

FIG. 2.—THE PLANNING GAP.

for a firm. The elements of this calculation are shown in Figure 3. As in the previous approach, a return on investment objective can be tentatively established for selected time periods. The analysis then begins by probing (in a fashion similar to that described above) what is necessary to achieve the objective. This approach is flexible in dealing with both short- and long-range factors in business life.

For many years, this has been the approach of the planning and control program of E. I. du Pont de Nemours & Company. It is, of course, usable by a small company as well. But a small company would find (as does Du Pont) the approach more useful when accompanied by other elements of planning noted in Figure 1.

Break-even analysis. The break-even point for a business is that point in production at which sales volume equals costs. At that point there is neither a profit nor a loss. Figure 4 shows a break-even analy-

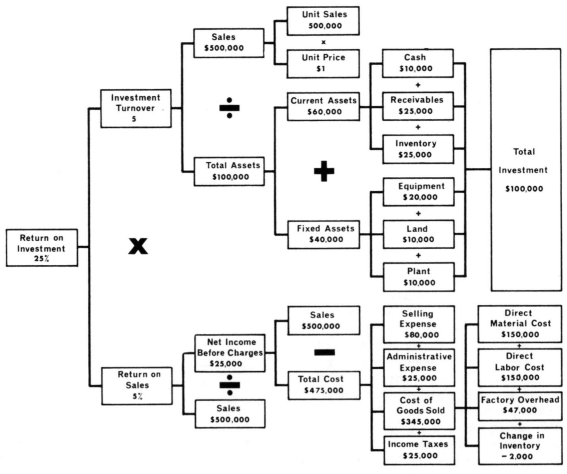

FIG. 3.—RETURN ON INVESTMENT.

sis. A simple formula will also yield the break-even point:

$$\text{Break-even} = \frac{\text{Fixed costs}}{100\% - (\text{Variable costs}/\text{Sales})}$$

The break-even analysis is a powerful tool to answer puzzling questions such as: What is the impact on profit if fixed costs rise 10 per cent and sales decline by 10 per cent? Or if variable costs increase by 15 per cent and volume drops by 14 per cent?

This is a simple method to get at some major issues important in company planning. If break-even analysis is used to ask a widening range of questions, as illustrated above, it can be the starting point for a long-range planning program.

Economists have criticized this tool because they rightly claim that cost curves are curves and not linear as drawn on the chart. Furthermore, the technique assumes many things that may not be true; for instance, that productivity remains the same over time, or that fixed and variable costs can be separated. This is not the place to argue the merits of such criticisms. It is in point here to observe, however, that within a "range of relevance," the functions of a break-even chart are rather linear. For many companies within a range of ten to fifteen per cent on either side of the break-even line, an assumed linear relationship can be approximated closely enough to form a solid basis for planning. Hence this is a useful short- and long-range plan-

ning tool. Its value does, however, decrease the longer the time span covered and the wider the ranges of output are.

Standard accounting statements. Standard accounting statements are excellent bases for developing long-range planning. They can be very simple for a very small enterprise or developed in complex detail in a comprehensive planning program.

In a simple approach, and one which is indispensable to proper management in small as well as large enterprises, cash forecasts are prepared. What is involved is the identification and forecast of all important future sources and uses of cash available to the enterprise. Table V gives an elementary arrangement of items to be forecast to determine net cash flows. A number of different formats are contained in Schabacker's *Cash Planning in Small Manufacturing Companies.*[6] Most commercial banks have developed cash flow forms which are available to businessmen. These forms can be used to forecast cash flows for any period of time chosen—daily, weekly, monthly, quarterly, or over a number of years.

The revenue-expense forecast can also be used as a beginning point for long-range planning. Table VI shows a simple revenue-expense forecast format. Here the task is to identify and forecast all important elements of cost and revenues. The difference will show profit or loss, and this in turn will provide the basis upon which simple or sophisticated rates of return on investment may be calculated. Revenue-expense forecasts can and should be prepared for each important product of an enterprise as well as for the enterprise as a whole. Revenue-expense forecasts for individual products should at least extend over the major part of the life span of the product.

An important feature of the revenue-expense forecast is that when depreciation is added to net profit the result is cash gain from operations. As noted in Table VI, this does not, however, represent net cash flow. So, when simple revenue-expense forecasts are used in planning they should be accompanied by cash flow analyses.

Complete balance sheets and profit and loss statements constitute a more complicated basis for developing long-range planning. When a company gets to the point where it can develop such documents for the length of time for which organized future planning is done, it has demonstrated high

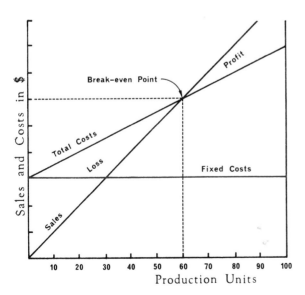

FIG. 4.—A BREAK-EVEN ANALYSIS.

TABLE V.—FIVE-YEAR FORECAST OF CASH SOURCES AND NEEDS FOR A SMALL BUSINESS

Item	First Year	Second Year	Third Year	Fourth Year	Fifth Year
Cash sources:					
Opening balance					
Revenue from sales					
Depreciation					
Borrowing on facilities					
Borrowing on inventory and receivables					
Total cash sources					
Cash expenditures:					
Direct labor costs					
Materials purchase					
Payments to subcontractors					
New machinery and tools					
Increases in inventory					
Increases in receivables					
Increases in operating cash					
Payments on loans					
Factory burden					
Officers' salaries					
Selling costs					
Taxes:					
Employer's share of Social Security					
Local property					
Income					
Total cash disbursements					
Net cash change					

capability for planning. Consequently, the company might just as well develop a more comprehensive formal long-range planning program in which these documents are included as parts.

As companies grow in size and experience with organized long-range planning, it becomes possible and desirable to have a more complete planning program than those discussed up to this point. The shape of the planning program follows more closely the conceptual model presented in Figure 1 and results in a comprehensive set of objectives and plans covering all major parts of the business.

Here is a brief description of an actual comprehensive planning program. This five-year plan was prepared by the president and his four major de-

partment heads, who worked evenings and weekends to complete it. The firm had less than $2,000,000 annual sales and about one hundred employees at the time the plan was prepared.

CORPORATE LONG-RANGE PLAN FOR MAGNETIC DESIGN, INC.

I. Corporate Purposes: the fundamental purposes of MDI. Two basic purposes are given, which is about standard. The four modifiers, however, are a little unusual.

A. Two prime objectives of MDI are:
• To improve earnings through productive effort primarily applied (but not limited) to the manufacture of magnetic devices and power supply equipment.

• To conduct the business in a manner that is constructive, honorable, and mutually profitable for stockholders, employees, customers, suppliers, and the general community.

TABLE VI.—FIVE-YEAR REVENUE-EXPENSE PROJECTION FOR A SMALL BUSINESS

Item	First Year	Second Year	Third Year	Fourth Year	Fifth Year
Sales revenues:					
Product A					
Product B					
Operating expenses:					
Direct labor					
Overhead					
Materials					
Selling expenses					
Depreciation					
Total					
Non-recurring expenses					
Total operating expenses					
Interest and loan amortization					
Net profit before taxes					
Taxes					
Net profit after taxes					
Cash gain from operations (net profit after taxes plus depreciation reserve)					

B. These objectives are amplified further:
• To earn a reasonable return on investment with due regard to the interests of customers, employees, vendors.

• To expand sales while increasing profits.

• To support the military effort of the United States by producing top quality products.

• To grow at a steady rate.

C. Departmental purposes: Administration, marketing, production and engineering, and finance. It is a little unusual for departmental purposes to be specified at this point in a plan; they are usually blended into specific goals set for their operations. Following are the objectives of the production and engineering department:

• Manufacture and design quality products with cost and delivery schedules which will be attractive to prospective customers.
• Stay alert to developments that promise new and improved company products.

II. Basic Corporate Five- and Ten-Year Sales and Profit Objectives:
A. The five-year annual sales and profit objectives are:

	Sales	Pretax Profits	Pretax (%) Profit	Federal Tax	Posttax (%) Profit
First year					
Second year		[Specified in dollars			
Third year		and percentages.]			
Fourth year					
Fifth year					

B. The ten-year sales and profit objectives are:
• After taxes, sales will be $5,000,000 and earnings will be $750,000.

III. Basic Premises: forecasts of future markets, technology, competition, and evaluations of internal strengths and weaknesses. A framework of premises, with illustrations from the MDI plan, follows:

A. External projections and forecasts:
• Survey of general business conditions, including Gross National Product forecast.

• Survey of the market for company products, based upon general economic conditions for industrial products and estimates of government spending for company products.

• Forecast of company sales based on the above two forecasts. (MDI made forecasts for each of the next five years. Since the company is in the Midwest, government spending for its products in the Midwest was estimated. Included were the Department of Defense, the National Aeronautics and Space Administration, and the Federal Aviation Agency.)

B. Competition: Because competition is keen for most companies, objective estimates of its strength are important. After looking at what its major competition was likely to do, the firm looked at itself.

• Several advantages have placed MDI several years in advance of competition in the magnetic devices equipment field. These are cryogenic magnets for commercial applications and high reliability power supplies for long-endurance military application.

• However, in order to realize fully the growth commensurate with the above advantages, several weaknesses must be overcome by developing an ability to construct crystals as well as developing more sophisticated test procedures.

C. Internal examination of the past and projections: Analyses of various parts of the enterprise, e.g.

• Product line analysis:
a. Product(s) performance (i.e., sales volume, profit margin, etc.).
b. Customer class served.
c. Comparison with major competitors' product(s).
d. Comparison with substitutes and complementary performance.
e. Possibilities for product improvement.
f. Suggestions with regard to new products.

• Market analysis:
a. Important factors in projected sales changes: product success; marketing organization; advertising; and competitive pressures.
b. New markets to be penetrated (i.e., geographical areas and customer classes).

• Financial analysis:
a. Profit position.
b. Working capital.
c. Cash position.
d. Impact of financial policy on market price per share.
e. Prospects for future financing.

• Production analysis:
a. Plant and equipment (maintenance and depreciation).
b. Productive capacity and productivity.
c. Per cent of capacity utilized.
d. Suggestions for: productivity improvements; cost reduction; utilizing excess capacity; and planning expansion.

• Technical analysis:
a. Research and development performance.
b. Suggestions for improving research and development effectiveness.

• Employees:
a. Employment and future needs.
b. Technical manpower deficiencies.
c. Appraisal of employee attitudes.

• Facilities:
a. Evaluation of current facilities to meet new business.
b. Machine replacement policy and needs.

IV. **Basic Objectives, Policies, and Strategies:** This covers every important area of the business, but most companies concentrate on A through F of the following:

A. Profits.
B. Sales.
C. Finance.
D. Marketing.
E. Capital additions.
F. Production.
G. Research.
H. Engineering.
I. Personnel.
J. Acquisitions.
K. Organization.
L. Long-range planning.

This list can be expanded. As noted elsewhere, the more concrete the specification here can be, the easier it usually is to implement the plans. It is especially important for a small businessman to know precisely what he is seeking and the method to be employed to get there. For example, MDI marketing objectives were set forth as follows:

• Increase sales of magnetic devices 100 per cent in the next five years. Increase sales of power supply equipment 200 per cent during the next five years.

• Increase the total volume of industrial sales from today's 25 per cent to 50 per cent of total sales at the end of five years.

• Penetrate the western market to the point where the company will control 10 per cent of it at the end of five years.

• Enter the foreign market within five years by a licensing agreement, a joint venture, or manufacturing facility.

For each of these objectives, the company prepared a detailed series of strategies ranging from a strategy to "sell custom designs directly to prime contractors in geographic regions where their main plants are located" to details such as special services to selected specified customers, training programs for employees, and top management meetings with customers.

Further strategies which might be included in

this section of the plan, with special regard to marketing, are organization, use of dealers, possibility of distributing products manufactured by others, salesmen's compensation plans, and pricing policy.

Drawing a proper line of demarcation between the strategic plans and the detailed operational plans is difficult. Ideally, the two blend together in a continuous line. This was the case with MDI, where those making the strategic plan also were the ones to implement it.

V. Detailed Medium-Range Plans: more detailed plans growing out of the above. For MDI these plans were developed for each of the succeeding five years:

A. *Pro forma* balance sheet, yearly.
B. Income statement, yearly.
C. Capital expenditure schedule, yearly.
D. Unit production schedule for major products, yearly.
E. Employment schedule, yearly.
F. Detailed schedule to acquire within three years a company with design capability in solid state magnetic devices.

VI. One-Year Plans: the next year's budgets. The first year's budgets for items A through N were, in the aggregate, the same for the first year of the five-year plan, but broken into quarterly time periods. In addition, MDI had other budgets, principally purchasing schedules for major components and raw materials and typical detailed administrative budgets covering such things as travel and telephone.

Comprehensive planning in decentralized companies. When divisions are established as profit centers, a new dimension is added to the planning process. At first, long-range planning is usually done for the entire company by the central office. But once the process is established the central office usually concentrates on over-all company objectives, strategies, and policies and leaves the detailed medium- and short-range planning to the individual divisions, reserving only the right of review and approval. Sometimes the divisional plans are aggregated into one composite company plan. The structure and substance of the plans parallel that given for MDI.

Help for the chief executive. One of the major problems of the chief executive in doing long-range planning is getting adequate help. It is important for the manager-owner of a very small enterprise, as well as the president of a medium-sized business and the chief executive of a large one, to recognize that help is available. Each needs only to understand what is available and to learn how to use it.

His own staff is a prime resource. A manager al-

ways can do the planning himself—almost obligatory for a very small firm. As firms grow larger, however, it becomes impossible. Growth leads to staff help. Methods which have been employed in using staff successfully are:

■ The chief executive can conduct a freewheeling "think" session to get long-range planning started. Many companies take their top executives away from daily routine to some spa to engage in thinking and planning about the future and conduct these sessions as part of a well-entrenched planning program. These sessions are useful to get the process started.

■ The chief executive can first prepare objectives for the firm and then ask each functional manager to prepare plans for his own area of responsibility.

■ The chief executive can ask each functional manager to tell him what his plans are for the future and then develop over-all objectives and strategies on the basis of them. Or, to initiate the process, he can ask each functional officer what he thinks ought to be done by the firm to get long-range planning under way.

■ The chief executive can assign to one functional officer the job of starting planning. This man can monitor the process in progress.

■ The chief executive can get together with his functional officers to form a committee to prepare strategic over-all as well as working plans for his company. This is what MDI did. As the number of employees increases, there may be great advantage to this method. A committee can offset some traits of chief executives, such as the desire for one-man authoritative control, making snap judgments, preoccupation with short- at the expense of long-run planning, and secretiveness which hurts the firm more than it helps it. Committees of this sort bring to the front different points of view, which is usually healthy. Better communications are promoted, and individuals are likely to feel more intimately associated with the prospects and problems of the firm.

■ When a firm gets larger it may be able to afford one person or a small staff to devote full time to planning. Such a staff is especially useful in decentralized, divisionalized companies. The staff coordinates work of the central headquarters' functional officers in the development of over-all firm objectives and strategies, aids the divisions in improving their planning capabilities, and helps the central headquarters management review plans. Sometimes the director of such a staff serves as the secretary to a corporate planning committee.

Outside sources of help are available, including consultants for all the major problems of the firm. These are well known and need no further analysis here. One of the most neglected sources of help, particularly for the small businessman, is his board of directors. Small businessmen should think seriously about the advantages of placing on their board one or more individuals with talents that can be used in actually performing long-range planning or advising the president about the use of outside consultants.

Summary. Many small businessmen do not engage in effective long-range planning because they are puzzled about how to begin the process and execute it so that its values exceed its costs. Many of these approaches have been tested by small, as well as large, firms, and they have been found operational and valuable in doing effective long-range planning.

REFERENCES

This article is based on a chapter from a book edited by Professor Irving Pfeffer, entitled *Financial Aspects of Profit Planning for Small Business*, to be published later this year.

1. For a fuller definition of long-range planning, see my "The Critical Role of Top Management in Long-Range Planning," *Arizona Review*, XV:4 (April 1966); and my "Long-Range Planning: Concept and Implementation," *Financial Executive*, XXXIV:7 (July 1966), 54–61.

2. For a profile of the successful small businessman, see Orvis F. Collins, David G. Moore, and Darab B. Unwalla, *The Enterprising Man* (East Lansing, Mich.: Bureau of Business and Economic Research, Graduate School of Business Administration, Michigan State University, 1964).

3. Delbert C. Hastings, *The Place of Forecasting in Basic Planning for Small Business* (Minneapolis: University of Minnesota Press, 1961), p. 23.

4. Roger A. Golde, "Practical Planning for Small Business," *Harvard Business Review*, XXIV:5 (Sept.-Oct. 1964), 151 f.

5. See my "Making Long-Range Company Planning Pay Off," *California Management Review*, IV:2 (Winter 1963), 28–41.

6. Joseph C. Schabacker, *Cash Planning in Small Manufacturing Companies, Small Business Administration* (Washington, D.C.: U.S. Government Printing Office, 1960).

CRITICAL STAGES OF SMALL BUSINESS GROWTH

When they occur and how to survive them

LAWRENCE L. STEINMETZ

Mr. Steinmetz is an associate professor, School of Business, University of Colorado.

A small business—if it is succeeding—is inescapably committed to living through three critical phases of growth. The only alternative to forced growth is the demise of the business and the probable loss of nearly 50 percent of the assets. The rewards of survival can be phenomenal. Phase 1 occurs in the direct supervision stage; Phase 2 in the supervised supervision stage; and Phase 3 in the indirect control stage, when the firm has "arrived" at last. What can the small businessman do to ensure his progress through these stages and ease his own development from autocrat to professional manager? If he does not solve the problems encountered at each stage he can expect to go out of business. This article pinpoints these problems; recognition of them is the first step toward their solution.

Are you working longer hours and enjoying it less? Has it seemed that your business expands but your profits do not? Are the "little guys" taking all the gravy business? Do you feel you have to do something, but you don't know what? Maybe an explanation is in order. .

Most men who have been successful in operating their own businesses seem to have been able, intuitively or instinctively, to figure out what causes waning profits, organizational headaches, and acute personnel problems. They have managed to revitalize their businesses when—if not before—such problems occur. Unfortunately, many small businessmen have not had such insight. For these, this article will describe the three critical phases of small business growth. These phases are critical because failure to live through them will result in the death of the business, either because the business must be liquidated or sold to another company because continued operations would be unprofitable.

THE TYPICAL GROWTH CURVE

It has been known for some time that the growth pattern of the typical small business is S–shaped. This growth curve shows the stages of a firm's growth and their critical phases (see accompanying figure). The three critical areas are Stage 1, which occurs in the direct supervision stage of growth; Stage 2, which occurs in the supervised supervision stage; and Stage 3, which occurs in the indirect control stage.

Stage 1 problems occur about the time the

29

Lawrence L. Steinmetz

Stages of Organizational Growth and Their Critical Phases

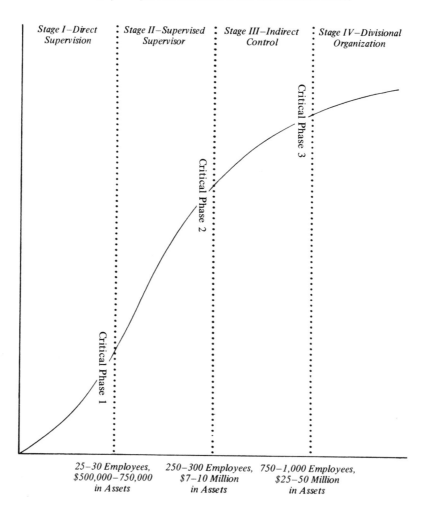

30

organization has 25 or 30 employees and $500,000-$750,000 in invested capital. If the organization lives through its problems and difficulties at this stage, it develops into a Stage II business. At this point, the organization experiences very rapid growth, increases in sales volume, additions of personnel, and improved profitability. Most organizations having between 30 and 300 employees, and with assets of perhaps $5-$10 million dollars, are in Stage II. It is far and away the most profitable stage of growth for the small business, the time at which the *rate of return* on invested funds will far exceed the returns in Stages I and III. Unfortunately, a critical point is reached in Stage II (when the firm has 250-300 employees, $7-$10 million in assets)—a point where the rapid rate of growth begins to hit its peak and, again, death of the firm may occur. Death here usually does not mean liquidation, but it does mean failure (usually via merger) and loss of identity of the original small business.

If the small businessman has enough foresight or luck, he will guide his business through this second critical phase and will arrive at Stage III. Stage III is delightful for the small businessman, because the odds of death of the business are now considerably reduced; the firm has "arrived" by most people's standards. It is characterized by total indirect control upon the part of the small businessman.

Now for the real question at hand: what are the tip-offs that should alert the small businessman that his business is approaching the critical phases in its growth, and what can be done to obviate the accompanying problems?

STAGE I–LIVE OR DIE

The prognosis for the small businessman just starting out—even if he is successful—is a fairly limited rate of return on his investment. At this stage the small businessman is a rather pathetic individual. As Collins and Moore have said:

The image of the entepreneur as a great inventor and great promoter or the great and daring risk-taker simply doesn't square with the facts. Reality is far less spectacular than this. In fact, the beginning entrepreneurship turns out to be a mundane affair and not at all heroic. There is the entrepreneur without capital resource, without apparent social skills, and without even a good idea. No respectable element in the community is even aware of him, let alone ready to help him.[1]

In short, the stereotype of the small businessman in the early stage of organizational growth is an unimaginative man who feels he has a good idea; whose role as a leader of his business is largely a result of his ownership rights rather than leadership talents; and who may or may not be able to develop a few loyal employees. Fundamentally, he is relying on

personal skills or a unique product (or method or market) of which he can take advantage. He is usually not concerned about the rate of return, being more concerned with keeping the sheriff away from the door. However, assuming that he is successful—that he is not among the 50 percent of the people who will lose their business and 44 percent of their savings[2] —he will experience a slow but sure increase in sales and profitability. Unfortunately, this is where his problems come in; he is at the threshold of the first critical stage in his organization's growth.

A critical stage in growth is reached at this point because prior to this time the business has been a one-man operation, experiencing no real management problems other than "buying low and selling high." However, as the level of business increases a myriad of problems develop: paperwork multiplies, personnel must be added to the payroll, promised dates are not met, facilities get crowded, and so on. At first, of course, a few extra working hours are sufficient to cope with these problems. However, if business is good these minor problems rapidly assume major proportions. Paperwork is not only time-consuming, but more and more is required; the Internal Revenue Service begins to demand more elaborate tax information; bills begin trickling in at all times of the month; and accounts receivable begin to lag merely because statements are not mailed.

Furthermore, the increasing number of personnel begins to complicate matters. First, of course, the manager must spend more and more time in recruiting, selecting, developing, and training new employees. Then there is the problem of maintaining an acceptable relationship with employees already on the payroll. Once enough employees are added, the small businessman must begin to comply with unemployment compensation, minimum wage laws, and so on. The problems confronted by the small businessman, once he achieves a

31

1. Orvis F. Collins and David G. Moore with Darab B. Unwalla, *The Enterprising Man* (East Lansing, Mich.: Michigan State University Press, 1964), pp. 242-43.

2. Lawrence L. Steinmetz, John B. Kline, and Donald P. Stegall, *Managing the Small Business* (Homewood, Ill.: Richard D. Irwin, Inc., 1966), p. 29.

Lawrence L. Steinmetz

modicum of success, may be enumerated brief-ly.

His organization becomes too large to permit him to supervise the efforts of all his people directly.

With inadequate supervision, some of his employees become disloyal and begin to resent the hard-driving attitude of the owner, thus creating motivational problems.

Competition sets in and gets keener be-cause others see a "good thing" going and sense the possibility of quick or easy profit.

The owner-manager (who heretofore has not had to be a real manager but just an owner-worker) is under increasing pressure to delegate work. He usually delegates ineffective-ly because he is not comfortable in this role.

Some of the growth pains of the success image begin to set in—the garage-factory gets too small, the rented facilities somehow seem cluttered, and new quarters seem to be urgently (and expensively) in order.

The market for the unique skill (or product or service) of the small businessman begins to dry up, shift toward some other skill, product or service, or, worst of all, is stolen by a (giant) competitor.

The manager is continuously pressed for "time to do what needs doing."

The manager experiences an overload of worry.

All difficulties become problems of crisis proportions.

These problems normally beset the small businessman when he is hiring between ten and thirty employees, and indicate the point on his growth curve where he faces the first serious threat to the continued existence of his busi-ness. And the facts are that if he does not begin to think in terms of overcoming these prob-lems, he can expect to go out of business. His competition will become increasingly strong, he will have more personnel problems, his account-ing and record-keeping problems will become a "stone around his neck," and he may find that he is being outstripped by other small busi-nesses or by a giant that "doesn't like him."

At this stage, unfortunately, either the small businessman will succeed or he will fail. Statistics show that he cannot stagnate and stay small, nor can he even entertain the notion of hoping that his business will stabilize. He must press on or his business will die. Of course if he

is a man who is aware of what it means to manage—to plan, organize, direct, and con-trol—he will pass through this critical phase, will move into Stage II, and become a capable supervisor of supervisors. If not, his business is doomed. But how does he move successfully into Stage II?

STAGE II—BEING A MANAGER

The activities of those small businessmen who successfully enter Stage II in the normal growth pattern of their firms are entirely different from those actions taken by the owner-worker of the Stage I business. The Stage II small businessman truly becomes a manager rather than a mere owner of his operation. He assumes a certain entrepreneurial aura, partly because of success (he has, after all, become successful) and partly because of charisma. Further, both of these images feed on each other and combine with the fact that normally he will be making more money than ever before in his life— probably more than 95 percent of the working population in his community.

Being a successful, charismatic individual is not the only characteristic of the owner of the small business during growth in Stage 11. Typically, he devotes a great deal of attention to being a manager. Suddenly, perhaps acciden-tally, he learns how to delegate. Furthermore, he learns how to delegate through one or two levels of command and develops good "lieuten-ants." Another characteristic of the manager in this stage is that he usually develops a new method or gimmick to enhance or capitalize on the unique skill, product, or service which he found so useful in Stage I. He may diversify his line or service, capitalize on the use of waste material, or perhaps even integrate horizontally or vertically.

In addition, he now becomes a far more adept financial manager and managerial expert. He becomes aware (by observing competition, talking to other successful small businessmen, reading, or other education) that there are accepted norms or standards of performance which he should be obtaining in his business.

Stages of Small Business Growth

He may discover, for example, that in his particular industry it is an accepted fact that a 12 percent return on investment is the minimum acceptable. Thus, he will begin to develop ways to measure his business performance, because at this point he will have left the stage of survival and can turn his attention to growth and expansion. Furthermore, his attention to the financial aspects of his business—like rate of return, profit margins, and so on—will take on a different meaning to him. Growth and expansion, for example, begin to concern him because at this point his income will have gone up enough in absolute dollars to allow him funds to plow back into the business; in addition, he recognizes that he must make a more formalized investment decision. Thus, at this stage, his actions become far more typical of those of the true entrepreneur, being more concerned with taking calculated risks than simply keeping his doors open for business.

Fortunately, although the Stage II business manager is far more willing to take risks, he still tends to be a bit conservative because he can remember the wolf at his door. Therefore, even though he is willing to engage in diversification of activities, he looks primarily for lucrative opportunities and is concerned with target rates of return. This thought pattern, in turn, causes him to engage in the practice of management by objectives, a technique he finds useful in managing men, materials, and machines, as well as money. Furthermore, the results he obtains from this technique generally are most satisfying both financially and emotionally.

Thus all would appear rosy in Stage II of the economic growth cycle of the normal firm. However, just as the firm in Stage I begins to sow the seeds of its own destruction, so does the small business in Stage II. The demon of success again emerges, and the resulting problems are serious enough in their own way to merit separate attention.

Rigidity of thinking   One of the first problems that crops up in Stage II is in the thought processes of the owner-manager. Whereas the very reason for his success is that he was able to change from the thinking of an owner to a manager in going from Stage I to Stage II, many managers at the same time become very rigid in their thinking or too speculative as a result of their previous triumphs. Any hang-ups in thinking at this point can ring the death knell for the manager because he will not continue to adapt with the times or will commit "speculative" errors.

Surreptitious actions by subordinates   A second problem that crops up in the supervised supervisor stage of small business growth is that the subordinates—particularly the lieutenants developed by the small business manager—often behave in ways not beneficial to the small business. This behavior manifests itself in several actions: fouling up projects and denying responsibility for it; becoming greedy and resenting the small businessman's financial success; fighting among themselves in an effort to enhance or establish individual positions; or the development of blind resentment of the boss's son (or wife, father, brother, and so on).

33

Business overhead growth   A heavy increase in business overhead is another tip-off to entry into the second critical phase of growth. This usually happens as a result of real financial success in the business and manifests itself in increased travel by the owner, grandiose ideas about building new plants, moving to a new location, and particularly, the construction of a lush office with all the accessories, like a refrigerated bar, good-looking secretary, and two telephones. Unfortunately, most of these fixtures are deemed essential only when they

Lawrence L. Steinmetz

are purchased, not being recognized as superfluous until it is too late.

The union moves An additional problem that tends to complicate the life of the small business man approaching critical Stage II is that of unionization. Ironically, the prospects of unionization tend particularly to unnerve the hard-charging, successful, charismatic small businessman. He feels insulted because his employees no longer look to him as the "great white father" and because the union's philosophy of the strong helping the weak is the very antithesis of his personal philosophy. Unionism per se runs against his grain, and he feels his employees have deserted him.

The informal organization gains power The informal organization becomes more and more of a burden to the successful small businessman in Stage II. The small businessman, who was successful in reaching the rapid growth phase of Stage II by learning how to be a manager, still has not learned how to be an administrator. That is, success through Stage I does not require human relations and employee behavior savvy by the small businessman, but success in Stage II does. He can no longer get by just by barking orders; he must truly learn to administrate.

Diseconomies of scale Diseconomies of scale form the sixth problem that normally accompanies movement into the second critical phase of economic growth. For example, H. O. Stekler has found that small businessmen in Stage II begin to encounter certain difficulties that theoretically should not even develop, but do.[3] For example, theoretically it is expected that the bigger the small business gets the more able it is to take advantage of such principles as buying in bulk quantities, selling at lower prices because of higher volume, and so on, and still make increased profits. However, the practi-

calities of life teach otherwise. Stekler argues that there is relatively no advantage with respect to economies of scale realized by firms the size of those in their second stage of growth. In fact, the opposite seems to be true: diversification of products and markets causes some losses, which tend to force a *reduced* rate of return over what had been previously experienced by the small business manager in the rapid growth phase of Stage II.

Production problems The glow begins to wear off the rapid growth phase of the small business as production problems arise. This does not occur because the manager fails to supervise his subordinates effectively, but because his organization has become big enough, with so many intermediate levels of managers, that some of them simply are no good. The manager may not know how to find out about any unsatisfactory performance on their part.

Family problems The final difficulty that arises for the small businessman at critical Stage II is that of family problems. The difficulty here can be capsulized: either the man, his wife, or his children have not managed to grow up with his income. It is not uncommon for the small businessman at the peak of his growth years to discover that he is making ten times what he had ever dreamed of, but that he is spending eleven times that amount, his wife thinks he is stingy, and he resents his "social obligations."

MAKING IT TO STAGE III

The foregoing may lead the reader to believe that it is almost impossible for the small business manager to pass successfully through Stage II of his organization's growth. In reality, many small businessmen easily cope with the problems enumerated and manage to enjoy the good life of the relatively stabilized small business. However, all that glitters is not gold, and, as in the other two stages of small business

---

3. H. O. Stekler, *Profitability and Size of Firm* (Berkeley: Institute of Business and Economic Research, University of California, 1963).

growth, the critical point arrives at Stage III when the small businessman must successfully overcome his problems or be absorbed by the giant organizations. Fortunately, however, the small businessman at this stage is no longer small, and he is far better equipped to fight giant industry than is the tiniest of the small businessmen. Ironically, however, it is not really the giants that cause him the trouble at this phase; rather, his main problems are created by other small businesses. Let's briefly evaluate these problems so that the aspiring small businessman may duly be forewarned as to what awaits him at the end of the road.

The greediness of others One problem that the small businessman must effectively cope with upon entry into the third stage in his organization's growth is the disloyalty of some of his divisional managers. If the businessman is successful in training his divisional managers to manage his small business, they will have learned to manage their own small business and may be induced to strike out on their own, leaving the small businessman holding the bag.[5]

New small businesses take markets This problem is partially an outgrowth of the first problem, but is nevertheless a singular problem in itself. If and when his divisional and departmental managers abandon ship, they usually end up in industries competitive with the business they have abandoned. When they do decide to take on the "old pro," they will do so in his most profitable lines because they know which ones are the most profitable.

The institutional toll Increasing overhead costs are a third nemesis of the larger business. These costs usually begin to mount when the small businessman feels the need for institutional advertising, "national" distribution, outlets, and so on. In fact, these costs are why real economies of scale never seem to be realized by the larger small-businesses, which one would theoretically expect.

4. *Managing the Small Business*, pp. 33-38.

The diminishing absolute rate of return The fourth problem of the small business in its plateau stage is that the rate of return on invested capital decreases. Innumerable studies attest to this fact, all of which add up to an "iron law" of small business ownership: once the small businessman has reached full bloom, a disproportionate and diminishing return on invested capital must be expected by the owner(s).[5]

Organization top-heavy with staff personnel Overstaffing, particularly at the middle-management levels, is a serious problem with most businesses in the United States, including larger small-businesses.[6] Furthermore, it appears that all businessmen at this stage of development seem to arrive at some point where they feel they must surround themselves with staff men who can "keep them informed." Obviously, such hired help are an expensive luxury and take a heavy toll on the newly-arrived small business' overhead.

The staff starts infighting As the business becomes top-heavy with staff personnel, most large small-businesses also experience a certain amount of infighting among personnel, which not only results in serious morale problems but sometimes causes vital breaks in their performance capabilities.

A full line causes some products to become unprofitable Growing businesses in the maturity stage must diversify in the products, or markets, or services they offer. This diversification, unfortunately, carries with it the inherent probability that some of these diversified lines

35

5. See, for example, *Profitability and Size of Firm*; Ralph C. Epstein, *Industrial Profits in the United States* (New York: National Bureau of Economic Research, 1934); William L. Crum, *Corporate Size and Earning Power* (Cambridge, Mass.: Harvard University Press, 1939); and Joseph Steindl, *Small and Big Business* (Oxford: Oxford University, Institute of Statistics, Monograph No. 1, 1945).

6. Charles Lupton, "Watch Your Management Weight," *Management of Personnel Quarterly*, I (Winter, 1962), pp. 11-17.

Lawrence L. Steinmetz

will fail, and, as Stekler[7] says, this creates a high probability that any given *marginal* project will actually yield a return which is lower than the previous *average* rate of return for the firm's other projects. This, of course, reduces the new rate of return realized by the business.

▰▰▰ There is no question that small businesses experience growing pains. The ability of the small businessman to cope with these pains will determine whether or not he will be successful. Unfortunately, however, he will never outgrow such pains and still be a small businessman. Therefore, those who undertake a venture thinking that all would be nice if he could stabilize his business at $2 million or

$10 million or $20 million may as well forget it. There will always be critical stages of growth for the small business.

Fortunately, these stages of growth arise only from success. Anyone who commits himself to managing a small business must recognize one irrefutable fact: the minute he commits himself, he is on the treadmill of forced growth, growth that requires his ability to change from an autocratic to a professional manager. Furthermore, there is no escape from this escalator unless he is willing to accept the demise of his small business and the probable loss of nearly 50 percent of his assets. On the other hand, the rewards for success are phenomenal and few successful small businessmen will fail to agree that it is the climbing of the stairs that is important, not the arrival at a plateau.

7. *Profitability and Size of Firm*, p. 82.

36

In sensory terms, one might say that people like Charlie Chaplin and Thomas A. Edison, though great artists, were scarcely print-oriented. In later life, Edison, while still in possession of his sight, switched to Braille as preferable to visual reading. . . . Charlie Chaplin was so deeply aware of the processes of his art that he frequently acted his scenes backwards, leaving it to the technicians to run them frontwards. Tony Schwartz, a sound designer, has a tape of Chaplin pronouncing words and phrases backwards. When the technicians reversed these sounds, they came out as ordinary speech.

—Marshall McLuhan and Quentin Fiore
War and Peace in the Global Village

STRATEGIC PLANNING IN THE SMALL BUSINESS

The procedure in three corporations

STEVEN C. WHEELWRIGHT

Mr. Wheelwright, a faculty member of the Harvard Business School, is spending the 1970-71 academic year at INSEAD (the International Institute of Business Administration) in Fontainebleau, France.

The importance and value of strategic planning is often discussed in management seminars and publications. However, few of the details of how a firm might approach the task of strategic planning have been investigated in a research setting. Taking the importance of strategy as given, this article considers some of the important characteristics of strategy and summarizes the findings of a recent research program on strategy at the Stanford Business School. The author then reports on the application of these research findings to three small but growing companies in order to develop strategies for them. Finally, the factors that should be considered, as a company develops its own approach to strategic planning, are summarized.

There are few industries in the world today where a company can achieve satisfactory profitability simply by meeting its competition head-on. This is particularly true for small, growth oriented firms; companies of this kind usually achieve success by developing an approach that gives them some competitive advantage in meeting the needs of the market. The development of such an approach, most often referred to as "a strategy," has been the subject of considerable discussion during recent years.

The reason for the tremendous interest in corporate strategy and strategic planning is twofold: first, managers realize that a good strategy greatly enhances the likelihood of a firm's success; second, a body of research results has been developed that can help a company to formulate a strategy and then evaluate it to determine how good it is.

Taking the importance of strategy as given, this article considers some of the important characteristics of strategy, summarizes the findings of a recent research program on strategy, reports on the application of these research findings to three small but growing companies in order to develop strategies for them, and finally summarizes those factors that should be considered as a company develops its own approach to strategic planning.

STEVEN C. WHEELWRIGHT

CHARACTERISTICS OF STRATEGY

The first aspect of corporate strategy that is of major importance is the identification of a set of criteria that can be used to evaluate a strategy. While the most accurate evaluation can be given only after the firm has followed a strategy for some time, this is of only minimal value to the firm planning a new strategy. What is needed is some method for evaluating corporate strategy before it is implemented.

The best approach available today for making such an evaluation is to use a set of questions regarding the strategy. A variety of questions have been suggested;[1] most of these relate to one of four basic areas:

How well does the strategy fit with corporate objectives and purposes?

How well does the strategy fit with the company's environment?

How well does the strategy fit with the company's resources?

How committed is the corporate management to the strategy?

Questions along the lines of the first three are based on the notion that a good strategy effectively matches the firm's resources with the opportunities and realities of the market in order to accomplish the goals of the firm. The assumption is that matching or fitting the strategy to the specific situation will result in a unique (differentiated) approach that will lead to the development of some kind of competitive advantage. The fourth question relates to how well (and how rapidly) the firm will be able to adopt the desired strategy, since the greater the commitment to the strategy, the more likely the company will follow it successfully.

A second aspect of strategy and strategic planning that is of major importance is the purpose it is to serve in a company. Since corporate situations vary widely, the role of strategic planning in the success of the firm also varies widely. At least three major purposes can be aided through the development of a strategy: the need for specialized skills and resources within the firm can be identified and defined; corporate activity can be focused and coordinated; and a standard can be established against which future performance can be compared.

RECENT RESEARCH

Identification of the specific purpose of strategy in a given firm is particularly important to the selection and development of an effective procedure for strategic planning. Recent literature on strategic planning has suggested a number of procedures that a firm might follow in preparing a strategy.[2] Since these procedures vary widely, one would expect that the resulting strategies would also vary.

In order to study the effect of various factors, especially the strategic planning procedure, on corporate strategy a program of research was carried out over a two-year period at the Stanford Graduate School of Business.[3] This research consisted of three phases.

---

1. See Edmund P. Learned and others, *Business Policy: Text and Cases* (Homewood, Ill.: Richard D. Irwin, Inc., 1965); George W. McKinney III, "An Experimental Study of the Effects of Systematic Approaches on Strategic Planning," unpublished Ph.D. dissertation, Stanford University Graduate School of Business, August, 1969; Seymour Tilles, "How to Evaluate Corporate Strategy," *Harvard Business Review*, XLI (July-August, 1963), pp. 111-21; and S. C. Wheelwright, "An Analysis of Strategic Planning as a Creative Problem Solving Process," unpublished Ph.D. dissertation, Stanford University Graduate School of Business, June, 1970.

2. See H. Igor Ansoff, *Corporate Strategy* (New York: McGraw-Hill Book Company, 1965); J. Thomas Cannon, *Business Strategy and Policy* (New York: Harcourt, Brace & World, Inc., 1968); Frank F. Gilmore and Richard G. Brandenburg, "Anatomy of Corporate Planning," *Harvard Business Review*, XL (November-December, 1962), pp. 61-69; Robert L. Katz, "Cases and Concepts in Corporate Strategy," Stanford University Graduate School of Business, unpublished, 1967; Robert F. Stewart, *A Framework for Business Planning* (Long-Range Planning Report No. 162; Menlo Park, Calif.: Stanford Research Institute, 1963); George A. Steiner, "Long-Range Planning: Concept and Implementation," *Financial Executive*, XXXIV (July, 1966), pp. 54-61.

The first phase of the program was strictly exploratory. Using two time-shared computer terminals, a number of business managers enrolled in the nine-week Stanford Executive Program (summer, 1968) were asked to use a computer program to help develop a strategy for a situation described in a business policy case. This interactive computer program acted like a consultant, probing the businessman (student) with questions to help him formulate and improve his strategy. The results of this part of the program showed that those who used the computer program developed much more creative and unusual strategies; in most cases, they felt that their strategies were improved significantly through use of the computer program.

Because the initial research was only exploratory, the second phase aimed at developing a controlled experiment that could effectively test the impact of an interactive computer program on strategies. This work, carried out by McKinney, not only tested a research methodology for examining some of the factors relevant to strategic planning, but also compared two complementary procedures for strategic planning recommended by Cannon.[4]

McKinney's work produced four major findings. *First,* it showed that the experimental methodology he devised was suitable for examining strategic planning. *Second,* by using the two procedures in sequence, as recommended by Cannon, students developed significantly better strategies than when using either of them separately. *Third,* the first procedure recommended by Cannon (referred to as opportunity oriented) led to better strategies than those developed without

A Model of Strategic Planning

following one of these set procedures. *Fourth,* the second procedure (referred to as tactically oriented) resulted in strategies that were inferior to those developed without following one of these set procedures.

Because the results of the second phase of the research showed that some procedures for strategic planning can be better than no set procedure and that some can be worse, it was decided that a natural third phase of the research program would be to examine at least two different procedures for strategic planning in more detail.[5] To help in identifying the important factors in this phase of the research, the simple model shown in the accompanying figure was developed. This model indicates that the final strategy depends not only on the procedure that is followed, but also on the strategic planner (his background, bias, and so on), the strategic task (the company's situation), and the general environment (the urgency and motivation for strategic planning, for example). While these factors overlap somewhat, they do present a scheme that is useful in designing research and in determining what type of approach would be best for a specific company to adopt.

The third phase of this research began by identifying two general classes of procedures for strategic planning—the synoptic and incremental. These two were chosen because a number of examples of each can readily be found in the strategic planning literature.

3. Henry B. Eyring, Edwin V. W. Zschau, George W. McKinney, and Steven C. Wheelwright, "Research in Methods for Formulating and Analyzing Changes in a Corporate Strategy: Progress Report No. 1, " Stanford University Graduate School of Business, unpublished, 1968; McKinney, "An Experimental Study of the Effects . . ."; and Wheelwright, "An Analysis of Strategic Planning . . . ."

4. McKinney, "An Experimental Study of the Effects . . ." Cannon, *Business Strategy and Policy.*

5. Wheelwright, "An Analysis of Strategic Planning . . . ."

STEVEN C. WHEELWRIGHT

Procedures that are synoptic in nature emphasize setting corporate objectives, generating a range of alternative strategies, and then using the stated objectives to evaluate these alternatives and select the best one. This type of procedure focuses on examining the entire range of possible strategies for the company and selecting the one that will best accomplish a stated set of objectives.[6]

Incremental procedures, on the other hand, generally consist of identifying the firm's existing strategy, examining the strengths and weaknesses of the firm, and the threats and opportunities of the environment (particularly competition), and then improving the existing strategy.[7] Thus the incremental approach does not seek a comprehensive analysis of alternative strategies as does the synoptic approach, nor does it involve explicit specification of corporate objectives at the outset.

The methodology used in testing these two classes of procedures was developed by McKinney.[8] The results of this phase of research were indeed striking. *First,* it was found that even though the strategies developed using the synoptic approach were more creative (distinctive) than those developed using the incremental approach, the incremental prepared strategies were better—over-all—than those prepared with the synoptic procedure. *Second,* it was found that the strategic planner, the strategic task, and the environment in which the planning took place each had an impact on the relative effectiveness of the synoptic and incremental procedures for preparing strategy.

Those planners who were "quantitative" in their general problem solving orientation (such as engineers and mathematicians) preferred the synoptic approach and thought it was most effective. Planners who were "nonquantitative" preferred the incremental approach.

Three different strategic planning tasks (three different corporate situations) were assigned. The company that was most successful and could follow a wide range of alternatives was handled best by planners using the synoptic approach; the company with the least amount of flexibility in its options was handled best by planners using the incremental approach.

The two aspects of the general planning environment that were examined were the motivation for planning and possible carry-over effects from the synoptic to the incremental approach. It was found that planning done in a supportive atmosphere, produced a much better strategy than planning in a nonsupportive atmosphere. There was no carry-over effect, indicating that using the synoptic and then the incremental approach is generally no better than using the incremental approach alone.

Since the results of this three-phase research program were very significant, the researchers felt the need to interpret these findings in terms of how they might apply to the practicing manager. This was one by helping three small, growth oriented firms to each develop a procedure for strategic planning and a strategy through application of these experimental results. (This was not a controlled experiment; it was simply an attempt to apply what had been learned.)

6. Alan R. Eagle, *Analytical Approaches in Planning* (Long-Range Planning Report No. 238; Menlo Park, Calif.: Stanford Research Institute, 1965); Ansoff, *Corporate Strategy;* Cannon, *Business Strategy and Policy,* and Steiner, "Long-Range Planning . . . ."

7. Robert L. Katz, "Cases and Concepts in Corporate Strategy," Stanford University Graduate School of Business, unpublished, 1967; Edmund P. Learned and others, *Business Policy: Text and Cases* (Homewood, Ill.: Richard D. Irwin, Inc., 1965); Robert F. Stewart, *A Framework for Business Planning* (Long-Range Planning Report No. 162; Menlo Park, Calif.): "Organized Entrepreneurship: a Network of Tasks That Produce a Coherent Chain of Reasoning," Stanford Research Institute, unpublished, 1969; and Eyring and others, "Research in Methods . . . ."

8. McKinney, "An Experimental Study . . . ."

STRATEGY IN THREE FIRMS

The three companies in which these results were implemented included a new enterprise in the computer peripheral equipment industry, a prominent firm in the urban planning field, and a well-established firm in the yearbook printing industry. Each of these will be discussed in turn by first describing the firm's situation in terms of the factors identified in the figure, then describing the procedure for strategic planning that was used in each situation, and, finally, reviewing the effectiveness of each of these.

Computer Peripheral Company (Company A)

This company was in its first year of operation at the time the author became involved in the development of a procedure for strategic planning. The company had been started by two "quantitatively" oriented members of a graduate business school faculty who were interested in meeting some of the needs of the unsophisticated users of computers. Thus the orientation of those involved in strategic planning for this firm was quantitative.

In terms of the general environment, the principals in the company were well aware of the need for developing a strategy to guide them in decision making, especially since they did not yet have an established set of operating procedures which could serve as a basis for most of their short-term decisions. The strategic task facing this company was indeed mixed in nature, since its managers could follow a wide range of alternative strategies; the risk of corporate failure, however, was very high because of the competitive nature of the industry.

The first steps taken by Company A in developing a procedure for strategic planning were essentially synoptic in nature. They focused on trying to state a set of objectives for the firm and formulating some alternative decide what some of the subparts of the strategy would be, strategies that could accomplish these objectives. While several ideas were generated during this phase, it soon became apparent that the range of alternatives had to be narrowed considerably in order to move forward in the strategic planning process.

This narrowing was achieved, first, by using the objectives to determine what alternatives were acceptable. Second, pressing problems were examined to decide what some of the subparts of the strategy would be, for example, what type of production facility to have, what type of marketing sales force to employ, and so on. The approach of making decisions on a subject of a strategy before the composite strategy has been stated would normally be risky, since it could easily lead to suboptimization in one area that would not fit into the over-all strategy at some later point in time. This did not seem to be a major problem in this case, however, because the company had examined a range of alternatives and these were still fresh in their minds as they began to make these decisions.

In the case of Company A, the major focus of the strategic planning process (after the initial search for alternatives) was the development of a strategic plan that could serve as a guide to action. This purpose was effectively accomplished in initiating the subparts of the strategy in such a way that they could be a guide in making the important decisions that the company faced.

Urban Planning Firm (Company B)

Unlike Company A, the urban planning company that was involved in this study had been operating for about eight years and enjoyed a solid reputation in the urban planning market. The firm had been built around the abilities of two men, each recognized in the industry for his skill in architectural design and urban planning. The president of the firm, who was professionally the better known of the two founders, was definitely "qualitative" in his approach, but had been very successful in his handling of the company's financial affairs, as well as in directing several of their consulting projects.

Company B had grown rapidly during the two years preceding this study and was close to doing $1 million in annual sales. The general environment was one in which strategy was little known in the terms

STEVEN C. WHEELWRIGHT

generally used in business. The firm chose to focus on strategic planning at this point because their recent growth had fully utilized their existing financial resources, and they recognized that they would either have to severely limit their growth or look for other financing. The second alternative would obviously commit the founders to staying with the company for some years, and they were not certain they wanted to make such a commitment.

The strategic task facing the company provided a wide range of alternatives, each of which appeared likely to be successful, but each of which would leave the founders in a very different position in three to five years. Thus personal objectives were extremely important in the selection of a strategy for the company.

The first step in the strategic planning process was to specify a suitable set of objectives for the firm, which the principals could agree on. The background of the planners seemed to suggest that an incremental approach would be best. However, a synoptic approach (starting with objectives) was used because of the importance of objectives in this situation and because the firm recognized the need for a major decision on strategy rather than a mere modification of existing strategy.

The firm identified a number of important objectives during this first phase; these were grouped into four areas so that the impact of various strategies on them could be more easily evaluated. It was particularly important at this stage of the planning to keep the process moving so that it would not get bogged down in attempts to resolve minor difference in the objectives.

Once the relevant objectives had been identified, it was possible to evaluate and compare a number of alternative strategies in terms of how well they accomplished the four major objectives. After some lengthy discussion and additional investigations, the company was able to agree on a strategy that would meet the majority of the firm's objec-

tives without overly constraining the principals who were involved.

Thus the major focus of strategic planning in Company B was to select a strategy which would ensure the continued success of the firm and be acceptable to the two founders of the company. Finding such a strategy was of critical importance in order to get the commitment of the entire firm to that strategy so that it could be effectively followed, and so that the decisions that were to be made in the next several months would be made in a consistent manner.

Printing Company (Company C)

The third company for which a strategy was developed as a part of this study was a family-owned printing firm. This company had originally been founded by two brothers. For approximately twenty years, the older brother had been president and in charge of sales, and the younger brother had been in charge of production.

About three years before the study was made, the older brother left the firm (selling his half to his brother) to become an administrator in a nearby university. Thus the younger brother suddenly became president and owner of the entire company. This man was knowledgeable in the production aspects of the business and systematic in his analysis of problems, but he felt somewhat unsure of himself in the sales area and as chief executive.

The company was quite aware of technological advancements being made in the industry and anxious to take advantage of them. The firm enjoyed a good reputation for quality in their geographical region, but had recently felt their position slipping somewhat as other firms seemed to be advancing more rapidly than they were. The management team (composed of five people) seemed to be convinced of the need for strategic planning but were uncertain of the procedure they should follow.

In terms of the strategic task involved, the company was anxious to maintain its position of prominence. There appeared to be at least two or three alternative strategies they could follow in order to do that. It was apparent from the start that a major shift in strategy did not seem feasible or attractive; rather, what was needed was a sharpening of strategy and a rounding out of some of the areas overlooked in the past.

An incremental approach to strategic planning appeared to be the most appropriate. Therefore, the first step was to examine what the company's strategy had been in the past. The management team of Company C spent three days (away from the office) examining their strengths and weaknesses, and the opportunities and challenges in the environment. Eventually, the team came up with a revised strategy. This strategy was stated both in simple prose and as a series of actions that were to be taken. Since many of these actions were spread out over time and since it was felt that other actions would have to be added as the strategy was adopted, the management team decided to hold a monthly planning meeting to evaluate their progress in implementing the strategy and to define these additional actions.

Thus in Company C, the major purpose of the strategy was to strengthen the corporation's position by focusing management attention on those actions required to implement the strategy. In addition, management was provided with a broader base on which to relate its many day-to-day decisions.

THE PLANNING PROCEDURE

A general approach for selecting and implementing a strategic planning procedure in a firm can now be suggested. Because of the complexity of most situations, the exact planning procedure that will work best is difficult if not impossible to specify beforehand. Nevertheless, it is possible to suggest some guidelines that will usually lead to the utilization of an effective procedure.

Important Variables in Strategic Planning

The planners

Their background

Their orientation in problem-solving situations

Their roles in the company (managers, professionals, owners, and so on)

The environment

The factors prompting the development of a strategy

The motivation of the planners

The urgency in completing the task

The strategic situation

The range of alternatives available to the company

The company's current competitive position

The range of alternatives the company might be willing to consider.

The first step in selecting a strategic planning procedure is to specify and define the three major variables that are relevant: the planners, the environment, and the strategic situation. Some of the factors that are important to each of these variables are listed in the accompanying table.

The second step in selecting a procedure is to identify the major purpose of strategic planning within the firm in question. The most common purposes are to:

Develop a strategy that will lead the firm to a strong competitive position

Focus and coordinate corporate activity on those areas that are most important

Establish criteria that can be used to guide decision making and to evaluate performance.

Rather than merely saying that all of these purposes are important in a specific situation (which would be of little value in selecting a planning procedure), it is important to state the one main objective of strategic planning in the situation in question.

Once the above two steps have been taken, the strategic planning procedure can be selected. The aim is to select a procedure somewhere between the incremental and the synoptic that will fit the company involved and will best help its managers to achieve their purpose.

STEVEN C. WHEELWRIGHT

Once a procedure has been selected, the major task of implementing it can be undertaken. The first phase of implementation is to assign responsibility for preparing, recording, and communicating the corporate strategy to the appropriate members of the management team. Obviously, the chief executive officer must take over-all responsibility for strategic planning.

The second phase is to start the task of strategic planning and to keep moving. This requires keeping the major purpose in mind so that if things start to slow down on a minor point, the chief executive can get them moving onto a more important part of the task. Staying on the move also requires that the planners be somwhat flexible in the procedure they are following so that, as unforeseen difficulties arise, they can make the necessary adjustments.

The final phase of strategic planning is to get the strategy in written form so that it can be communicated to others and easily be referred to. The plan is not complete until it is in writing.

In order to ensure that the company adopts the strategy which it develops, it is important that the written strategy be translated into a series of specific actions so that the completion of these actions can be measured. This evaluation of adoption of the strategy will be most effective if the firm establishes a series of periodic planning meetings (monthly or quarterly) to review progress in the adoption of the strategy and to solve special problems as they may arise.

The importance and value of strategic planning is often discussed in management seminars and publications. However, few of the details of how a firm might approach the task of strategic planning have been investigated in a research setting. This article describes how the recent program of research on strategic planning conducted at the Stanford Business School has been related to three corporate situations. The procedures used in these three situations and the general approach for selecting and implementing a strategic planning procedure are intended to help the small, growth oriented firm achieve satisfactory profitability.

TWO IDEAS ON EXECUTIVE DEVELOPMENT IN SMALLER BUSINESS

By A.A. Imberman

One of the popular ideas being generated among smaller business presidents today is the notion that if department heads are brought together regularly to deal with company problems, the resultant clarification of ideas will lead to more fruitful planning and better company policies.

Together with this notion is another idea: if various types of executives — good, bad or indifferent — are brought together in such group meetings to exchange ideas, such men would be improved by the process.

I would like to suggest — in the light of my long association as a teacher and as a consultant to smaller businessmen — that these two notions may not be true, and that it may be hazardous, indeed, to embark upon such a method without careful thought.

To evaluate this method — which I would like to call the Group Decision Method — one must look at executives first, since the advice of department heads in a weekly conference would be no better than the executives themselves. What kind of executives attend these weekly meetings, and what do they have to contribute?

A company that manufactures widgets has a management staff composed of three kinds of executives: a production chief, a sales manager and a financial man.

PRODUCTION EXECUTIVES

Let us look at the production people first. The production executive is mainly engineering-oriented. He is engaged in setting up production plans, quality controls, tooling plans and machines, in model-making, etc. Usually he is an executive engineer — he initiates action, coordinates work, supervises and delegates, and he reports this to other men of broader responsibility.

Production-minded executives usually perceive the world as a complex but mechanistically patterned place. The ambition of the production-minded executive is to understand and thus to manipulate the patterns, to bring about changes in the order and position of things. He is a "realist" in a special sense. He is fact-oriented and does not readily believe that words or feelings are facts. He is prone to restrict his attention to the observable fact, and he has a very real tendency to regard people as complicated machines that differ from his tools primarily in two ways — they are harder to renovate and they may cause some trouble through the union.

Making decisions is usually not difficult for the production executive. When he has assembled the facts, the decision follows in an orderly way. Most often he knows where to find the facts, and which ones to exclude, or if he doesn't, he can test them. Handling his work in the same way, he delegates and supervises in an orderly way, looking at production figures, testing excellence of work, and reasonableness in his subordinates. He is likely to be strong in his authority.

Toward his superiors, he is businesslike, respecting their knowledge (it is easier if they share his scientific or engineering interest) and accepting his tasks as a unit of a larger job. He wants to learn from his superiors, and to be respected as a professional person. He wants differences to be settled with real facts — he is often at a loss when they cannot be. He sees production as central to company goals, and production should be protected.

His company goals are usually quite concrete — to design a machine that will speed up or increase accuracy in a certain operation, to convert to non-human form some previously human activity (e.g., mechanizing some hand operation), to rearrange a production unit for less movement of parts and supplies, etc.

Unfortunately, the production executive also has to deal with people. He meets with colleagues who understand him very clearly, but do not operate as they should — they make mistakes, ignore specifications, restrict output, play politics, and consider him too big for his britches. To the extent that he is able to do so, the production executive usually handles such problems by insisting on "facts" and orderly performance. Consequently, the work of being a production executive is most likely to stimulate conservatism and inflexibility in dealing with life. In a management conference, he insists on facts — and only facts. He is not apt to be influenced by any grandiose visions of company expansion not solidly grounded on facts. And the facts must be verifiable.

SALES EXECUTIVES

Is the production-minded executive different from the sales executive in the same firm? The sales executive — either directly on the firing line or on the management staff — is mainly a salesman at heart, with administrative duties in addition. The sales executive's ambition is often competitive in its composition; his self-esteem is fed by knowing that he does something better than other people do, and by knowing that, he is the dominant person in direct contacts. He is prone to see the world as a place filled with *people* (rather than facts), and the world is provided with a variety of objects that can be traded and sold, contributing to the pleasure and welfare of people.

He is impressed with the importance of influencing people, with the vagaries and whimsies demonstrated by the human being, and by the certainty with which people will succumb to persuasiveness or exemplary conduct.

Formal procedures (so valued by the production executives) are primarily tolerated by the sales executive as a useful way of keeping the background in order, but only in order that the essential activity of dealing with people can be fully attended to. The sales executive thinks accumulating and distributing merchandise important. He thinks designing and producing are important. But neither of these is important enough to absorb his entire energies. Anything that is non-human cannot absorb the full interest of the sales executive.

The real stuff of this world — as far as the sales-minded executive is concerned — is people. And he thinks of his work and of his company as a way of dealing with people — constructively, profitably, and satisfyingly. He is concerned with efficiency in distribution and service, with production keeping up with his needs (and suitably dying down when consumer activity declines), with providing plant facilities, keeping the clerks from quarreling with customers, with accounting and inventories, etc. But these activities are looked at as secondary or subsidiary to *his* goal. More important to him is to achieve a realistic evaluation of people — seeing them dispassionately but acutely, learning more and more about how to judge their motives, characters, and the implications of their behavior, so that he can sell his merchandise.

In his work, the sales-minded executive is oriented toward a considerable amount of autonomy, and is likely to be resentful of close supervision that is highly directive. Dealing with people is still an art, and the man who makes people his business expects to be given leeway to pursue his style and talent. He expects his superiors to help him develop and to give him opportunity to perfect his skill. He respects them for their personal characteristics, and for their proven capacities to handle other people.

He usually comes to the conclusion that a great part of executive work lies in making decisions, and he is likely to make a decision at the drop of a hat. Assertiveness, leadership, salesmanship, and decisiveness are all rolled into one neat package, often called "the positive approach." Decisiveness is often overdone in these executives in distribution and sales. As a result, their errors are more numerous than those of the production-minded executive.

Over a period of years, the sales and distribution executive is likely to become something of a "risk-taker." With experience in his field, he is impressed with the potency of the unforeseen and the uncontrollable. He therefore places greater emphasis on his hunches, on feelings that this or that *will happen* — and some very great (and some very mistaken) predictions have been made by leaders in this field of management. Systematic risk is the order of his life, so that he most nearly fulfills Barnard's statement that the job of an executive is "to make decisions about matters he knows nothing about." In contrast to the production-minded executive, who usually becomes more confident, the sales-minded executive is likely to become surer of uncertainty.

In the management conference, the sales-minded executive is more interested in the future than the past, and more interested in what can be done than in what has been done. He is more optimistic about growth and expansion than the production-minded executive, and is often not deterred or discouraged by facts. His hunches and experience are to him better guides.

FINANCIAL EXECUTIVES

Now what about our third type — the financial executive? The financial executive is more like the production executive than the sales executive. Finance proceeds in an extremely exacting way. There is no function in our society that is so regulated, or so resistant to revolutionary change. The product handled by financial executives — money — is expected to be handled with 100% accuracy at all times (even engineers are allowed a "tolerance" for mismeasurement). Finance is the only field in which honesty is required by law. The company hands its more cherished function to the gentlemen in the treasurer's office, and in the credit and accounting departments, and then watches these gentlemen with a jaundiced eye.

The financial executives who find satisfaction and opportunity for self-expression within this structure are quite homogeneous. Among the executives, the financial men find a consistent interest in status and in titles. They keep a considerable distance from other people, and are more certain about what's right and what's wrong. Most of the executives in a treasurer's office are serious men; the world is an arduous place, and life is earnest. They view work as a technical affair, to be handled by rules and regulations, to be dispatched concisely and immediately. Their world is numbers — not facts, as with the production executive, not people as with the sales executive, but numbers that can be added and subtracted and shown on a balance sheet or on a credit report.

The financial executive in a treasurer's office, in credit and collections, in accounting, etc., prefers to work in a business-like way with supervisors, and not to be drawn into personal relationships that might call for loyalty and extra curricular duties. He wants a superior who is competent, who keeps the lines of communication open, who works in an orderly movement, who knows what to ask for and what to expect.

Most of the financial men accept the policies of the company and its prescribed methods without question. Indeed, they would not know quite what to do if the company did not make clear the order of the work. Their own goals and their own habits of solving problems are likely to be unformulated. Left to their own devices, these men often mull over a *non-financial* question without being able to define it precisely or to come to a definitive conclusion. They know they want constructive work, they want to be useful and productive — but they are usually uncertain of how to go about it until they have been taught specific techniques in a concrete job. Most of their academic schooling is devoted to a study of specific techniques.

Once they are trained, they are likely to be inflexible about following the directions. Some are out-and-out rigid — insensitive to new ideas, resistant to changing interpretations or methods. The financial executive is likely to be conservative when he starts, but will accept a broader viewpoint only if his sphere of knowledge and range of judgment are radically enlarged.

Making decisions for the financial executive might be called an "all or none" proposition. When the methods and goals are clearly established, and the problem is financial, he is quick and terse in coming to conclusions. When the methods and goals are not clearly established, he is likely to "wool-gather" and to over-think without being able to decide. He may cling only to one opinion, over and over again, or he may get lost trying to make up his mind which of the many *non-financial* possibilities is the right one. He often loses sight of the major problem as he explores the details of minor, subsidiary goals.

Working in finance, credits or accounting will develop his confidence and his speed in handling concrete problems. He often develops striking efficiency at collecting data and reaching conclusions of "yes" or "no," of handling this snarl this way, expediting that matter that way.

PRESIDENT'S PROBLEM

What does all this mean to a company president? If he endeavors to put in practice the group decision method, he will call his department heads for weekly meetings and there is an exchange of ideas from which planning and policy follow.

If one were to peek over the transom to see what actually goes on at many of the group decision committee meetings, one might go away with something far from the idyllic picture painted by proponents of the technique. While it is assumed that a group of executives will come to a better decision than any one individual alone, in many cases we find that a group decision often is a compromise between different points of view, or between conflicting personalities. A group decision may not represent the best solution to a problem, no more than a public election always elects the best candidate.

In many other instances, the group often grapples with problems outside their areas of knowledge and prejudice. In many such cases they are not even aware of their bias and of the limitations of their knowledge, so they do not know when to turn to experts. For example, we find company executives coming together to determine what ought to be the best line to follow in a forthcoming advertising campaign. But the personnel director has no interest or knowledge of the problem, the production chief is indifferent; the treasurer is interested only in the cost. Can a group decision based on such reasons be more effective than a decision reached by the sales manager, the ad agency and the president?

Of course, group decisions are sometimes better than any individual decision. For example, group discussion of a problem in an area in which all participants are competent, or a group of specialists trying to cooperate on a problem, often leads to solutions better and faster than any one alone would produce. The interchange of ideas, the stimulation of discussion is one fruitful road to problem solving. But this only occurs where the individuals are absorbed in working out a solution, not in sparring among themselves.

In some situations the group process results in the avoidance of decision. In many committee meetings, the participants feel no compulsion to bring things to a conclusion. Some executives substitute words for action, and sometimes confuse one with the other. They attend meetings, they discuss, they go away, with no feeling that they have further responsibility. The real decision is left for the other fellow — in the last analysis, the president. In some companies there seems to be an endless succession of such meetings, leaving the executives feeling bored and frustrated, often wishing that the boss would go ahead and decide without so much talk.

The growth of the entire field of human relations has demonstrated the value of stimulating men through positive and cooperative motives. Committee management has the strong appeal to Americans because it appears to be eminently democratic, giving voice and consideration to men below the top level.

This very appeal makes it difficult to evaluate the group decision method. If one brings its disadvantages to the fore, there is the danger of seeming to favor autocratic, overbearing management techniques. If one argues for group management, there is likely to be a "do-good" quality in the arguments, which makes the listener less critical.

There is no doubt that business executives have learned a great deal from the group decision technique. It is an important and valuable tool of management, one well worth learning how and when to use.

But it is still only a *technique* of management. It does not replace the need for executive judgment, and it cannot displace the responsibility that falls on the top executive. Unless the members of management have good judgment individually, the group techniques cannot endow them with a wisdom they did not possess before.

By and large there is no substitute for sound and seasoned judgment, for conclusions that are based on knowledge, and for forward planning that is based on distilled experience. If the president of a company doesn't have those, then a management committee will not be able to save his hide. Management committees, however, can save wear and tear on his temperament, can save his time by amassing facts and making recommendations, and can generally serve as his right arm. But the management committee can't serve as his heart and brain.

BROADER EXECUTIVES

What *can* save a president's heart and brain are executives who have broadened *their own* knowledge so that they can contribute to the problems of other departments in their company.

There is no way, for example, in which a production boss can learn to make decisions in the area of finance, or sales, if he has had little practice grappling with such problems. The same applies to sales executives and financial officers in dealing with problems outside their departments. In short, the top man in a small business must seek some way of broadening the knowledge and experience of his executives, if he expects them to be able to contribute to each other, and to management, in decision conferences.

Short of literal experience, there is no other way of acquiring this knowledge except by schooling. But it has to be schooling of a certain kind. It cannot be schooling devoted simply to studying principles. The schooling must involve a liberal dash of case work — where participants are confronted with a variety of problems and asked to provide solutions.

At the Illinois Institute of Technology, where I have directed the Management Seminar for Smaller Business for many years, we go further. In addition to case work, we bring in the top executive of a major company every week to discuss some aspect of his company operation — in short, to serve as a living case. The facts are laid out, the problem discussed, the solutions attempted — and the outcome frankly unveiled. Sometimes the outcome is a bust. One executive regaled the class last year with an account of his company's plunge into a new marketing program on a product. In addition to winning three awards for package design, etc., after $300,000 expenditure the company concluded the endeavor was a mistake. The reasons were discussed in class.

Several universities have endeavored to follow this pattern where case studies are supplemented by executive accounts of company actions. But even where the latter are unavailable, merely the case studies by themselves have value in training sales managers to understand financial problems, training production chiefs to understand sales problems, and training financial officers to grapple with sales and production data.

It is only when small business executives are broadened in this fashion that their contribution to group decisions has merit. When such enlightenment is accomplished, it cannot be measured in dollars. But it can be measured in company growth and increased strength.

CHAPTER 6
THE MATURITY CRISIS

The business has now reached a level of maturity that presents new challenges to the entrepreneurial management team. Since the initial start-up, the firm has changed from having an almost complete concern for the production and marketing of a product to a more people oriented, professionally managed and more risk averse organization. If the entrepreneur-founder is still with the business, then he also will have changed — most noticeably from an autonomous leader to a delegating manager. He will have learned to work from reports and meetings, rather than from direct day-to-day interaction with marketing, production, and financial personnel.

The entrepreneur faces many difficult personal choices during the maturity phase of the business. If a successor to the business must be found, then he must prepare a plan for the non-interruptive transfer of his duties during the maturity crisis. If he is either not competent as an executive, or finds his motivational needs unfilled, then he is likely to sell his interest in the business and start a new venture. May I suggest the reader refer back to section one, Who is the Entrepreneur?, for the article reprinted from Forbes, entitled "The Incurables." Fairchild and Lear, two of America's premier entrepreneurs, chose to remain as active business starters rather than live through the maturity and transition phases of business.

It is during this maturity stage that business firms will outgrow their ability to generate sufficient cash from internal operations to finance expansion in plant and equipment, or development of new products, or the addition of new markets — some or all of which may be required to meet major competitive forces or increased consumer demand. Several alternatives exist for securing this financing, each having its advantages and disadvantages. There can be the outright sale of the firm, resulting in the entrepreneur becoming either an employee of the purchasing firm or unemployed. Alternatively, a merger may enable the entrepreneur to retain some control over the combined business while providing the necessary capital and resources for expansion required to meet the new company's business objectives. But the merger transaction may be difficult to complete, especially if the company's stock is closely held and not readily marketable.

A public stock offering has many advantages if it has been successfully completed before the maturity crisis. One advantage is that the market value of the firm will be clearly established, enabling a realizable value to be placed on the stockholder's investment. Establishing the liquidity of the stock will also make any future acquisitions or mergers a more viable alternative to expansion, especially for the small high growth company. A successful stock placement will bring an influx of capital; however, the entrepreneur must trade-off some control over the destiny of his business for this new capital.

Auren Uris provides insight into the roles entrepreneurs play and how they are differentiated from other business executives. For the prospective entrepreneur who has an innovative idea, situational factors may influence his decision to actually start the business venture. Germane to the situation are the risks in divulging the idea to another company, the employability of the individual (ie., health problems), the relationship of the intended business to a previous hobby, prior specialized experience, and the need for money.

Uris presents certain personal traits that further differentiate the entrepreneur from the organization man. The data is from a study by Collin and Moore of over a hundred small manufacturers in the midwest (published in their classic book: The Enterprising Man, University of Michigan, 1958).[1] In this pioneering study, entrepreneurs are seen as rebels, self-made, highly driven, and creative men. The entrepreneur appears to shed the route of formal education and instead prefers the immersion in real life experiences which encompass people interactions and pressure situations with few constraints. Organization men are generally more highly trained and more role directed, according to Uris.

What is particularly important in describing the entrepreneur's philosophy is the data on the entrepreneur's perception of his place in his environment. Essentially, he sees himself as an integrator of talented people to aid in furthering his objectives by exploiting his idea. The executive is more of a user of men and this skill is the ingredient which aids his rise up the corporate ladder.

A business doesn't get started by itself. It is the entrepreneur who takes the risks and is willing to face devastating failure. Failure to the company executive, according to Uris, may mean little more than locating a new job, perhaps at an even higher salary. The organization man is usually preconditioned by his social contacts — or interested only in a specific field, and therefore is not affected by such factors. Not so for the entrepreneur, claims Uris. In a book entitled, Executive Breakthrough (Doubleday & Co., 1967 Uris), devotes a chapter to "Entrepreneur versus Organization Man." The differences and similarities between internal and external entrepreneurs are spelled out clearly by Uris. Looking at 21 people who have made it to the top, he contrasts executive motivation and involvement in big and small companies.

The next three articles by Golde, Gallagher, and Gilmore offer insight into the planning process. Each presents the issue from a different viewpoint. All three articles taken together can have considerable value to a manager of either a large or small company. Planning is now the necessary skill to manage a mature business. Those that do it well succeed, those that don't are never able to control the business.

The successful entrepreneur will be able to shift his leadership styles to match the changing skills required at various stages of the company's life cycle. The article by Lawrence Steinmetz presents a business growth model to analyze the three crisis phases of development. Using the conventional "S" curve, Steinmetz takes the reader through the slow start-up stage, involving direct involvement of the entrepreneur in every facet of the business; to the high growth stage, involving the transformation of the entrepreneur into a manager; and to the final maturity stage, where the entrepreneur-manager has divested himself from direct operating control. Each of these stages ends in a crisis involving personnel, expansion, competition, operating and profitability problems.

The first stage ends with the entrepreneur faced with an over-burdening work load. Steinmetz's second stage crisis results from an excessive business overhead growth, power plays in the organization and production problems. At the last critical stage, significant competitive forces exist, the rate of return on invested capital decreases, unprofitable products exist, and large amounts of capital resources are needed for national expansion. If the owner-founder is to remain in control of his

company, his actions must be managerially and administratively effective throughout these three crisis stages, according to Steinmetz.

During the second and third stages of the business growth cycle, new products must be ready for replacing those which no longer contribute appreciably to profit, or for diversification of the existing product line. Small businesses fail to develop products that are based on advanced technology during this initial phase according to Steinmetz. Barriers are thought to exist which prevent small companies from pursuing this potentially rewarding and less competitive type of high risk involvement. Most product innovation in small companies evolves from present or known levels of technology.

Informal planning by the entrepreneur may omit major factors affecting the growth of the business — omissions which in some cases may result in a business failure. A more formalized and comprehensive examination of the company and its environment is required to minimize these unnecessary risks. The need for product development and organizational, marketing and financial changes in the company should come as no surprise if sufficient forethought is being given to the firm's operations. The last two articles present a discussion by George Steiner and Steven Wheelwright on approaches the small businessman can use to do long and medium range planning.

How, other than through a systematic planning process, will the entrepreneur be able to take advantage of all profitable opportunities which may occur in the future while avoiding major crises in the business? He must strategically plan to effectively achieve future company goals and objectives. What resources are available to the firm to handle these growth crises? How will changes in the future environment influence the firm? What will be required to meet future product promotion and distribution goals to take advantage of market opportunities? Steiner presents a conceptual model depicting the steps in the business plan for implementing and monitoring the actual operating procedures to help the entrepreneur get started in the planning process.

Identifying strengths and weaknesses of the business; noting anticipated changes in the company's objectives and resulting changes in the corporate strategy; determining return on investment; and preparing cash flow analysis and pro forma financial statements are a few of the planning procedures that Steiner suggests. To

ensure that the value from the planning process
exceeds the planning costs Steiner concludes
that planning tasks should be minimized to satisfy
the entrepreneur's situational needs. Steven
Wheelwright's article articulates these same issues
for three small but growing firms. His paper grew
out of work being done at the Stanford Business
School.

[1] Updated in their second book "The Organization Makers" --
University of Michigan, Ann Arbor, 1970.

THE USE OF ACCOUNTING TECHNIQUES IN SMALL FIRMS

There Are Still Chief Accountants Who Disclaim Even An Awareness Of Cost-Volume-Profit Analysis, Operating Budgets, And Responsibility Accounting

By Gardner M. Jones and
    Saber A. Awad

This article reports the findings of an inquiry into the use of contemporary accounting techniques by small and medium sized manufacturing firms. The authors investigated the extent to which these firms accepted eight specific accounting techniques, the various characteristics of the firms, characteristics of the accountants employed by the firms, the "agents of change" who were able to introduce new techniques, and finally, the role of consultants in introducing accounting changes in these firms.

The survey was made during 1970 and consisted of in-depth interviews with the chief accounting officers of 35 small manufacturing firms located throughout Michigan. The firms represented a variety of industries, including eight producers of durable goods and five of nondurable goods. Because there are many different definitions of "size of firm," they were classified in five different ways. When the five size definitions were combined, a composite measure of size produced 25 of "small" and 10 "medium" sized firms. (See Exhibit 1.)

The accountants interviewed were usually heads of the accounting function. As was expected, there was no uniformity of titles or of assigned duties, although the titles of treasurer and of controller do predominate. The various characteristics of these individuals are shown below. These characteristics are significant, where relationships between age, and educational development correlate with activity in introducing "new" accounting techniques into the subject organizations.

Titles
V-P Finance	2
Treasurer	6
Treasurer and Controller	2
Secretary-Treasurer	4
Secretary	1
Controller (or Ass't. to)	16
Chief Accountant	4
	35

Education
Less than H. S. diploma	1
H. S. & Junior College	6
B.A. or B.S. in Business	17
B.A. or B.S. plus M.B.A.	10
Other	1
	35

Service in Firm
Under 2 years	6
2-4 years	15
5-9 years	9
10 and over	5
	35

Professional Affiliation
NAA	9
AICPA	14
NAA and AICPA	11
None	1
	35

Ages
Under 35	8
35-39	6
40-44	7
45-49	7
50 and up	7
	35

G. M. JONES

Lansing *Chapter* (Baton Rouge 1955) *is Professor of Accounting at Michigan State University. Dr. Jones, who holds B.B.A. and M.B.A. degrees from the University of Michigan and a Ph.D. degree from Louisiana State University, is a previous contributor to* MANAGEMENT ACCOUNTING.

S. A. AWAD

Is a University Faculty Member in the United Arab Republic. He completed his doctorate at Michigan State University.

Techniques Investigated

The techniques investigated included "planning" techniques such as cost-volume-profit analysis, capital budgeting, linear programming and network analysis; "control" techniques such as standard costing, contribution margin analysis, and responsibility accounting; and operating budgeting which serves equally well for planning and control. Of the eight techniques, linear programming was selected to be a surrogate for the whole class of operations research techniques; if an accountant is familiar with any of them, he is familiar with linear programming; if he does not know linear programming, he probably does not know any of them.

"The average company used only three of the eight techniques."

Findings Of The Study

EXTENT OF APPLICATION. Among the small and medium sized manufacturing firms, modern management accounting techniques are not as widely used as one might expect. The average company used only three of the eight techniques. No company used all of them, and only one used as many as seven of them. Two companies used none at all. The extent to which the eight techniques were used is as follows:

	Number of firms	Percent of sample
Operating budgeting	22	63%
Capital budgeting	20	57%
Standard costing	19	54%
Cost-volume-profit analysis	18	51%
Contribution margin analysis	10	29%
Responsibility accounting	10	29%
Network analysis (PERT/CPM)	6	17%
Linear programming	1	3%

ENVIRONMENTAL CONDITIONS UNDERLYING NON-USE. When the respondents were questioned as to why their firms did not use some of these accounting methods, the replies ranged all the way from managements' perceptions of what a management accounting system is supposed to do, to the accountants' own qualifications, to the cost of doing detailed analysis, to organizational resistance to change. Exhibit 2 is a breakdown of reasons given by respondents.

Surprisingly, the size of the firm bore no statistically significant relationship to the number of accounting techniques used. Although accountants themselves sometimes said "our company is too small to use such a sophisticated technique," evidence of such use did exist in smaller companies. The only exception was standard cost, where size did have a bearing on use.

NATURE OF OPERATIONS. Another sometimes mentioned reason, for non-use is the nature of business operations. Seven of the 35 firms did not use standard costs for this reason, and for each of the other techniques, there was at least one firm which didn't use it because "our operations are different."

TOP MANAGEMENT ATTITUDE. Cited most often by the respondents as the reason for non-use of these techniques was top management attitude. Resistance to change on the part of top management was given by 13 respondents as the reason for not using responsibility accounting, and it was given by 10 as the reason for not using contribution margin reporting.

ACCOUNTANTS' ATTITUDES AND PERCEPTIONS. Another reason for non-use may be attributed to the accountants' own attitudes and understandings. Among the elements which make up his attitude are the following:

1. The accountant's perception of managerial information needs and what accounting constructs and presentations will best meet those needs
2. The accountant's perception of management understanding of accounting data and of the extent of management reliance on it
3. The accountant's perception of top management attitudes toward changes—particularly change in the accounting system

---

Exhibit 1

SIZE CLASSIFICATION OF SAMPLE FIRMS

Size of Firm	Very small	Small	Medium	Large	Totals
Annual employment	1	27	4	3	35
Annual sales	0	23	11	1	35
Total assets	1	20	13	1	35
Number of product lines	3	18	10	4	35
Number of producing departments	3	12	13	7	35
Composite measure		25	10		35

Note:

A weighting scheme was used to establish the composite measure, i.e., each company was identified as very small (weight = 1), small (weight = 2), medium (weight = 3), large (weight = 4), according to each of the following criteria: employment, sales, assets, products, and number of departments. An example of the weighting for a particular company might be: (3 + 3 + 4 + 3 + 3 = 16) divided by 5 (factors) to give a weighted size of 3.2 as a composite measure for a medium sized company. Interestingly enough, no company rated "large" by more than 2 of the criteria, thus, even the "large" companies were not really large when all factors were considered.

Exhibit 2

REASONS GIVEN FOR NOT USING ACCOUNTING TECHNIQUES

Reasons given	CVP analysis	Contribution margin	Standard costs	Operating budgets	Responsibility accounting	Capital budgeting	Linear programming	Network analysis	Mentioned
Management resistance to change	8	10	9	6	13	7	3	–	56
Nature of operations	4	1	7	2	1	1	2	–	18
Size of firm	3	5	2	3	5	4	7	4	33
Accountants' satisfaction with existing techniques	6	7	2	5	8	4	2	1	35
Shortage of qualified staff	4	6	–	5	9	2	1	2	29
Pressure of time	7	11	3	7	7	2	5	2	44
Lack of guiding publications	–	–	–	–	–	2	9	2	13
Lack of computer	–	–	–	–	–	–	3	–	3
Too costly to use	1	3	4	2	2	–	2	–	14

Values given are frequency of mention.

4. The accountant's satisfaction with the existing system and his motivation toward modernization
5. The accountant's technical competence
6. The accountant's age and duration of service with the firm

Technical competence (and the accountant's own confidence in it) is of course difficult to measure. In the absence of any absolute measure, it is possible to substitute such evidence as formal training (degrees held), participation in professional workshops and seminars, and activity in professional accounting organizations. The data for these companies show that younger accountants, with more degrees held, are found in the firms which use a larger number of the techniques; conversely, older accountants with fewer or no degrees are found in the firms using fewer of the "modern" accounting techniques.

Age was a directly related factor. In the firms which used more than an average number of the techniques, all the respondents were under 40 years old. In the firms found to have a below average application of these methods, 67 percent of the respondents were over 40.

As to familiarity with the methods, most of the accountants interviewed did have basic knowledge of the "traditional" techniques, but 13 of them knew little about linear programming and 11 knew little about network analysis. Most accountants who did know about the latter techniques felt that they lacked the analytical ability that was, of course, necessary to put them to use.

In summary, then, the composite management accountant in the firm which has come to use more of the contemporary accounting techniques, is likely to have the following characteristics:

1. He is perceptive of management information needs and is able to adapt the accounting techniques to meet them.
2. He understands management's attitudes toward change and is able to secure acceptance of change in the accounting system.
3. He is not satisfied when the system is outmoded.
4. He is better educated, with a B.A. or B.S. degree, and may have an M.B.A. degree.
5. He is about 35 years old and a member of a professional organization, and probably active in it.

AVAILABILITY OF RESOURCES. A shortage of qualified management accountants appears to be the reason for not adopting responsibility accounting, contribution margin reporting, and capital budgeting. Some accountants (who evidently have not been following the literature) complained of lack of available publications describing the "newer" techniques and how they could be adapted to situations. The resource lack most often mentioned, though, is the lack of time. The pressure of daily routine work typically stood in the way of studying alternative methods and procedures, even where admittedly some potential existed for worthwhile use. But two accountants did say that where they are convinced of the value of a new technique, they will create time for planning to apply it.

COST OF APPLICATION. Another, but minor, reason given for nonapplication of some of the techniques is cost of application. At least one person said this about every one of the techniques.

"Technical competence (and the accountant's own confidence in it) is of course difficult to measure."

Exhibit 3

AWARENESS AND USE OF ACCOUNTING TECHNIQUES

Adoption stages	C-V-P analysis	Contribution margin	Standard costs	Operating budgets	Responsibility accounting	Capital budgeting	Linear programming	Network analysis
Unaware of technique	2	1	–	1	3	2	13	11
Aware of technique	12	16	11	11	14	11	18	18
Interest and evaluation	3	8	5	2	8	2	3	–
Use of technique	18	10	19	21	10	20	1	6

Values are number of firms reported at each stage.

Exhibit 4

AGENTS OF CHANGE

Reported sources of the Innovation

	C-V-P analysis	Contribution margin	Standard costing	Operating budgets	Responsibility accounting	Capital budgeting	Linear programming	Network analysis
Management accountant	12	4	10	10	6	7	–	1
Top management	2	3	6	7	2	4	1	3
Management accountant and top management	3	1	–	1	1	5	–	2
Management accountant and outside consultant	–	–	–	–	2	2	–	–
Top management and outside consultant	1	2	3	4	1	3	–	–

Values are frequency of mention by respondents

Awareness of Techniques

Exhibit 3 shows the four stages of development of interest in "new" techniques and the standing of the firms in those four stages. It is not surprising that few accountants have reached the adoption stage for linear programming and network analysis, but what is surprising is that there are still chief accountants who disclaim even an awareness of cost-volume-profit analysis, operating budgets, and responsibility accounting.

We found only two companies that had tried a technique and given it up. In both cases, linear programming was tried and found to be unsuitable for use in the circumstances. The high rate of retention of all other techniques, once they were tried, indicates the probability of actual use once the awareness and investigation stages are achieved.

Agents of Change

Three kinds of agents of change were identified in the process of securing acceptance of accounting techniques. These were the management accountant himself, top management, and outside consultants. However, in many cases, the techniques which had been in use for some time could not be attributed to any one influence. In other cases, the accountant had brought the method with him from some prior employment. As might be expected, he took credit for introducing most traditional techniques. Even here, top management played an important role, as shown in Exhibit 4. In actual application, though, the accountant was the "figure specialist." He was the key man in providing the analysis in the more traditional accounting techniques, shared the analysis with others in capital budgets and in operating budgets, and sometimes was involved in network analysis.

Outside consultants were felt to play a minor role in the diffusion of accounting techniques. Only five companies called on management consultants frequently, 15 firms said they never employed them.

Conclusion

The level of knowledge of "new" techniques by some accountants themselves appears to be deficient, in spite of the literature available and the educational efforts of NAA and CPA groups. Managers, also, cannot be persuaded of the worth of accounting techniques. The evidence points to a need for continued efforts by NAA and other professional organizations in providing continuing education at the local level. Although accountants cannot change their managers, there is much to be done by accountants themselves in upgrading their own knowledge, skills, persuasive talents, and appreciation of their role in their own environments.   □

Gerald A. Sears

Public offerings for smaller companies

Underwriting and 'after-market' guidelines to help growth companies realize the potential benefits of public ownership

Foreword

As a way to raise capital, diversify the owners' investment, or accomplish some other goal, "going public" is not the best answer for many smaller companies, the author warns; if growth slows, for instance, additional capital may be hard to get. But for the company whose continued growth results in steady market appreciation of its stock, public ownership can help stimulate that growth while permitting management to obtain capital gains. The author explains the process of underwriting and the operation of the over-the-counter market.

Mr. Sears is Vice President of Glore Forgan, Wm. R. Staats, Inc., Chicago, and participates in underwriting activities as a member of the firm's Corporate Finance Department. He previously has been Sales Manager of an agricultural products processor and Manager of the Corporate Development Service of the Chemical Bank New York Trust Company.

In recent years, stockholders of small, closely held companies have increasingly chosen to sell their interests to larger, publicly held companies in order to get a more liquid holding. This has resulted in a fast-paced merger and acquisition momentum that is unparalleled in the history of the United States.

A public offering of part of the stock can often be a better solution, because it permits the owners to retain control of their company and reap the benefits of an increasingly more valuable equity position if the company continues to grow. Moreover, "going public" can sometimes result in getting a higher long-term price than selling out to a single buyer.

In this article I shall discuss the pros and cons of going public and offer some suggestions on establishing a public market and selecting an underwriter for the consideration of stockholders of privately owned companies who wish to create more liquidity for their investment.

Not every firm a good bet

There are three main reasons why owners of companies sell their interests to a publicly held corporation or make an offering of a portion of their stock to the public:

1. They desire to diversify and take some of their eggs out of one basket.

2. High federal estate and income taxes force the owners to alter the foundation of their estate so that they can leave their heirs with maximum assets.

3. Because of expanding markets and new

technology, many small companies suffer acute growing pains and need infusions of capital beyond their own resources and the credit available from financial institutions.

The need for working capital was by far the most important motive for a public offering given by 209 presidents of small companies in one survey.[1] The results are shown in *Exhibit I*. A need for operating cash was the impetus behind one third of the stock issues of these companies.

Half the presidents gave corporate financial needs, including working capital, as the primary reasons for their public issues. This is not surprising; we are a technology-oriented society, and as long as one or a very few men can together push the state of the art in any technology, small companies will be formed to capitalize on this ability. Their growth can be rapid, creating acute cash needs.

But whatever the motives for making a public offering, success in doing it is limited to companies that meet certain criteria. I shall list these criteria and describe what happens after the offering to a company that fails to meet each one:

The company should have a growth rate higher than its industry if it is to attract investors. Consider the small company that staggers on from year to year showing below-average growth. Since the stock market is mainly a vehicle for capital gains—few investors nowadays buy equities for dividends—the slow-growth or no-growth company soon falls into that vast wasteland of "lost" public issues.

Financing becomes difficult to obtain. Because the company's price/earnings ratio is very low, a great amount of stock would be needed in a subsequent offering to raise even a moderate amount of cash. And when the market price of the stock falls near or below book value, debt financing can be impaired as well. The result is that the company has few of the advantages of the public market.

Owner-managers, accustomed to answering to no one in running their businesses, must be able to adjust to operating in the sometimes uncomfortable spotlight of attention. The creation of a public market brings with it the "financial crowd" of brokers, analysts, auditors, and stockholders. They feel they have a right to be given certain information about the company, and

1. Cited in Solomon J. Flink, *Equity Financing for Small Business* (New York, Simmons-Boardman Publishing Corporation, 1962), p. 87.

Exhibit I. Reasons for going public given by 209 small-company presidents

	Percent of total
To meet company objectives	
Financial needs	
Working capital	36.0%
Fixed capital	9.5
Research and development funds	5.7
Investment activity	
Establish market for later offering	
by shareholders	9.5
Probable purchase of another firm	3.8
Contemplated merger	2.4
To meet owners' personal considerations	
Minimize estate taxes	13.4
Resolve personal conflicts	2.4
Provide "nest egg"	4.8
Diversify investments	4.8
Take advantage of a bull market	3.8
Other reasons	3.8

some of them place no reasonable limit on this right. Management can find itself in the annoying position of fielding myriad requests for explanations about actions that previously have gone unquestioned.

When the company's performance is good, management can bask in the applause. But it may not be easy for onetime entrepreneurs to handle critical questions on operations, on executive salaries, or on stock option plans, not to mention explaining a downturn in the business. Often they react to such questions as if they were personal reflections on them. If management is uncomfortable in the spotlight, the result can be strained relationships with the financial community which can cause more harm than the public market does good.

The effect of public disclosure must not be to compromise the company's business. In a case where concealment of profit margins, share of market, and so on, is essential for competitive survival, the required disclosure of these facts by a company issuing a prospectus can spell disaster. This is particularly true for a one-product business. Even with a multiproduct company, however, disclosure of sales by product or product group—increasingly demanded by government agencies and investors—can affect the company's competitive position.

A public offering is not appropriate for a small company with slow growth, a company whose

Harvard Business Review: September-October 1968

owner-manager is a prima donna, or a company dependent on a single major, nonproprietary product with a high profit margin and large share of the market.

The proceeds from a public issue of stock can flow to either the company or the selling shareholders, or both. With some investors there remains a lingering suspicion of an initial offering that mainly benefits the selling shareholders. This stems largely from the "bail out" theory—the idea that management has information on a future downturn for the business. Though this occurrence is rare indeed, the suspicion lingers. A wise management will think twice about proceeding with an offering if it will benefit only the principal shareholders' personal interests.

Advantages of going public

The advantages of a public offering are not always clear. Small-company owner-managers who are considering selling their interests, or a part of them, generally hold certain beliefs about selling to another company which in my view are erroneous. Let us use the case of "Mr. Jones," who sells his company to "Big, Inc.," a publicly held corporation, to illustrate these largely unfounded beliefs:

☐ Jones believes he should get a price based on as high an earnings multiple as he would have obtained if his company had gone public. But Big, Inc. recognizes that if comparable publicly held companies are selling at 10 times earnings, Jones's lack of a public market should knock down the price a few multiples to 8 or 9 times earnings. In short, Big, Inc. will avoid "giving away" the many expenses it incurs as a publicly owned company, maintaining a market liquid enough to attract Jones. As a rule, the more liquid the buyer's stock, the greater the discount the seller must accept from the buyer's price/earnings multiple.

☐ Jones's contemplated position with Big, Inc., as either an executive or a consultant, gives him a security that often turns out to be false. Big, Inc. has control after the sale, and Jones's position continues only at the company's pleasure.

☐ Jones's only certain stream of income is from the investments he makes with the cash proceeds of the sale. But if Jones takes Big, Inc. stock in exchange for his with the idea that he will have a "management-free" investment in a marketable stock, he will have traded the un-

certainties of running a small business for the vagaries of the market.

☐ Jones may have elected for a private sale because it is supposed to be quicker than a public offering. While the preparation for a new public issue can take as long as a year, a private sale seldom takes less time and can take longer. The initial contact, the evaluation, research, investigation, and negotiation precede the sale. A small company seeking the best deal often goes through this procedure from two to six times before it concludes a satisfactory sale. The duration of the courtship with each prospect is seldom less than three months and often is five or six months, meanwhile draining enormous amounts of top-management time.

Rising market values

On the other hand, entrepreneurs like Jones can find in a public offering a potentially profitable alternative to outright sale of the company. The success of the offering depends on creation of a liquid public market, which takes time and good management of the new issue and the all-important after-market. The time factor poses a greater risk for the company than is present in an outright sale, but the rewards can outweigh the risk.

In the last few years the demand for equities has made the public market increasingly attractive to smaller companies. Institutions are putting more of their portfolio resources into seasoned equities, creating a market shortage of them that spurs investing in less-tested issues; mutual funds, feeling an urgency to show "performance," are looking harder for stocks with high growth potential; the sales forces of brokerage firms have grown substantially in size, resulting in pressure to build greater retail volume; and the long economic boom, coupled with inflation, has stirred investor interest in common stocks (which, in bull markets, has caused rampant speculative fever).

That small companies have taken advantage of these conditions is evident from a look at the over-the-counter market. Some 10,050 issues were quoted in the National Quotations Bureau's daily listed services as of early this year. This figure compares with 7,930 as of early 1959. That is an average annual growth rate of 3%. But a 1966 study for the National Association of Securities Dealers showed that unlisted stocks have declined rapidly in both volume of trading and dollar value compared with volume and total values on the stock exchange.[2] This indicates that the OTC market has become one of the smaller publicly owned companies.

A sample of OTC companies by market value and assets, taken from the Securities and Exchange Commission's study of the securities markets in 1963, supports that conclusion.[3] The results are shown in *Exhibit II*. The companies

ly held firm must pay him almost twice the amount of cash.

Cash salaries come out of company earnings, while stock option gains are "paid for" by the rising market value. The exercise of options may have a slight effect on earnings per share, but none on aggregate earnings. Moreover, one of the better ways to encourage good perfor-

Exhibit II. Sample of issuers of over-the-counter stocks, classified by market value of outstanding stock and amount of assets

Market value and total assets (in thousands of dollars)	Market value			Amount of assets		
	Number	Percent	Cumulative percent	Number	Percent	Cumulative percent
$1-$249	238	14.6%	14.6%	105	6.5%	6.5%
$250-$499	153	9.4	24.0	111	6.9	13.4
$500-$999	229	14.2	38.2	161	10.0	23.4
$1,000-$4,999	449	27.8	66.0	483	29.9	53.3
$5,000-$9,999	166	10.3	76.3	245	15.1	68.4
$10,000 and over	308	19.1	95.4	504	31.1	99.5
Not reported	75	4.6	100.0	9	0.5	100.0
	1,618	100.0%		1,618	100.0%	

whose assets totaled less than $1 million, for instance, comprised 23% of the total, while those concerns whose stock had a market value of less than $1 million made up 38% of the total.

By-products of a public market

Once a small company's stock is in the public domain, and if the company's growth continues at the same rate, the company derives some benefits other than the rising market value of the stock:

☐ Since the advent of stock option plans and high personal income taxes, privately held companies have been at a competitive disadvantage in compensating management, as all executives know. Beyond a certain level, higher cash compensation enriches the tax collector more than the recipient. Because of this, managerial talent has tended to migrate toward companies that offer less heavily taxed compensation through stock option plans. To net an executive the same after-tax income as the option-compensated officer of the publicly held company, the private-

mance is to make the rewards to an extent depend on how valuable management makes the stock.

☐ Obviously, a company can sell additional stock more easily in an already established market. Another source of financing growth is the increased borrowing capacity which is a result of the public market.

The company has increased its borrowing ability to the extent that lenders use a debt/equity ratio as a guideline. The sale of stock increases paid-in capital and therefore net worth, or book value. Thus borrowing capacity has been enhanced, if lenders use book value as a yardstick. If the company's stock enjoys a high price/earnings multiple, lenders using market equity value as a guideline will be even more receptive to meeting the company's capital needs.

Moreover, the strict reporting requirements for publicly owned companies give lenders more confidence in their financial statements, resulting in a better reception for their managements. Finally, in addition to having a greater borrowing capacity, management can be more flexible in its borrowing, using the public debt market for both straight and convertible debt. Convertibles, in particular, can help to free management from the shackles of tight money.

☐ Because of the tax laws, sellers are more

2. Booz, Allen & Hamilton Inc., *Over the Counter Market Study* (August, 1966).

3. *Report of the Special Study of the Securities Markets*, 88th Congress, First Session, House Document 95.

interested in a tax-free exchange of stock than in a taxable cash transaction. The acquisition business is intensely competitive—a seller's market. So the ability to compete is enhanced by having a marketable stock.

Smaller public companies may even have a certain advantage over large ones in this competition, since they are generally interested in acquisition of even smaller companies ignored by many large corporations. I am not making the suggestion that every small private company should go public and then set out to build another Litton empire. But frustration at seeing their suppliers, competitors, and customers acquired has led many small company owners to "sell out" themselves. Creating a public market and using the stock for growth through acquisition can combat this trend.

☐ Even if a small company plans an eventual sale of the assets after it has gone public, the market value of the stock can provide a base for negotiations by establishing a minimum price that the buyer must pay. In that event, assuming that the initial offering and after-market have been handled competently, the final net price to the selling shareholders can be considerably higher than if the stock had been disposed of another way.

☐ The first time a company goes to the equity market, great interest is created in it. Customers, suppliers, and competitors treat the company, its products, and services with a new respect. The reputation of being substantial, which most publicly held companies enjoy, also may enhance consumer acceptance of their products. While it is difficult to tie increased sales to the publicity arising from the market, it seems to do the recipients of this attention no harm.

Broker and underwriter

In considering whether to go public, and in order to understand better the mechanics of the market, the owner of a small company should be familiar with how the over-the-counter market functions and with the role of the underwriter.

The float

The buyer of a security wants the market for that security to have sufficient depth and liquidity. He must feel assured that he can buy the desired amount of stock at a price he is willing to pay; and when and if he decides to sell his shares, he will want assurance that he can find a buyer with little delay and sell to him at a fair price. Brokers, of course, make markets in OTC stocks to facilitate these transactions, adding a markup to the price in lieu of a commission.

The market must be capable of handling a volume large enough to cause little or no change in price in each transaction. This is ideal liquidity. Between the ideal and the inability to trade at all are an infinite number of shades of liquidity. In its Special Study of the securities markets, the SEC reported on a sampling of the National Quotation Bureau's daily price quotations of OTC stocks (known as "the sheets"), from which it tried to determine what proportion had a liquid market. Over a 10-day period, two or more dealers entered quotations on 161 of the 300 stocks sampled, or less than 54%. By this measure, only about one half of the OTC securities have a reasonably liquid market, since one measure of liquidity is both a bid and an offer on a firm basis from two or more dealers in the sheets. (Since the sheets quote stocks with a degree of national investor interest, there is no telling the extent of liquidity of the thousands of issues traded only locally over the counter, nearly all of which are small companies' securities.)

The liquidity of a small OTC issue depends directly on the amount of stock changing hands —"the float." This is the stock held by short-term investors or speculators that comes into the market regularly (obviously, the stock held by long-term investors seldom comes into the market). The ratio of the float to the total shares outstanding depends on such factors as the type of company the issuer is, whether or not it has a few controlling interests, its growth potential, and so on.

To understand better the nature of competition in the OTC market, it is helpful to look at the market from the dealer's standpoint. He advertises his willingness to buy and sell for his own account by placing a bid or an offer in the sheets. In doing this, he is in direct competition with other dealers who are in the sheets in the same stock and in potential competition with all dealers who may decide to make a market in that stock.

If the dealer has no competition, he will make the spread between his bid and offer wider, in order to compensate for possible losses from inventory and make his profit equal to what he is gaining from more liquid stocks. He will probably also keep his inventory very low, which, with the wide spread, can result in poor liquidity. If the float should increase, more dealers would be attracted to make a market in the stock.

To enable two or more dealers to make a competitive market, the float should be a minimum of 50,000 shares. This is not an absolute figure, but it is difficult to maintain a market if the amount of float declines below that figure. It is a general rule of small OTC markets that the annual trading volume is about three times the float. So, assuming that two dealers are equally sharing a 50,000-share float market, each will trade about 75,000 shares a year and will probably have an average spread of about ¼ to ½ of 1% (25 to 50 cents per share). This would be a trading gross profit of $18,750 to $37,500, before expenses and inventory losses, for each.

Selecting an underwriter

Until about 50 years ago, the underwriting function was the principal source of income for the securities industry. Since that time, firms for which underwriting is a principal source of income have declined to only 1.7% of the total broker-dealer community, according to the 1966 OTC market study for the NASD. The principal activity of 80% of the 2,483 firms reporting was

---

Exhibit III. Percentage of new issues at or below offering price one month later, by size of underwriters

Adjusted net capital of underwriters (in thousands of dollars)	Percentage
$0-$9.9	33.8%
$10-$24.9	40.9
$25-$49.9	35.3
$50-$99.9	22.7
$100-$499.9	31.2
$500 or more	30.5

Source: Securities and Exchange Commission, *Report of the Special Study of the Securities Markets*, 88th Congress, First Session, House Document 95.

---

selling existing securities; firms retailing listed and OTC stocks accounted for 45.6%, while 34.4% dealt primarily in mutual funds.

Substantially all the underwriters in this 1.7% are large organizations; it is difficult to name more than a handful of small underwriting firms. So there are very few bases of performance comparison between large and small. *Exhibit III*

shows the percentage of new issues that were at or below the offering price one month after the offering, broken down by size of the underwriting firm. It indicates some tendency for a more favorable after-market performance as the size of the underwriting firm increases, but not enough to make a direct correlation between market performance and size.

The typical national underwriting house requires a company to have had at least $750,000-$1,000,000 in net earnings before it will consider a public offering of the company's stock. A regional house with underwriting capability will generally scale the minimum down to $500,000 or $400,000. This income may be either for the fiscal year completed just prior to the contemplated offering or for the year ending immediately thereafter. In the latter case, it is assumed that there has been a record of earnings growth in previous years.

Many large underwriting firms have a continuing financial advisory relationship with their large clients, but this is not as common in the case of smaller firms. The NASD study attempted to classify these relationships by size of firm. Large firms indicated that they have been the underwriters, if not managing underwriters, of about one third of the issues in which they maintained active trading markets. The firms were asked about other traditional relationships—a directorship, a financial advisor, and past underwriters for the same issuer. Less than 8% of the small firm market makers had had any one of these three relationships, compared with 14% of the medium-sized firms and 43% of the large firms.

Selecting an underwriter is not an easy job. Not only must the issuer make a decision as to the underwriter's technical ability, but he should also try to find an underwriter who is familiar with and understands the issuer's industry. In addition, the underwriter should have the ability, either alone or through correspondent relationships, to distribute the stock in a geographic pattern that closely follows the geography of interest in the stock.

There are very few other business relationships which reflect as much deep mutual understanding as that of the issuer and the underwriter. The Special Study included a statement by one underwriter that expresses well the nature of this relationship:

"We are frequently asked to help new issuers with general problems of a company going public for a first time, such as advising them on the

Harvard Business Review: September-October 1968

basis of our experience on handling stockholder relations, meetings with the investment community.... Related to this, we are a sounding board as to how the financial community and the public generally might react to proposed corporate actions.... We advise the company on a broad range of their financial problems, including such matters as the need for new financing, the methods of obtaining new financing, either publicly or privately, dividend policy, the desirability of mergers, acquisitions.... We feel a responsibility for seeing to it that an orderly after-market in the security is maintained so that persons who have purchased the issue will be able to liquidate or increase their investments if they desire."

Underwriting remains a very personal business. The "personality" of a firm is directly attributable to the one or two key people in the organization who decide underwriting policy. So a firm's policy on the size, industry, and other criteria of companies which it is willing to underwrite can change as fast as the makeup of the top echelon changes.

Often there are not enough comparable publicly held companies to arrive at a clear-cut determination of the public's interest, the issuer's industry, and an estimate of its potential for growth. Nevertheless, the underwriter must make a judgment. The judgment about public reception is an area where reasonable men can differ. This is particularly the case with small new issues, where public receptivity to the issuer's industry is crucial.

An underwriter may have managed one or more public offerings in the issuer's industry, so he would be a likely prospect. But the underwriter might be precluded from managing another offering in that industry because of conflict of interest. Because of the constantly shifting underwriting marketplace, the best course of action for a small company is to rely on the advice of its auditor, banker, and lawyer in suggesting two or three underwriters. After interviewing them, the company will select one as the managing underwriter.

Preparing the offering

Making an initial public offering of stock is a complex process. *Exhibit IV* lists the major functions of an underwriter in preparing for the offering. Some of them are entirely the underwriter's responsibility; in others, he works with

lawyers or auditors; and, in this example, the firm is managing the offering in association with other underwriters. If the offering is more involved than the relatively simple one illustrated in *Exhibit IV*—presenting tax considerations, for instance—the 40 steps could easily be increased

to 100.[4] It has often been said that the underwriter must know his business and understand the issuer's. From this list, some appreciation can be gained of the technical complexity of the underwriting business.

Many questions about the offering naturally will occur to the company's management. For instance, if the underwriting is done by a syndicate, how should the stock be distributed to its members for sale? What is a reasonable gross spread or underwriting commission? How much information should be included in the prospectus? Should the managing underwriter be represented on the board of directors? What part should the company play in determining if the underwriter and other market makers are inventorying enough stock?

Any one of these questions requires far too much detailed analysis to be addressed within the scope of this article. Company management, however, should bear these points in mind:

☐ The underwriter takes the same civil and criminal risks as the company for the representa-

4. For a discussion of the complex subject of taxes, see James R. Wimmer, "Tax Effect of the Privately Held Corporation 'Going Public,'" *TAXES—The Tax Magazine*, December 1967, p. 932.

Exhibit IV. Managing underwriter's selected steps in preparing a new issue

1. Review with company SEC rules regarding public statements.

2. Decide on financial data to be included.

3. Prepare underwriters' memorandum.

4. If offering to employees or other special persons, determine price, liability for unsubscribed stock, time schedule, subscription and confirmation mechanics.

5. Prepare S-1 registration statement.

6. Decide on form of stock certificate.

7. Obtain indemnity insurance policy, if appropriate.

8. Prepare prospectus.

9. Prepare agreement among underwriters (AAU).

10. Prepare underwriting agreement (UA).

11. Prepare underwriters' questionnaire to make sure they have not recommended the stock.

12. Prepare blue-sky memorandum (preliminary).

13. File registration statement with SEC.

14. Clear proposed underwriters' comfort letter with company's auditors.

15. Advise as to the number of copies of preliminary prospectus ("red herring") necessary.

16. Clear with NASD.

17. Issue invitational letters to prospective underwriters.

18. Determine makeup of underwriting group.

19. Coordinate with syndicate department for any directed sales to officers, other employees, stockholders, or creditors.

20. Compile summary report of the distribution of the red herring and amendments thereto.

21. Furnish own accounting department (for closing) with tentative time schedule, copies of prospectus, AAU, UA, and other pertinent documents.

22. Arrange "due diligence" meetings with company and underwriters.

23. Arrange (with underwriters, company, auditors, sellers, and counsel for underwriters) inspection of company's facilities, time of signings of underwriting agreement, and requested effective date of SEC registration.

24. Prepare memorandum to salesmen.

25. Prepare copy of published announcements and schedule of publications and tentative dates.

26. Determine where offering will be advertised.

27. Clear deficiencies with SEC and revise documents.

28. Send red herring distribution list to SEC.

29. Request SEC acceleration.

30. Establish final terms.

31. Prepare sets of AAU and UA and sign with underwriters and with company (and with selling stockholders, if any).

32. Recheck final prospectus.

33. Release offering for sale on telegraphed receipt of SEC clearance and after confirmation of good standing from state of incorporation of company.

34. Send copies of prospectus to underwriters, selected dealers, financial services, publications, and others.

35. Send copies of agreements to underwriters who gave power of attorney.

36. Decide on closing date with counsel, auditors, transfer agent, and registrars.

37. Advise underwriters and own accounting department as to stabilization of stock in after-market and closing arrangements.

38. Send legal opinions, comfort letter, and other closing papers to underwriters.

39. Take steps to get new issues quoted in newspapers and listed in stock guides.

40. Advise company of its responsibilities after offering.

tions made in the prospectus. So he will be careful to make adequate and truthful disclosure. (And in an important recent federal court case, lawyers, outside auditors, and company directors have also been held liable for false information in the prospectus.[5])

□ The prospectus is by law the underwriter's only permitted selling document. Therefore he will make sure it is well done.

□ While the terms of an underwriting will vary widely according to the size and industry of the issuer, any aspect of an offering has

5. *Escott v. Barchris Construction Corp.*, 283 F. Supp. 643.

enough published prior practice so that the underwriter should be able to show why he is making a particular recommendation. Whenever company executives are uneasy on a point, the underwriter should be able and willing to show them sufficient evidence of prior practice for companies of comparable size in the same industry. Enough information is available in any situation so that reasonable men should not differ.

Perhaps the most severe test of the underwriter-issuer relationship comes at the time of pricing

Harvard Business Review: September-October 1968

the new issue. Although it is not always immediately obvious, the goals of the underwriter and the issuer are the same. Both are concerned that the offering price be sustained in the intermediate and long-term market. But since the long-term market is very difficult to forecast, the responsible underwriter is usually most concerned with pricing for the foreseeable future.

The pricing decision is largely based on comparability. The underwriter is strongly influenced by the price/earnings ratios at which comparable companies are selling in the public market. An issuer can obtain a range of his probable P/E ratio by doing this analysis himself. It should encompass at least 6, but preferably as many as 12, comparable companies, and it should include information on their growth rates, balance sheets, cash flow to earnings ratios, proprietary products, and depth of management. A comparison of this type will show why companies sell at significantly different P/E multiples. It will also show the issuer's management where the company stands relative to its industry.

This comparative "spread" is one of the major tools any underwriter uses for pricing. Since no two companies are alike and no company is exactly like an average, however, the final decision on the P/E ratio must depend on the underwriter's judgment.

Concluding note

The public market gives the smaller company an opportunity to expand with its own resources.

Not every such company, however, meets the growth, management, and product requirements for success in that market. For the company that does not, a public offering can have a devastating boomerang effect. For those that do, it can bring substantial long-term capital gains. When a small company meets the criteria for a public offering, an outright sale of the stock to another company can be equivalent to selling the horse for the money to buy its feed.

The underwriting fraternity is increasingly recognizing that its customary reluctance to take on small-company public offerings needs reevaluation. Smaller companies will always be more vulnerable than large ones. But the demand for equities, as well as a lack of other suitable vehicles to enable investors to participate in the exploitation of new technology, is lowering the size minimums.

SMALL BUSINESS ADMINISTRATION   ●   JOHN E. HORNE, Administrator
— U. S. Government Agency —

Management Aids FOR SMALL MANUFACTURERS | 142 |

Washington 25, D.C.   July 1962

SOUND OBJECTIVES HELP BUILD PROFITS

By **T. Stanley Gallagher,** *Business Analyst,*

Management and Research Assistance, Small Business Administration, Philadelphia, Pennsylvania

SUMMARY

Many small businessmen try to guide their companies toward certain business objectives--ones that help build profits. Some of these men carry their objectives in their heads while others use a written statement of objectives. This Aid discusses the desirability of formulating and formalizing company goals, as well as the continuing need for reviewing such objectives in order to keep them current and sound.

Periodic review is necessary because marketing conditions change, and an objective set 12 months or more ago may not be entirely valid today.

By setting up specific business objectives, small businessmen can provide their organizations with an efficient blueprint to guide company progress in an orderly manner. By reviewing objectives, periodically, small businessmen can learn: (1) whether their objectives need to be adjusted, and (2) what, if any, policy and procedure changes are needed in order to achieve current goals.

Most successful businessmen have determined their business objectives, at least in a general way. They appreciate the value of specifying business objectives, even if expressed only in such general terms as "increasing profit next year."

Small business often has an advantage in determining objectives. This is true because a major strength of many small companies lies in the business ability and acumen of their owner-managers. These men and women are familiar with all aspects of their businesses.

Often because such owner-managers are the major decision-makers, they carry in their heads such matters as statement of company objectives and the accompanying operating policies and procedures. This lack of a formalized statement can be dangerous.

Large corporations are aware of this danger and work to overcome it. In the large company, to insure communication and uniform interpretation all along the line, the top managers write out in detail the company's objectives. Much research, consideration, and discussion go into preparing these statements. And they become the starting point for company planning, policy formulation, and the development of operating procedures which will help to build profits.

Such detailed research and formalizing of business objectives sometimes may seem unnecessary to small owner-managers who can carry the information in their heads. However, these men often forget that this information is lost if they become critically ill or otherwise incapacitated.

● Changing Conditions

Perhaps even more important is the fact that objectives established several months ago may no longer be valid because of changing conditions. Small businessmen in increasing numbers realize they are operating in a complicated world. They know also that management of small companies has long ceased to be a simple affair.

But they live so close to their business that they sometimes overlook changes--some of which are undesirable and detrimental.

One way to prevent this is by making a periodic review of business objectives. And the trend seems to be in that direction among the more progressive businessmen.

ASPECTS THAT NEED REVIEW

These men are examining their written statements of objectives against today's marketing conditions. They are looking at such fundamental aspects as:

"What is my place in my industry?" "How do I carve out a better competitive niche?" "Are we known as a quality house?"

In terms of the consumer market, "Are we attempting to serve class or mass?" If we are in the industrial market, "Are we in any sense a 'captive plant'?"

"What is our company image to customers and prospects? To the general public?"

"Do we specialize in serving only a limited number of industries? Why?" "Should we consider developing a line of proprietary products?"

"What are our specific goals with regard to profit improvement--to lowered cost of manufacturing and distribution?" "Do we have any plans for new product development or acquisition?"

- 2 -

Businessmen who ask those questions are comparing their goals with their companies' actual performance--currently and in the future. This procedure should result in their giving improved direction to the company's daily efforts.

The examples point to this: Before trying to review your objectives get them on paper. If they're already written out, so much the better.

RE-PLANNING TO MEET CHANGES

Chances are when you review your business objectives you'll find that certain changes are in order. Conditions may have shifted somewhat since you determined objectives several months or years ago.

Your problem today then is to re-arrange the plans you've been using for the accomplishment of these goals.

One consumer-durable's manufacturer, for example, had the goal of making his company an industry leader. To do it he needed to achieve a targeted share of the market within a designated period of time. His approach was to improve the quality of his product, to style it to the needs of the market, to price it competitively.

However, during periodic review it became clear that the company was not capturing the additional share of market which it knew existed, and on which its sales goals were based. Although the company was producing a quality product, that was priced competitively and marketed aggressively, it was styled above mass tastes.

As the designer of this fine line remarked, "All these years I've been designing this line for the department store buyer (and prestige stores, at that) only to learn at this late date that three-fourths of this product's sales moves through furniture stores."

This owner-manager realized that he had "missed the boat." He had failed to research the consumer adequately.

Reviewing objectives showed him the need for re-planning. His new plans included marketing research which demonstrated that the buyers in many furniture stores were looking for something styled quite differently.

Look for a few moments at what is involved in re-planning as done by a manufacturer in the industrial market. Not infrequently, the business objective is stated very generally as: "Next year, our goal is to increase sales by 10 percent; in 5 years, we expect to be producing and selling 35 percent more units than this year."

This manufacturer arrived at these figures after considerable investigation, research, and discussions with key personnel representing all major functions and operating divisions of his company. Moreover, better market information developed through more objective investigation and evaluation pinpointed the need for a drastic overhaul of current sales policies.

At periodic review time, therefore, the owner-manager realized that certain aspects of his operations had to be re-planned.

ADJUSTING SALES POLICIES

This company had to re-plan its sales policies. Even though its statement of sales objectives rested on a factual basis, improved knowledge of the markets indicated that the sales forecast should be reviewed, in order to take full advantage of the new profit opportunities which better communications had opened up.

Such a review was logical because the sales forecast is the keystone on which other company forecasts, such as financial, manufacturing, and purchasing, are based.

This company had a useful and accurate forecast--one that has been made up: by product line, by sizes and other pertinent detail, by industry, by customers' plants, and by sales territory. The company had also developed product market potentials in these same terms so that it had a practical foundation for sales forecasting.

The owner-manager was using his sales forecast as the basis of his sales quotas. He was also using it to improve the quality of sales effort by channeling such effort into the areas (geographic, customer-prospect, product, and so on) of maximum sales potential.

In like manner, he was using the sales forecast to guide the other marketing efforts: advertising, sales promotion, merchandising, and publicity. Achievement of his business objectives, then, depended upon a valid sales forecast, which, in turn, rested on a bedrock of facts.

This industrial company had also developed comprehensive product market potential data by user-industry, by company (customer and prospects), and by sales territory.

This data indicated a situation that is fairly representative in an industrial market, namely, that of a small number of plants representing large volume usage of the product. (Not infrequently for many industrial products, 10 percent or less of the number of plants may comprise two-thirds or three-quarters of the total market for the specific product.)

Many companies (and their salesmen) divide their selling efforts and time by the number of accounts. However, the more enlightened companies, having at their disposal marketing facts of this type, can direct their salesmen to spend their time in relation to sales potential.

Moreover, if the market potential data, (as well as that of the sales forecast "grassroots" information), are developed in terms of product classifications, it becomes possible, first, to identify, and then to cultivate, those accounts which will yield, in the aggregate, the most profitable sales volume. Profitable for two reasons: (1) Salesmen maximize their exposure to top-volume business, (2) Field selling expense is drastically reduced. This epitomizes the approach to sales known as "selective selling."

A further refinement, labelled "executive selling," carries this one important step further. Where large volume profitable product usage is identified through marketing research, sales negotiations can be carried on through the executive officers, or major officials. Under this system, the president of the supplying company would deal with the president, or executive vice-president, or vice-president for purchasing of the user-company.

Some of the advantages which come out of this arrangement are: (1) More advantageous prices; (2) More dependable sources of supply; (3) Product improvement and other innovations.

A company's decision to institute such a system of strategic marketing should be formalized in a sales policy.

You should also spell out new products development in policy statements. New products, increasingly, are becoming important major additions to a company's net profit. Some companies for years have spent considerable money to develop new products, and their investments (based on orderly programs) have paid off.

Other companies have found that technological change and shifts in consumers' tastes have decreased or eliminated the demand for their product. Thus they were forced to look for new ones. Such new product programs were often of the "crash" variety and were not always the most successful.

NEW PLANS INVOLVE MANY AREAS

In like manner, owner-managers often find upon periodic review of their objectives that many other operating areas of the business demand re-planning. They see a need for shifting their policies on manufacturing, purchasing, finances, and personnel.

Such is true because policy determination makes possible a reasonably uniform approach in the conduct of business. It provides for the solution of problems by different members of the same organization. In addition, policies help owner-managers to keep the company headed in the direction they want it to go.

They prepare company policies, by and large, in terms of company functions. Thus, there are manufacturing policies, purchasing policies, financial policies, personnel policies, and so on, in addition to sales policies.

● Manufacturing
A marketing-oriented approach can be helpful when re-planning manufacturing policies. Suppose, for instance, that this objective sales approach results in obtaining customers with individually-larger volumes. Usually such a product mix results in improved production volumes of individual items (more "production" runs).

Review of objectives and policies may indicate that the distribution of present manufacturing and warehousing facilities need to be changed. For example, review may demonstrate that certain of these facilities are not in the right places from the standpoint of service and freight costs.

Thus a company objective that was stated simply as a goal of an additional 10 percent next year, and 35 percent 5 years hence, may cause a considerable reshuffling, including a need for new equipment, and new bricks and mortar in different places.

Important, too, in the consideration of greatly increased sales volume, is the fact that quantity discounts pare the gross profit margin. Periodic review here helps to see that production is kept efficient so as to offset the lower, more competitive gross profit margin. It also helps you to consider replacing obsolete machinery in specific locations in order to maintain or improve the targeted net profit margin.

● Purchasing
The impact of an increased sales volume could affect current purchasing philosophy. First, it might cause the company to look for new suppliers in different geographic areas, as well as industrial lines.

Even more startling, the system of reciprocal buying, which quantity customers may insist upon, may result in drastic changes in purchasing procedure.

● Financial
Each of the three functional areas already mentioned has one thing in common--they will increase the financial needs of the company. It will need more capital for investments in plants, machinery, and inventory in meeting the heavier load on operating funds required by increases in personnel (especially in sales and manufacturing), in advertising, and in materials procurement.

At review time you'll want to re-examine such financial requirements and commitments to see if they need re-planning. For example, because of changed conditions you may need more money in the next 6 or 12 months than you'd planned on having available. Or you may need less.

USING OUTSIDE HELP

Sometimes, when some businessmen review their objectives, they find problems they cannot handle. These problems may be either outside their experience, or require more time than they or their men can devote to them.

Some of these problems are of a one-time, non-repetitive nature, and thus they lend themselves to the use of outside specialists. Here an industrial engineer, management consultant, marketing research specialist, or accountant can render a real service.

For example, look at the detail of market and sales planning involved in a planned expansion of sales. A skilled marketing management consultant can develop the basic product market potential data. He can also develop the

- 4 -

sales forecasts, set up proper sales territories (and sales quotas) and assist the owner-manager in writing the sales policies and the selling plan. He can, moreover, train the company's personnel in methods to be followed so that the benefits of his comprehensive marketing research may be brought up to date periodically.

Or the marketing specialist might be asked to evaluate the marketing and selling methods presently pursued. He might be called on to select a new plant site (in many businesses, the site should be chosen from the standpoint of nearness to market).

In some cases, the owner-manager may have problems in manufacturing: obsolete equipment, poor plant layout, or a variety of other similar problems. A management engineering firm, with specialists such as industrial engineers, is available to perform services as required.

As in the case of the marketing management consultant, the benefits of the know-how of the manufacturing specialist can be spread over many years. Savings and increased profit can be the result. And these will, in all probability, more than pay the consultants' costs. The small owner-manager can thus buy these services as he requires them, just as easily as his wife buys groceries in the food store.

TAKING ACTION IS IMPORTANT

The owner-manager can make his periodic review of business objectives a fairly simple process or a very elaborate one. It is, however, better to refrain from making such review too complicated.

Rather try to keep your review process as clear-cut as possible. Thus, it will be easier to use, and you will be more apt to apply it at the designated time. Make your review at frequent intervals.

The main reason for this is: Marketing conditions sometimes change QUICKER than you think.

Therefore, when you review your objectives you can stay on top of shifting conditions. This helps you to do two things: (1) replan to correct mistakes, and (2) replan to take advantage of new opportunities.

Taking such action should help you to keep your procedures based on sound objectives which will help build profits.

FOR FURTHER INFORMATION

Businessmen interested in exploring further the subject of sound objectives may be interested in the references indicated below. This list is necessarily brief and selective. However, no slight is intended toward authors whose works are not included.

"How To Set Realistic Profit Goals," by Bruce Payne. *Harvard Business Review*, September-October 1958. Harvard Business Review, Soldiers Field Station, Boston 63, Mass. Single copy, $2. Reprint, $1.00.

Marketing, by Theodore N. Beckman and William R. Davidson. Ronald Press Co., 15 E. 26th St., New York 10, N. Y. 7th ed. 1962. $8.00.

Marketing Management, by Kenneth R. Davis, Ronald Press Co., 15 E. 26th St., New York 10, N. Y. 1961. $8.00.

Planning the Product, by D. M. Phelps, Richard D. Irwin, Inc., 1818 Ridge St., Homewood, Ill. 1947. $4.50.

"Sales Forecasting," by Lewis A. G. Martorano. *The Journal of Accountancy*, August 1960. American Institute of Certified Public Accountants, 270 Madison Ave., New York 16, N. Y. Single copy, 85 cents. $8 a year.

Small Plant Management. McGraw-Hill Book Co., 330 W. 42d St., New York 36, N. Y. 2d ed. 1960. $10.50.

Filing Classification:	*Administrative Practices*

─SMALL BUSINESS ADMINISTRATION─
U. S. Government Agency

MANAGEMENT AIDS No. 179

for small manufacturers

| Washington, D.C. | First printed September 1965 | Reprinted October 1972 |

BREAKING THE BARRIERS TO SMALL BUSINESS PLANNING

By **Roger A. Golde**

President, Golde Management Services, Cambridge, Massachusetts

──── SUMMARY ────

Most small manufacturers do not use long-range planning even though they could gain much from it. Planning can, for example, help owner-managers to provide lead time for necessary actions and to use resources effectively. With such benefits in the offing, why do small business owners neglect this management tool?

In many instances, certain barriers get between owner-managers and long-range planning. Some do not plan because of fear of the future or because of the inexactness of the future. Others fail to think systematically about where their companies may be 2 or 3 years hence because of the lack of proper time and place for planning or because of the lack of planning knowledge.

This Aid dicusses these barriers to small business planning and offers suggestions for overcoming them.

Many small business owners feel that they are doing enough planning when they use short-run sales forecasts, expense budgets, and other short-range planning tools. They shrug off the idea of long-range planning by saying, "That's for big companies."

Such owner-managers couldn't be more mistaken. Because of the rapid rate of change in today's world, present production methods may be totally inadequate next year or the year after next. Or present products may be dead or dying a few years from now.

In either case, which small company will have the best chance of survival --the one whose owner-manager neglects planning because he is busy with today's crises? Or the one whose owner-manager tries to plan ahead?

Small companies need to plan as thoroughly if not more thoroughly than large ones. Few small firms have enough resources to overcome their future problems with aggressive financial force. Few can afford to underwrite the loss that can occur while adjusting to an unexpected change when they depend on a single product or on a few key customers.

Essentially, long-range planning is the process of systematically and consciously thinking about the future of an enterprise as an integrated whole. It, therefore, is a vital tool for competing effectively and for trying to reduce future crises.

BENEFITS FROM LONG-RANGE PLANNING

When an owner-manager systematically thinks about the future of his company, he stands to gain certain benefits. The planning process helps him: to provide lead time for necessary actions; to make decisions where there are long-term effects; to use resources efficiently; and to improve current operations.

● Lead Time. Doing things in business takes time. The owner-manager must anticipate not only the changes that his business will need but also the time required to make these changes.

For example, if you expect that one of your products will become obsolete, you probably couldn't think of trying to develop a new product, produce it, and market it in only 30 days' time. You know that a development project for a new product may take 1 or 2 years, or longer. Therefore, you start early-- while the product destined for obsolescence is still marketable--to develop its replacement.

Other examples of business activity that require lead time are: building a new plant; beefing up a sales force; and putting together a promotional program. With specific plans for such activities, you can see what actions will be needed and provide the lead time for getting them done on schedule.

● Long-Term Effects. Planning helps make decisions where there are long-term effects. Many management decisions involve investments, that is, expenditures of time, effort, or money in the present in order to achieve benefits over a number of years in the future. As automation and mechanization increase, the number of investment decisions is also increasing. If money is to be spent on a machine that will last for 5 years, it is vital to think about the 5-year future of your business to be

- 2 -

sure the purchase is really justified. Mistakes in investment policy are costly and difficult to rectify.

● Efficient Use of Resources. Planning can help you provide for the efficient use of your company's resources--an especially vital area when they are scarce. When money, personnel, or facilities are limited, you have to be careful in using them.

You have to make choices as to what will be done as well as to when it will be done. You have to consider alternatives and weigh their impact on the prosperity of your whole company. Planning is necessary if the best choices are to be made.

When you look at long-range planning as a matter of choices, it is an extension of an ordinary activity, such as scheduling a day's production. There you have to decide which orders should be first. Similarly, in planning for next year, the year after next, and so on, you have to decide what activities are most important. Then you have to schedule these activities in a way that produces the best possible results per dollar of expense.

● Improved Operations. Another benefit which you may get from planning is improved current operations. Because planning often involves making periodic evaluations of the company as a whole, it can show up areas which need improvement.

For example, you might discover that your salesmen spend too much time selling the product with the lowest profit margin. Or you might find that a slight cut in your cost of raw materials could increase profits more than the increase which could be made by hiring another salesman.

BARRIERS BLOCK PLANNING

Even though they are aware of the advantages of long-range planning, many small business owners fail to do it. In fact, most small companies do little, if any, long-range planning.

Why do most owner-managers neglect trying to look ahead--in an orderly and detailed fashion--for at least 2 years? Life being what it is, certain barriers tend to discourage them from planning.

Among these barriers which block attempts at long-range planning are: fear, inexactness, changeability, lack of proper time and place, and lack of planning knowledge.

OVERCOMING THE BARRIERS

Recognizing that such barriers exist is an important step in overcoming them and moving along toward some long-range planning. Keep in mind also that only one of the five barriers may by itself be enough to impede planning in a small company. For example, the barrier which blocks one owner's planning efforts may be the inexactness-of-2-years-from-now

while-fear-of-the-future is the barrier which bothers another.

● Fear. Even though most people don't talk about it, fear is a barrier to many kinds of activity. It is especially a roadblock to planning, and it may be the biggest hurdle for most owner-managers.

Fear, for example, causes some owner-managers to feel that careful thought about the future of their companies will bring to light a host of trouble. "I've got enough worries without trying to cross bridges ahead of time," is a normal reaction.

Somehow it seems easier to live with vague apprehensions about a fuzzy future than it does with reasoned expectations. When the owner-manager has no clear description of the problems and opportunities, he tends to feel that his company can get by with token measures.

Yet such token solutions are often just "whistling in the dark." They remind one of the story of the executive who snapped his fingers as he paced up and down outside his plant. Asked what he was doing, he replied, "I'm keeping away the lions."

"But there are no lions around here," an observer said.

The executive nodded, smiled, and proclaimed, "Then it looks as though I'm doing a good job, doesn't it?"

A ridiculous story, perhaps, but it does show what can happen when a person doesn't recognize fear for what it is. Fear is a natural reaction. Realizing this fact is important in overcoming fear as a barrier to planning. The events, the problems, and the opportunities of the future cannot be taken care of with a snap of the fingers. They have to be faced. And the real fear which the owner-manager should have is that of facing the future without a plan--without a set of alternatives to choose from when a possible event occurs.

● Inexactness. Another barrier to the planning process is inexactness. One small business owner sums up this barrier by saying, "Planning is so inexact that it doesn't seem worth doing. No matter how carefully I plan, things often do not work out according to the plan."

And what he says is true--to an extent. Planning is an uncertain thing because, among other reasons, the future is uncertain.

However, the important fact is to realize that business operates in a world where certainty is impossible but where probability is sufficient to govern action. Essentially businessmen are bettors trying to find out the best way to play the odds. The job is to make the best possible decision before a series of uncertain events, not after.

One way of illustrating long-range planning is to look at a die which carries the numbers "1 through 6." When you roll this die, the probability of any one number--for example, 4--coming up is only 1 out of 6.

- 3

Now suppose that you find a special die. Upon scrutinizing this die you find that the number "4" is on 5 of its sides and the number "2" is on the sixth side. When you roll this die, the probability is that the "4" will come up 5 times out of 6. However, you are not surprised if the number "2" comes up instead of a "4." In the long run, it is bound to happen 1 out of 6 times.

The important thing in this example is taking time to learn the odds--to determine what is likely to happen. And so it is in business. The problem is getting some idea of the odds. For example, what are the odds that more customers will need your type of product 2 years from now? Ten years from now?

You formulate that idea by planning--by developing a description of what will probably happen. Then you plan what you want to happen within the framework of those odds. If your plans do not materialize, does that necessarily mean you should not have made them? Does it mean you should not have taken the time to examine your company and its environment in order to discover how best to bet on its future?

● Changeability. Often small businessmen complain that plans and goals change too frequently to make planning worthwhile. "I no sooner make a plan than something happens, and I have to modify it. Or I have to make a completely new plan."

Of course, this can be a serious problem. However, the solution lies in the frequency and flexibility with which you plan, rather than in the rejection of planning altogether.

If the situation changes rapidly in your company, review your long-range plans periodically--and alter your original project to the changing situations. Perhaps you should not try to plan 5 years ahead but only 1 or 2 years in the future.

However, in most small businesses, the time scale of events demands that you look ahead at least a year or two. Rare is the industry where some significant change does not occur within a period of 1 or 2 years. It is also hard to find the company in which certain necessary projects do not require a year or more to be completed.

Part of overcoming the barrier of changeability lies in flexibility. Make flexible plans. Do not plan for one narrow set of possibilities. Rather, consider how you might alter plans if a change materializes. For example, in thinking about building a new plant you should consider: (1) What would I do if the demand for my product turns out to be substantially less than I expected? (2) What would I do if the demand turns out to be much greater than I had predicted?

● Lack of Time and Place. Many small business owners say that the lack of proper time and place is an obstacle to planning. Quite often, however, this statement is just a way of avoiding a task which they do not really want to do.

Then, too, it is easy to let planning slide when you are busy. Many owner-managers do not plan because they feel that they cannot be spared from daily operations--from the day-to-day crises. They tend to forget that their plants and salesforces operate successfully when they are out sick for several days.

Like many other vital aspects of management, the owner-manager has to make a conscious effort to find the time and place for planning. In the normal run of affairs, the time for planning just will not turn up by itself.

Special conditions are needed for planning. You also need some peace and quite--some protection from continual interruptions.

Some owner-managers create an environment for their planning by doing it in the evening at the office or on Saturday. The president of one small company rents an office at the other end of town and uses it to get away from the daily crises of the plant.

Setting a schedule for planning is another way to help get it done. For example, you might decide to spend 1 hour every Wednesday evening on planning. Or you might set aside every other Saturday morning for thinking about your company's future.

● Lack of Knowledge. Lack of planning knowledge can be a most serious barrier to planning. Even when the owner-manager has a proper time and place, he must have some idea of how to go about planning in order to do it effectively.

One common approach to planning contains three steps: (1) set goals and objectives, (2) develop plans to achieve the goals, and (3) assess progress towards the objectives. Yet this approach is often confusing to the owner-manager who has never tried to plan.

Essentially, the important thing about planning in small business is getting started.

GETTING STARTED

If you've never planned, start by getting a complete picture of your operations. You may know some of the details individually, but the chances are you need more information to get the complete picture.

● Five Written Statements. Here's the type of information you need to stimulate your planning thought.

(1) A brief description of your company's present practices in all important areas such as products, purchasing, storage, quality control, labor relations, training, sales outlets, advertising, and research and development.

(2) A brief description of your present management procedures, reports, and organization (including informal job descriptions along with an organization chart).

(3) A list of the main factors exterior to your firm which affect your company the most. Areas to be considered include government, the

- 4 -

national economy, your competition, the community in which you do business, scientific advances, and overseas markets.

(4) A list of the changes you expect in any of these factors in the next few years.

(5) A list of the main strengths and weaknesses of your present operation (based on items 1 through 4).

It is essential that you write down your thinking because (1) getting something on paper is at the heart of any formalized kind of planning, (2) writing things down clarifies your own thought. Written plans are also helpful in conveying your ideas to others who will play a part in implementing them.

You probably noticed that several of the five items above refer to your business as it now exists. Planning for the future starts with the present. You have to have a clear idea of where you are before you can think about where you want to go. Only then can you select a few specific goals to work toward.

• The Right Frame of Mind. In trying to get started, remember that the right frame of mind is important. Most of the barriers to planning stem from one basic situation: Planning represents a vastly different type of activity and approach from the one you use in the day-to-day management of your company. Because long-range planning is so different from dealing with daily brush fires, the owner-manager needs to make a conscious effort to plan on a formal basis. Otherwise proper planning will not get done.

The owner-manager's attitude is important. It can make or break planning. In order to plan effectively, your attitude should be one that is unafraid of discovering what the present state of your business really is. It should also be one

that is not afraid of trying to learn what the future might bring.

Such an attitude can help you to clarify problems and plot solutions. And once you have developed possible solutions, following through on your plans is largely a matter of management--of doing what is needed at the proper time. Keep in mind that a very important part of making plans work is reviewing periodically performance against plans.

FOR FURTHER INFORMATION

Readers interested in exploring further the subject of long-range planning may wish to consult the references indicated below. This list is necessarily brief and selective. However, no slight is intended toward authors whose works are not mentioned.

Planning for Company Growth. Bruce Payne. 1963. $8.95. McGraw Hill Book Co., 330 West 42d St., New York, N.Y. 10036.

Customer-Oriented Planning. Robert W. Ferrell. 1964. $9. American Management Association, 135 West 50th St., New York, N.Y. 10020.

"How to Evaluate Corporate Strategy." *Harvard Business Review,* July-August 1963. $10 per year; $2 per copy. Graduate School of Business Administration, Harvard University, Soldiers Field, Boston, Mass. 02163.

"The Hierarchy of Objectives." *Harvard Business Review,* May-June 1964. $10 per year; $2 per copy. Graduate School of Business Administration, Harvard University, Soldiers Field, Boston, Mass. 02163.

"Practical Planning for Small Business." *Harvard Business Review,* September-October 1964. $10 per year; $2 per copy. Graduate School of Business Administration, Harvard University, Soldiers Field, Boston, Mass. 02163.

Long-Range Planning for Management. David W. Ewing, editor. 1964. 2d ed. $8.75. Harper and Row, 49 East 33d St., New York, N.Y. 10016.

When Companies Reach the Awkward Age

F. W. COPELAND

What should a small manufacturer do when operations reach a point beyond one-man supervision but not large enough to support an integrated organization? This is the period of adolescence separating the men from the boys.

Today there are thousands of small, specialized job-shops producing billions in total output. The small technical manufacturer renders such a useful service in handling semi-developed and short-run parts and assemblies that he has little trouble getting all the business he can handle. But the problems of growth strike before he has had time to gain management experience or capital. Then, like Mr. X—the composite character whose woes are chronicled here—the small manufacturer more often than not feels the pinch of corporate growing pains.

FIVE years ago, Mr. X was earning $20,000 a year as an engineer with a big defense manufacturer. Then he quit to launch the XYZ Company. It grew from a staff of three, working in his garage, to a force of 50 people turning out billings of $40,000 a month in a 10,000-foot leased shop. Getting orders was the easiest part of the operation. Mr. X could quote fixed prices on jobs that were headaches for a prime contractor because of mysterious "bugs," or because the quantities were so small. Purchasing agents were tickled pink to get the order off their desks, and a "fixed price" instead of "cost-plus" in their over-all cost estimates. Mr. X figured material cost at $50 per unit and quoted $500 apiece for a lot of ten. Nobody batted an eye. Then he devoted the brains and skill of a $20,000-a-year man to the task of designing and making a successful prototype. He worked, ate and slept with the problem until he either licked it

or decided it was hopeless. In the first case, he had a good chance of getting the pre-production order of 100 units at $200 apiece. If he failed, he lost nothing but his own time and a little material. When he had a $20,000 backlog, he leased more space and hired a few people. In due course, Mr. X's special training plus the cut-and-try experience at customers' expense made him known as an expert in his specialty field. Inquiries and orders began to come automatically.

In flexibility and speed of quotation and delivery he could run circles around larger competitors, because he personally initiated, specified and implemented every phase of design, procurement, and production. He could quote a lower price yet make a wider margin of profit because he had no overhead except rent, utilities, and the salary of a part-time bookkeeper. Another advantage was in income taxes. If he considered it good business to charge off a 100

per cent tax reserve against work-in-process inventory and all drawings, special tooling, jigs, fixtures, and so on, and this happened to wipe out all or most of his operating income, nobody could challenge him, for there were no cost or turnover records to contradict his pessimism (But if somebody asked him to put a value on his company for sale or merger, how fast those values soared!)

Mr. X enjoyed another extraordinary advantage—the microscopic amount of capital required. Since his operation consisted largely of assembling small, light pieces, his fixed assets were few and inexpensive. The principal outlay was for testing and inspection equipment, some of which could be borrowed, some bought second-hand and some included in the cost estimate of the first jobs and charged off accordingly. The only inventory required was for specific orders, self-liquidating on completion. Accounts receivable were low because the large customers were sympathetic, paid promptly or prepaid. Suppliers and even bankers gave very liberal terms of credit, hoping to win the gratitude of the little company if and when it orbited. Although it was impossible to figure the net worth of the XYZ Company, it appeared to be turning its capital ten to twenty times a year.

The Great Divide

When the company hit the 50-employee mark, Mr. X was unaware that he had reached a milestone—the limit of his capacity to do everything and boss everything himself and the loss of some of the important advantages of smallness. He did, however, realize that although he was enormously proud of his accomplishment, and rated locally as an industrialist, he was running breathlessly

44

on a treadmill. Mrs. X was complaining that for five years she had had no husband. His children hardly knew their father, and his doctor had hinted of ulcers.

Mr. X pondered three alternatives: to disregard the doctor and leave it to chance whether the business would expand or shrink, to cut back to a comfortable volume based on his personalized efforts, or to take the plunge —to think big, act big, grow big. Of course, he picked No. 3.

As a starter, Mr. X hired a "management consultant" with a degree from a famous business school, two years as a junior employee of a nationally known management firm, and three months on his own—admittedly young, but eager and cheap. Mr. X told him to study the picture carefully and bring in a complete set of recommendations for an expanded operation, based on an annual gross income of $1 million. "If we can do $500,000 a year with me doing all the selling, it's a cinch to do twice that with a real sales organization."

Man with a plan

The expert returned a month later with a 50-page report and a wall-size organization chart elaborately diagramming an impressive array of management functions. The book of procedures outlined in detail the exact duties and responsibilities of each department head and tactfully quoted from various reports that stressed the need for the president to delegate authority and refrain from breathing down anyone's neck.

The organization chart fascinated Mr. X, and it pleased his ego that it should take all these people to accomplish what he had been doing all by himself, but he was appalled at the prospect of spending so much money unproductively. Still, the expert showed him figures proving that billings of $80,000 a month, with a normal margin of gross profit, would absorb all costs and expenses and leave a net of 15 per cent before taxes. Groggy but game, Mr. X said he would buy the package—but would select the personnel himself.

The employment agencies were excited when he said he wanted five department heads immediately, though when he limited salaries to $500 a month, and said he expected "damned good men," the applicants seemed to fall into two categories: elderly men with long lists of jobs and lukewarm references, and young men with excellent references but in positions well below department head level.

When the smoke cleared, the XYZ Company had engaged five men at $500, two girls at $300, and one trainee at $200. Some 1,000 feet of additional floor space had been leased and two toilets added. There was a great deal of new office equipment, a switchboard, and an intercom system.

Although he suffered nightmares of apprehension, Mr. X kept his hands off the reins. Theoretically he was supposed to keep in touch through reports from the controller, but the latter was honest enough to admit that his monthly P & L reports and balance sheets were unreliable until his newly established systems of jobcosting, perpetual inventory, depreciation etc., could build up a historical record.

One evening Mr. X was surprised to receive, at his home, a phone call

---

How Small Is Small?

I have been impressed by the fact that smallness has many advantages, if the operation is planned and kept small. But anyone discussing a subject related to "small business" must first define what he means by "small." The Small Business Administration has recently stated that 95 per cent of the 4,684,000 businesses in the United States are now officially small. Presumably this excludes only the "untouchables," the big companies whom it is politically more expedient to attack than defend. The absurdity of lumping together the very small companies (more than 3 million businesses employ fewer than four people), the medium small, the small and the large-small (400 to 500 employees) is obvious but appears to be part of two carefully nurtured misconceptions: 1) that Uncle Sam is looking after most of us; 2) that a business has only to prove it is "small" to get longterm loans from the SBA, or equity financing from the nearest Small Business Investment Company. I prefer to define the "small" manufacturer as one who employs from five to 50 workers.

---

from the loan officer at the bank. The officer asked him to drop in for a chat, without bringing the controller.

When Mr. X appeared the next day, the banker said: "Please understand, Mr. X, we have great confidence in you and only want your assurance that this tight-money situation is due to a temporary surge of business and is self-liquidating." Mr. X was deeply hurt and indignant. He explained in detail his expansion program and showed the forecasts of income and profit. The banker spent the next hour patiently explaining the difference between credit and capital. What the XYZ Company needed was a base of permanent capital, and since the amount would be in excess of collateral and beyond expectancy of early repayment, it should be considered "risk capital." If the company contemplated marketing proprietary items in addition to its custom business, this would mean substantial amounts tied up in finished inventory. And if the largest manufacturers in the country could not turn their capital more than three or four times a year, the XYZ Company had to figure on at least $200,000 net worth if they anticipated doing $1 million a year.

Waking up to realities

Mr. X staggered back to his office in a daze, called a staff meeting that included the management expert, and told them what the banker said. "What the hell have you done to my company?" he shouted. "It looks as if we were broke."

The management expert asked quietly, "Where is that income of $80,000 a month?"

The sales manager said, "How can I get sales when it takes a month to get a price and delivery to quote?"

The chief engineer said, "How can I design, or even write up specs when the sales department keeps me swamped with cockeyed inquiries? Why doesn't somebody sell something standard now and then?"

The production manager said, "How can I turn out production when the engineering department won't release specifications, the purchasing department won't bring in enough material, the inspection and quality control departments are always feuding, and the financial department keeps me so busy with paperwork that I can't get into the shop?"

Each department head had been so fearful of deviating from the system that he dodged taking any responsibility. Although the backlog of orders was building up to record figures, little was being shipped and all the cash was frozen in inventory.

Did Mr. X fire the lot and go back to one-man supervision? Did he keep on doggedly and go broke—or get an angel to finance him for a while? Or did he compromise by keeping one or two of the department heads, taking back from them the authority he had delegated?

In any case, Mr. X had to look for new capital unless he wanted to sell out or merge. It is a safe bet that he went to the Small Business Administration and asked for a long-term capital loan—and was quite properly turned down for lack of either collateral or an earning record. He probably went to one or more of the small business investment companies for a debenture loan and was told that his operation did not have enough glamor to assure a resale market. The investment bankers shied away when they saw his figures. He flirted with a small-issue specialty house, but backed down when he learned the cost. Private investors offered him the capital he needed but demanded a straight equity position and control (Mr. X said he would "burn down the plant first "). If he did solve his problem it was probably via a face-saving compromise: For a substantial sweetener in free common stock, an outsider loaned him the money on a term basis, retaining control until repaid. Under this arrangement, Mr. X kidded himself that surrender of control was only temporary.

The root of the trouble

Mr. X was not a stupid man. His mistakes were due to wishful thinking, oversimplification, and possessiveness. What could have appeared more coldly logical than the assumption that if he was turning away as much business as he was accepting he could double his volume by doubling his production force? The expense scared him, but the cleancut figures of the expert would be impressive to any layman, particularly when they confirmed his aspirations. Nor should he be blamed for ignoring the need for an expanded capital base under expanded volume: He had been besieged by "deal men" hinting they could raise $299,000 for a third interest, and by mystery men representing undisclosed principals with

---

The ABC's of Expansion

Many a tycoon will say that he owes much of his success to what he learned from his first bankruptcy. There is no better teacher than experience—but it is still unfortunate that so much time, money, effort, and illusion are wasted by young pioneers who go broke and have to start all over again because nobody taught them the fundamental rules of business:

● It takes money to make money. A substantial increase in the size of any business calls for more capital, and if the owner cannot supply it, he must solicit outside investors. Any program of raising capital should go after an amount that will tide the company over a period of deficit operations as well as expanded volume.

● When the owner accepts impersonal capital, he must adopt an entirely new philosophy as well. It may be that the new stockholders will be humble sheep who never question or criticize, but smart management will put someone on the board of directors to share responsibility. An educated director is better than a troubleshooter sent in later by disgruntled stockholders.

● Instead of introducing more system than the company needs, more overhead than it can afford, and depriving the company of his personal talents, the owner should hire an associate who is strong in the areas where he is weakest. If they divide the executive duties between them, each can be planner, supervisor, and doer in his own bailiwick. Systems and subordinates can be added as the business grow

---

unlimited funds to invest. Even his bank had phoned him periodically to ask if he couldn't use more credit.

It is doubtful that any one had risked Mr. X's displeasure by preaching two simple facts of business: 1) It takes money to make money, and if the owner's ambitions carry him beyond his own personal resources, he must attract outside money by offering inducements comparable to the risk. 2) Good management is as important as capital, and when an operation gets too large for one-man dominance it must be strengthened from the top down, not from the bottom up. The $500-a-month departmental worker is as essential to a manufacturer as the non-com is to the army, but in today's market, one can not get a proven, competent executive for that figure.

But if Mr. X ruined his company by too much salaried overhead, how can he be criticized for not employing bigger men? The answer to this apparent riddle is that if, instead of Mr. X and five subordinates, the XYZ Company had had two topnotch men of Mr. X's caliber dividing the func-

tions of engineering, sales, production, and finance according to their respective aptitudes, they could have kept up the skills, flexibility, and speed of the company. They could have continued doing this until the force had reached 100 or even 150. And there is a strong probability that Mr. X could have found his counterpart in a junior executive in a large company—who, for a chance to bet on himself, would have been willing to accept a 50 per cent cut in salary.

For a small manufacturer the problems of acquiring growth capital and executive help are not insurmountable if the owner is willing to share with both investor and executive the possible fruits of success. But the possessive owner who insists on retaining all the glory, all the profits, and all the ownership can only succeed if the glory, profits and ownership are kept small.   END

A former company president, the author since retirement has carved out a new career as a Pasadena management consultant and writer.

CHAPTER 6
THE IMPOSSIBLE TRANSITION

Several separate and distinct articles are presented as part of this section to indicate the complex conditions that surround the entrepreneur during this transition period. His business venture has long passed from being a one man show. It is now a successful and probably large enterprise, having needs totally unlike the needs of a new venture.

Managing a mature organization does not satisfy the entrepreneur's need to achieve. He prefers the challenge of taking his vision of a new product and building a profitable business from nothing. He is willing to take the high risks involved. His rewards from innovating are more meaningful, and often more profitable, than filling a slot in a large corporation. It is during the transition stage of the entrepreneur's life cycle, after his venture has been a success, that he is most likely to choose the alternative of reaping the reward, bailing out, and attacking the business environment from a new venture formation.

If the entrepreneur is nearing the end of his active career, he should now be planning a successor to take his position. For the family-owned company, this may present special problems. In a non-family business, the transition of the executive function will usually be uneventful if the successor is at least as competent as his predecessor, and if the organization has had previous turnover in this position. Not so for the family business.

The first article by Prof. Levinson "The Conflicts that Plague the Family Business" offers hints on how to keep the emphasis on the business rather than the family. In an easy to read but insightful manner, Mr. Levinson, a leading author on management subjects, presents solutions to family business problems.

The article by F.W. Copeland portrays an entrepreneur-founder during a period of changing long term needs for his business. He has successfully developed his idea for a unique and better product into a profitable venture, which over time has grown modestly in number of employees and dollar sales. But now the entrepreneur is faced with his first major personal dilemma. The autonomous owner must now become the managing owner who delegates major responsibilities to the newly hired managers in an expanded organization. Copeland's story about the composite Mr. X is very real in the events that take place. The consultant who proposes the gold-plated plan, without establishing an adequate means for implementation; the hiring of managerial types to assume major departmental positions, but restricting the selection by imposing unrealistically low salaries; and then, after choosing the best man from the selection available, falsely assuming that the business is in the responsible and reassuring hand of managing "experts". The lack of intra-departmental communications and feedback monitoring almost bring Mr. X's firm to a state of collapse. Although originally written 15 years ago, Copeland's message and moral are equally true today.

There are several significant points covered in the Copeland article. If additional capital resources are required beyond what is presently available to the firm, outside capital must be raised. The availability of whatever funds are needed must be ensured before major expenditures on expansion begin. But no amount of capital resources will result in a successful expansion unless the new organization is staffed with competent men who continually monitor marketing, personnel, product and finance progress. The only factor that measures the worth of the small business' struggle for survival is its profitability. An over-zealous owner can endanger his company by too many frills resulting in too high an overhead and insufficient capital resources to support this overhead.

The two articles which follow, by Davis and Inbermann address similar issues with two different views. Inbermann offers a framework for company presidents to conduct more positive meetings. During this trying stage of development, the conduct at meetings becomes an even more central issue. On the other end of this same question, Mr. Davis discusses "Entrepreneurial Succession." Once an entrepreneur has opted to untie the company from his control, how can he make the transition more tolerable. This article is best read before one faces the dilemma. Before the overbearing emotions set in, how can one prepare for the eventual but inevitable separation?

In addition to reorganizational problems involving the adding of more personnel to meet increased customer demand for the company's product, the small business that has effectively exploited its product idea may also find that success has resulted in greater competitive pressures. Maintaining or expanding the rate of company growth under this threat may require the addition of distribution channels and warehousing, or horizontal integration in the form of additional manufacturing capacity. Sufficient capital and management resources may not be available for implementation of these necessary changes. Edward Fillon, in "A Way Out for Small Business," proposes mergers as a viable alternative in meeting and overcoming these competitive threats.

A merger may also be a way for the entrepreneur to profitably liquidate his investment. Fillon reviews the need for careful consideration of the operational and management needs of the business, and legal and tax requirements imposed by the government. One of Fillon's main points is that mergers should be considered in a positive sense as a strategic technique to use in achieving planned business objectives. Merging should not be viewed as a stop-gap measure for saving the business after the errors of management have already been made — although it may very well provide the only means for survival.

If the entrepreneur is still relatively young, then he is faced either with making a reassessment of his abilities as an effective manager — if this has not already been done by stockholders or other creditors — or selling his interest in the business and re-investing his talents and funds in starting a new venture. Similar periods of personal self-assessment occur at different times in everyone's life. In the first case, the entrepreneur may find that he no longer has the qualities and attitudes conducive to the profitable managing of the mature enterprise. His decisions may not be optimum in terms of the company's needs. His choice is to either attempt the learning and application of the required managerial skills, or to leave the business.

The second choice is somewhat difficult because the entrepreneur perceives a constrained environment where he is an ineffective manager and consequently makes the choice to be free from the bureaucracy of the business. He must seek to regain his autonomy, and his freedom to more actively participate in the innovation process by establishing a new business venture. I have called this predicament the impossible transition. It must be dealt with after the entrepreneur has made his impossible dream come true.

A WAY OUT FOR SMALL BUSINESS

By Edward P. Fillion, Jr.

When a small business has serious doubts about future operations,
——————————*risk can be eliminated or minimized — through merger.*——————————

Talk to almost any economist, corporate planner, or corporate president, and a generally pessimistic outlook as to the future of small business is forecast. While varied substantiations are put forth, most could be paraphrased as the dominance of size.

Many manufacturing companies are scurrying to grow faster than their competitors; others, already gigantic, are continuing to grow at a rate that is somewhat embarrassing to their management. While in most cases a portion of this growth results from expanding markets, no small amount is coming from increasing market share — to the detriment of small business. U.S. Department of Commerce figures state that the average monthly rate of business formation in 1964 was 16,477. Business failures during the same period were almost 10% of this figure.

Most of the business failures occur early in corporate life for a number of well-publicized reasons, but what is not pointed out is the growing number of businesses failing after a ten year life. In 1953, of all business failures, 14.8% occurred after 10 years. By 1963, the percentage had jumped to 22.9%. How many of these faltered because they could no longer compete? While the figure is sizeable to begin with, not included are the small businesses which do not die, but which hang on indefinitely to only a marginal existence. For every one failing, we suggest there might be 50 going nowhere.

Undoubtedly there is ample opportunity for the formation and growth of certain types of small business. The July 31, 1965 issue of *Business Week* pointed out opportunities in service businesses. However, their statistics and outlook for the future of small manufacturing companies were far from enthusiastic.

Marketing Problems

Probably the major deterrent to growth is inadequate or incomplete distribution. Most small companies sell only regionally, or in cases where there is national distribution, it is spotty and at a high sales cost. While this can be corrected by adequate financing, the dollar figure required to bring the sales message to the total market is staggering.

A case in point is the experience of a West Coast specialty soap manufacturer. After running through six figure investments on two occasions, the company, although considered to be successful, had made no market penetration east of the Rockies. It required sale to a large eastern company, well-known in the consumer goods field, to achieve its real potential. The parent was willing to commit substantial sums to television and other consumer promotion programs because the high profit margin of the product would return the advertising budget quickly. Other selling costs would decrease because the buyer had an existing national sales force and warehouse system which could move the product rapidly. In five years, sales volume went up about 1000 percent. Alone, the West Coast company could not hope to approximate these results.

Another marketing problem is created by too short a product line. This is particularly true in the industrial market, where increasingly complex assemblies require consideration of entire systems.

A Midwest metal products company developed a very high pressure hydraulic pump which was reputed to be excellent. The pump did not sell. Being small, the company had to rely on "reps." The reps did not have the background to provide the application engineering required. Potential customers stated they would rather buy a lesser pump from a company offering additional components and able to take responsibility for the entire system.

These and other examples in our files point out that today it is not enough to have a good product to achieve success. Of course, if limitless funds were available, distribution, product development, and management could be purchased, but what small company has access to funds of that magnitude? Slow growth of a product financed totally from within, may only invite Chinese copies.

While any given company may prove to be the exception, Department of Commerce statistics show that in the 15 year period 1947-1962, the two hundred largest manufacturing companies increased their percentage from 30% to 40% of total value added through manufacture. In 1958, four companies in each field controlled these percentages of total output:

Vacuum cleaners	70%
Transformers	71%
Primary Batteries	84%
Domestic laundry equipment	71%
Surgical supplies	54%
Abrasive products	58%

Faced with the growing pressures of bigness, what can the small business do? No one answer is without objection, but the following are suggested:

1. Pick a small localized market area. Stay put and be content to remain small. The large company, with its greater overhead and administrative costs will not find it economically feasible to attempt to invade your area. In certain cases this may not work, as the dominant companies in the industry may enter your market for non-financial reasons.

2. Seek a big brother. If a portion of your production capacity is unused or is returning an insufficient profit, the solution may be to find a captive customer. The very nature of contract manufacturing removes merchandising and distribution burdens from the manufacturer. Many companies have achieved substantial growth by being pulled along as their customer grows. There also are many cases where the opposite is true. The customer fails or at some point decides it makes more sense to perform the manufacturing function in-house. The small company may not be able to recover from the loss of business on which it is dependent.

3. Completely forego current enjoyment and plough all funds back into the company. Most small businesses are under-capitalized to begin with. The creation of capital is compounded as each succeeding profit is reinvested, and internal growth should accelerate. When all available funds are devoted to increased research and development, advertising, or in support of new salesmen, little is left for management compensation. It may be extremely difficult to attract the much needed competent middle management talent on only the promise of added compensation at some unspecified future date.

Stock options may be an answer, but of course the owner's equity is diluted. In practice, many businesses find it hard to adhere to such a Spartan plan. The hard working owner of a business may not resist the temptation to show off his success. In addition, as the equity grows, the risk of actual loss increases even though the degree of risk remains unchanged. Events outside the control of the business, such as the merger of a competitor with a big power, may show the prior frugality to have been in vain.

4. Join a big company through merger. The problems of remaining small are side-stepped by becoming big. The steadily increasing number of mergers between manufacturing companies attests to the logic of such a move. The question of small size versus bigness is relative and depends on the particular industry.

Not long ago, the chief executive of an auto parts manufacturer said that there was no place in his industry for a company of its size. At the time, annual sales were in excess of $60 million. The company subsequently merged and is now a division of one of the country's fifty largest corporations. While a transaction can be geared to answer practically every other requirement, the chief objection to a sale or merger is loss of independence.

Merger Considerations

What constitutes independence is as relative as size. One company president who championed his independence had to clear every decision with his bank and a factoring company. At the same time a substantial customer and the local union dictated many operations. The "independence" was wholly in the owner's mind and was a fallacy. In another company, which had gone public, the stockholders found themselves locked in, although the public issue had been made to get more flexibility.

If viewed objectively, there are many positive reasons to consider merger with a larger company. Excluding an incentive type transaction, the doubts of the future are resolved at the time of the closing. The liquidity or marketability of the seller's investment is improved. In one motion he has capitalized his past successes and realized the fruits of his labor. Dependent on his willingness to accept new risk, his funds can be reinvested in anything from government bonds to speculative real estate.

In a high percentage of cases, the owner who merges his company, receiving stock of the acquirer, will lighten up by selling some of these new shares to get diversity of investment. The recent success of exchange type mutual funds attests to the desire to spread the risk. Prime targets for exchange fund salesmen are stockholders of recently merged companies who would rather have a dozen blue chip stocks than one.

After the business owner has fully explored the personal benefits of a merger, he may then consider the benefits to his company. Can he develop a proposal for his business which will better enable his company to grow? The merged operation may result in marketing, production, or clerical economies for both parties, but in all too many cases the cost of coordination of activities outweighs the savings. It is important to pick the right partner and evaluate each operational phase of the combined business.

Since the major part of any negotiation involves the "coming to terms" between the owners, operational considerations often are skipped over lightly. When buyer and seller sense a deal in the making each is hesitant to rock the boat by bringing up points of possible dispute. Obviously the buyer takes the responsibility for making the merger work, but if the seller is going to continue in any capacity, he also should be very certain that the business combination is on sound footing. With or without outside advice, the seller should satisfy himself that he has picked the right prospect before entering into serious talks.

Management of a company interested in making an upstream merger must first determine its requirements. Specifically, what do they hope to accomplish operationally? In the area of marketing, they may seek a national system of warehouses, direct selling or jobber contacts among a new class of customers, or additional promotion or advertising funds. In production they may be interested in vertical help — by associating themselves with a company processing at a more basic level, such as the spring company that merged with a wire drawing business. It may be wise to merge with a company nearer the ultimate consumer. This generally would involve merger with an existing customer. A horizontal combination is indicated where additional manufacturing capacity is required.

Other requirements which may dictate consideration of merger are insufficient research and development facilities or talent, lack of depth in management, or need for additional working funds to support growth. All of these requirements are positive ones indicating growth problems of the smaller company. The time to merge is when the company is healthy and growing but could grow faster with help.

An entirely different set of requirements exists for the company that waits too long and has started to experience the problems of shrinking market, product obsolescence, burdensome financing charges, and flight of competent middle management. Regardless of the circumstances, the situation must be faced squarely and the requirements objectively drawn.

In addition to operational requirements, there are those of management. Should the company continue to operate with its personnel intact, do some wish to leave the business, or should some be replaced? Must the company look for a prospective parent able to supply some talent, or should the company seek a buyer able to utilize its rising stars who will go elsewhere if greater challenges cannot be found?

Governmental Requirements

A third requirement area of growing importance is observance of government policies. Anti-trust and taxation requirements are a substantial concern today, and may in the future override operational and management considerations. Governmental requirements are negative, requiring a broad knowledge of limitations. A good deal of confusion exists as to the inner workings of accounting, legal, and taxation aspects. The term, "pooling of interests," is often used to describe a tax exempt deal, but a pooling of interests really only has to do with a method of accounting.

Owners seeking a "tax free" deal generally think the exchange must be purely stock for stock or stock for assets. If, however, a statutory merger (legal basis) is accomplished, a pooling of interests can still be used (accounting basis), and tax exempt treatment will result on any stock exchanged (taxation basis), yet a substantial portion of the price can be in cash. Coordination of effort of the corporate attorney, accountant, and tax counsel are essential in any merger negotiation. This coordination must stem from top management or its merger specialist advisor.

Management also must clearly understand the impact of Sections 1245 and 1250 of the IRS code of 1962, dealing with taxation on depreciation. In the past, only legal considerations dictated whether stock or assets of a company should be sold. Today the tax implications of the two procedures are great, and may have a substantial impact on the selling price.

Another problem which will greatly affect merger strategy in the future is the handling of goodwill from the SEC standpoint. The effect of the new requirement is to benefit the buyer's earnings when the seller is merged below book value. If goodwill is involved, the results are opposite and may have a terrifically depressing effect on reported earnings per share. In most mergers today, the price paid is in excess of book value, adding to the complexity of making a deal.

The Proper Approach to Mergers

Once armed with a set of requirements, and a list of prospects fitting the requirements, the next step is the proper preparation of underlying data. When a company goes public, it issues a prospectus. When interested in merger, a document should be prepared which makes the prospectus look like a first grade primer. A full description of the business, the requirements, and the way in which it is felt the requirements can be met is necessary. This does not mean that you have to wear your heart on your sleeve. Properly prepared, such a report can tell what is necessary without becoming intimate to the point of destroying the romance.

A proper approach to the prospective buyer is equally important. Big companies don't have time to play cat and mouse. At the same time the smaller company does not wish to appear too eager. If all the proper groundwork has been laid, the company approached will be impressed with the businesslike manner, thoroughness, and logic of the exploration.

As talks are being held, it becomes equally important for the seller to analyze and evaluate the buyer. If the seller takes the buyer's stock, he has not sold out, he has traded. What is he getting? If a cash transaction, the seller still must evaluate the position his company will continue to hold unless he is one of those owners who doesn't care what happens as long as he gets his share. In many cases the buyer may think it presumptuous of the seller to pry into the buyer's motives and philosophies, but not if the preparation and approach have been properly handled.

Once buyer and seller are at the hand holding stage, someone has to ask the big question — what price! In a business marriage virtually every transaction hangs on the ability of the two parties to reach a fair and equitable price. Stated simply, it means compromise. Generally it is reported to the press that a merger is in the wind, "subject to working out the details." That little phrase is comparable to the part of the iceberg above water. There are many technical problems which must be worked out, but these are small in relation to the problem of reaching agreement as to price.

The price a company should sell for depends on the nature of the transaction, the compatibility of buyer and seller, the existing conditions in the industry, and the state of the economy. The price a company does sell for depends on the personalities involved. Recently several "how to" books on merger have been published. Each attempts to supply answers to the question, at what price should . . . No one gives more than passing treatment to the question, at what price does . . . This is understandable because the culmination of any negotiation represents a total of all the tangible and intangible relationships that have developed in the exploration. The accountant, attorney, production or marketing analyst is the catalyst in arriving at the tangible answer. A catalyst for the intangibles may be a great deal more important. Generally this function is filled by an intermediary.

The Role of the Intermediary

The intermediary may not be a third party, but few companies have successfully developed one internally who can retain third party objectively. Merging companies may ask a banker, investment banker, business broker, finder, or other outside party to act as intermediary. In many cases the intermediary is ineffective, because he has not been involved from the inception of the idea. Someone called in at the last minute has not experienced the total intangible relationship.

The proper intermediary is one who is willing to provide, and is capable of providing, a full range of services. These include advice as to the requirements of a company, the screening of prospects, development of background information, making the approaches, analyzing the buyer, being knowledgeable in tax and accounting matters, and to no small extent having the experience of many past transactions. With this background, the intermediary is then in the best possible position to act as a sounding board, keeping the exploration and negotiation alive — avoiding the problem of face to face confrontation

from which one party must retreat. Without a sounding board, many mergers have not taken place because of injured pride; or worse, they have taken place with one or both parties later discovering that "the deal was not what it seemed."

A great deal of criticism has been leveled at the broker or finder. Much of this may be warranted, but in a large number of cases the buyer or seller thought he was retaining an intermediary when such was not the case. The finder has no capability to evaluate or analyze. The accountant or attorney is not versed in marketing or production problems. The management consultant generally prefers not to become involved in the negotiation. The banker is not equipped to find or analyze. The proper intermediary is a merger specialist, knowledgeable in all these areas. In many cases, the principal, himself, may be to blame, for being less than completely candid with his representative.

Most intermediaries work, at least in part, on a commission basis. Compensation is predicated on success. We find no fault in the statement that the intermediary's prime concern is to see the deal, any deal, go through. This is precisely why he was hired. Fees vary widely and are a source of irritation to the principals and intermediary as well. In every case, the fee schedule should be agreed to in advance, at the same time the range of services to be performed is determined. The fee should be considered as part of the investment or sale price as the case may be. Certainly a deal looks better the lower the fee is, but it is a mistake to tie up the intermediary in compromising a fee at the very time the intermediary should be working for his client to compromise the price. Select the right intermediary to begin with and then devote all effort to the acquisition.

For a small businessman, consideration of merger often is not given serious attention. While merger may not be the answer, it should be viewed as objectively as a make-or-buy decision. In a great many cases merger is not considered until it is too late — when there is no other way to go.

Viewed objectively, a merger should be neither more nor less than a tool for achieving primary corporate goals, i.e. a means for expanding production, developing existing markets or pioneering new ones, increasing productivity of fixed assets, or better utilizing key personnel. Its degree of effectiveness in any small business situation often is determined by counseling talents available to the seller, as well as by the nature and timing of exploration made in his behalf.

The decision to merge, if approached only on a "if all else fails" basis rarely represents a decision at all. Being the last "independent," next door to a division of a major competitor, can be awfully lonely.

The Incurables

There are men who so love being entrepreneurs that even great wealth can't cure them of the itch. FORBES found nine of them and asked what made them the way they are.

A GOOD MANY Americans dream about starting their own companies, but most of them never get beyond dreaming. They're simply not entrepreneurs. There are others, however, a handful, so thoroughly entrepreneurial they're not satisfied with starting one company and spending the rest of their lives running it. They start company after company. For these people, entrepreneur-ing is a way of life.

Neison and Irving Harris of Chicago built the Toni company from scratch, then sold it to Gillette for $20 million. That was in 1948, when $20 million was as good as $30 million is today. And what did the Harris brothers do? Retire? No, they bought an old corporate shell and turned it into a $64-million-a-year industrial products maker called Pittway Corp. At that point, more money was the last thing they needed, yet they kept going. "Retire?" snorts Neison Harris. "I just don't know what the hell I'd do in the morning if I couldn't go to work."

The Harris brothers are not unique. In recent weeks, FORBES Reporter Alex Block has talked with others like them, outstanding examples of the entrepreneurial breed, individuals who have started not one but two or more successful enterprises. He found them a diverse lot. Some were born to wealth; others rose from poverty. Some were salesmen, some technicians, some plain businessmen. They operated in widely diverse fields, from pet foods to jet aircraft, from publishing to transistors. But they had, he found, certain things in common:

They were not interested primarily in money but in creating and building companies. In several cases, when they sold a company they had started, they received so much stock for it they could have taken over control of the company to which they sold it. They didn't, because that wouldn't

have been any fun; they would be running something that somebody else created. They would be managers, not entrepreneurs.

The companies they created and built were substantial and profitable but hardly in the billion-dollar class. They did have the base on which to build a billion-dollar conglomerate, but, again, that would have meant taking over businesses established by others. That's not for them. They have an ill-disguised disdain for the men who put together conglomerates. Such men are not creators.

Ask them why they refused to retire, and the usual answer given is, "How would I spend my time?" That obviously is not the real answer, because there are dozens of ways in which a retired man can spend his time—in public service, in politics, by going into Wall Street, by going fishing. To the born entrepreneur, building a business from scratch is a way of life. It's not only his occupation; it is also his vocation and his relaxation.

The classic example of the entrepreneurial breed probably is Sherman Fairchild. His father was a founder and the largest shareholder of International Business Machines. Obviously, every door at IBM was open to Sherman. He turned his back on the company. It was not that he scorned his father's money, but that IBM was his father's baby, already grown to manhood. He wanted to build something he could proudly call his own. He founded Fairchild Camera & Instrument, then Fairchild Hiller Corp., then Fairchild Recording Equipment. Money? What did he need money for, especially after his father's death, when he became IBM's biggest stockholder? He had an urge to create that has grown stronger with the years. He says: "The truth is that the man who just thinks of making money usually

doesn't make much money. You've got to have your eye not on the money but on the job. I've never met a real entrepreneur for whom getting wealthy was the sole object."

Superficially, no one could seem more different from Fairchild than Jeno Paulucci. Yet, basically, they are alike. Jeno Paulucci, son of an immigrant iron miner is, by his own estimate worth about $100 million at the age of 51. In 1966 he sold Chun King to Reynolds Tobacco for $63 million and began building a corporate shell he had held for several years into a brand-new food business, Jeno's, Inc. He gets to his Duluth, Minn. office at 6 a.m. and often works seven days a week. Paulucci says an entrepreneur is a man "who sacrifices everything to his work," not just for money, but for a burning desire to meet a challenge. The money's just a way to measure how successful you are.

William Lear comes from a very different background. A school dropout in the eighth grade, Lear started out as an airplane mechanic for the U.S. Airmail base at Grant Park in Chicago. But he agrees with Paulucci that the entrepreneur can do things no big company can.

"I want to be in a position where I can put an idea into effect," Lear says. "I don't want to have to sell it to four or five different levels of people. If my idea loses *I* lose. If it wins *I* win. You can't do that in many big corporations."

Says Jeno Paulucci, echoing Lear's dislike of depending on others: "I can't wait even a few days to convince people that what I'm doing is right. I'm in a hurry even when I may be wrong."

William Lear **founded** Lear, Inc., a manufacturer of aviation electronics; sold the company to Siegler and founded Lear Jet; sold that to Gates Rubber and now runs Lear Motors.

Sherman Fairchild: *"My mother wanted me to go into IBM and I wanted to build aerial cameras. Our general manager in Europe was talking to us one day and he said; 'Gee, give him a couple of hundred thousand dollars and if he loses it he will still be a better businessman.' That is what I started with. I never did use the money that my father had left to me. That would have been like playing golf and moving the ball."*

Bill Lear: *"Look at me. I couldn't get a job anywhere based on my engineering degrees, yet I've got a string of unbroken successes in engineering." Lear is right. Despite having ended his formal education in the eighth grade, his accomplishments include an innovation in radio sets that made possible the first multistation home radios in the Twenties; the first workable car radios; the Lear jet and a compact stereo tape system for cars.*

Neison Harris: "I've got five divisions and I know what's going on. I have a friend who heads a company with 35,000 employees. It'll take him ten years to know the names of all his vice presidents. I want more out of life than that."

Jeno Paulucci: "I think there's too much of the old gray flannel ethic, the 4½ day week, a lot of security. That's why I hate New York. The work we get out of New York is half what we get out of the same people in the Midwest."

Jack Kent Cooke: "Wouldn't you like to be in sports? Damn right you would. At whatever age reason assaulted me, I used to think, by golly, it would be wonderful to be in sports. And I'm sure the same applies to anyone."

His background is just as different from Paulucci's as Paulucci's is from Fairchild's. But he agrees with Paulucci that money is secondary. "I think I'd work even harder if I had a *trillion dollars*," says Bill Lear. "When I see a good thing that needs doing I want to do it. Like the thing I'm working on now, steam power plants for automobiles."

For a while Lear headed a good-sized public company, Lear, Inc. But he quit in frustration when his board of directors refused to let him build his now-famed Lear jet. "Why I might as well have been the janitor there," he says. "At least the janitor could decide on his own where he wanted to sweep."

Jack Kent Cooke, a Canadian, sold his interests in radio and publishing in 1959 when he was 47 and came to Los Angeles to retire. "I found I missed the fun and hurly burly of business," he says, "and in 1965 I went back to work." Cooke is president and owner of the L.A. Lakers basketball team, the L.A. Kings pro hockey team and the Forum, a new $16-million sport arena.

With a personal wealth estimated at nearly $40 million, Cooke could easily have bought control of a large business and tried to make it bigger. But that wasn't what he was after. "I need the feeling that I'm in effective control of the business. That's what makes me different from the professional managers. I guess it isn't fair to call them mercenaries, but their attitude is different from the entrepreneur's."

"They Are Stooges"

German-born Max Ries, 68, has started successful companies on both sides of the Atlantic. In 1940 he fled from Hitler. "I had to make a living here," he says, "and so I started peddling cheese from store to store from my car." Before he was finished, Ries had built his company, Reese Foods, into a $7.5-million-a-year seller of specialty food items. He sold it to Pet Inc. in 1964. Two years later he was back in business, partly because he was bored and partly because he disapproved of what the new owners were doing with his old company. "These big companies," he says in his German accent, "they are very funny. They are stooges. They're more interested in showing what *can't* be done than in what can be done." Ries is now in the snuff business. He says: "All the kids in England

are using it, soon they will be here also."

Richard Rich, 38, got a degree in business administration from NYU before entering advertising. After bouncing around several agencies he helped found the now-famous Wells, Rich, Greene advertising agency which he left this past April. Rich, who still holds several hundred thousand shares of Wells, Rich, Greene stock valued at over $3 million, is now starting his own advertising consulting service. Work for someone else or be part of a big agency? "Would you ask Howard Hughes that? I've been at the very top of the most glamorous agency ever to hit Madison Avenue. I couldn't see myself working for someone else." Says Jeno Paulucci: "As soon as Reynolds acquired my company and put me on salary I felt inhibited. So I left."

Eduard Baruch sold his Heli-Coil to Topps Industries in 1956 and bought it back 13 months later. Since then he has built its sales from $2 million to $20 million. "These big company people," he says, "are good to move into an organization that already has been created. But they haven't had the exposure to run on their own. They learn about business in graduate

THE BUYERS AND THE BUILDERS

Why do big corporations prefer to pay fat sums to buy a small company with an established product line? Why not start their own? "It takes the gamble away," says Max Geffen. "When they go to the banker with something that's pretty good, he isn't gambling in the dark." "The start-up pains are fantastic," says entrepreneur Eduard Baruch. "If I see a target of opportunity in mind today, I'll pay more than its worth just because they have broken the ground."

"I think it's kind of a healthy situation in that it gives the spark of life and hope to the young en-

trepreneur whereas he would be hopelessly sunk in a big corporation," says Bill Lear. "He gets an idea and he gets two or three friends to agree with him who can contribute something to the idea. They each have $15,000 and they put it together and they've got $45,000. They go out and they work day and night and Saturdays and Sundays and they put this little company together.

"Pretty soon it begins to generate some profit. Very likely the requirement for working capital gets out of hand, and they find themselves having to expand and then, they either go to the market

and get some money or borrow some. But in the long run they have a pretty well-defined product and it's successful. They're then ready for acquisition because now they can turn their ideas into something which their wives can spend. They look forward to having 'security.' In other words having money in the bank.

"Now you say, why can't a big company do that. Well, if a big company were taking that same group of fellas and said, now you go to work on that same idea, they would rarely work Saturdays and Sundays. They would take forever to get the job done." ∎

Richard Rich: *"I've had two great triumphs: the Alka Seltzer campaign, and the Benson & Hedges campaign. It's been absolutely marvelous. I made a lot of mistakes at the beginning. But I learned an awful lot."*

Eduard Baruch: *"I think you always learn from your mistakes. I think if I had not made them I'd probably be more stupid than I am today. I can't tell you which was the greatest mistake. I've made so many of them I can not keep track."*

Max Geffen: *"I'm embarrassed now because more people bother me about publishing ideas than ever before, they think I'm a magician. I look at them all, including a lot of dogs, but it gives me a great deal of pleasure.*

school but they haven't actually been out on their own. They should get out and work on the factory floor and get out in the field and sell and find out how people think—what motivates them."

Max Geffen (FORBES, *Apr. 15*) has started two successful magazines and several companies and sold them to bigger companies, including McGraw-Hill where he is one of the biggest shareowners He is currently launching a new magazine, *Family Health.* Geffen is worth maybe $50 million and, at 73, needs another business like a hole in the head. But he says, "Working is so much more fun than sitting around."

Geffen, too, scorns the idea that money is the main motive for the successful entrepreneur. "I always start a publication when I think it can perform a public service. That's the only kind that makes money. If you're doing a good job, then somebody wants it. Otherwise you're just forcing it on the public, and that's no damned good.

"I never started anything to make

money. I've been wealthier than I want to be for 20 years. I don't want to be Charlie Allen or Howard Hughes. I know some of these really rich men and they haven't got anything I can't have. I play golf with a man who is worth about $1 billion and I walk down the fairway with him and he hasn't got a thing I haven't got. In fact, I have to give him strokes."

Dreamer vs. Doer

What are the qualities that an entrepreneur needs? Perhaps these people aren't the most objective observers but we asked them all the same.

"They have to have vision," says Sherman Fairchild. "As contrasted with just having a dream. We have lots of dreamers. Not so many entrepreneurs. The dreamer figures, 'Wouldn't it be nice to have so-and-so.' But he doesn't have any idea how he is going to accomplish this. Real talent has organized vision. The fellow who says, 'Wouldn't it be nice to have an automobile that ran on

half the amount of gas? Think of all the money it could make' is a dreamer. I say to him, 'Come up with an idea how you are going to accomplish this.'"

Bill Lear says: "I'm not a good manager. I have an enormous distaste for management. Every minute I spend on it makes me just much less useful at what I am good at.

"What I'm good at is interphasing. That's not the same as being an inventor. An inventor thinks of things that have never been done before. An interphaser is a guy who puts things together that already exist and makes new and better combinations." Lear regards his Lear jet as an example of interphasing. "I wanted to make it so bad I could taste it," he says, explaining why he quit the chairmanship of Lear, Inc. when the board of directors refused to let him go ahead with the project.

Jeno Paulucci says much the same thing in different words. "It's not just a question of long hours and hard work. It's guts. You have to go at it

(Continued on page 60)

CHAMPION INCURABLE

"GENIUS is one per cent inspiration and ninety-nine per cent perspiration." The genius speaking was Thomas Alva Edison, chairman of the board of the Edison Electric Light Co. and partner, president or franchiser of more than 200 companies and several entire industries. He was perhaps the most incurable entrepreneur of all time.

Edison regularly paid key employees in stock rather than with cash. He was one of the few men ever to form a company solely for "research and development."

In September 1878, with a reputation based on an improved stock ticker, the phonograph and several minor inventions, Edison granted several newspaper interviews claiming he was ready to produce an efficient electric light. In fact,

he had barely begun his research, but investors jumped at the bait and provided Edison the $250,000 that he needed. Later when the light was ready to be manufactured, Edison's backers wanted to sell the rights and take their profit. Edison insisted on manufacturing it himself. Edison's upstate New York factory is today's General Electric Co.

Edison, like his fellow entrepreneurs, was interested in money chiefly as a tool. "I always invent," stated Edison, "to obtain the money to go on inventing." He liked to tell close associates that if he hadn't made money off his crazy inventions the authorities would have put him into an insane asylum a long time ago.

Perhaps Edison best summed up

his own feelings for business in talking about financier Jay Gould who used Edison's telegraph patents to help wrest control of his Western Union Co. "Gould had no sense of humor," Edison wrote. "He took no pride in building up an enterprise. He was after money and money only. Whether the company was a success or failure mattered not to him. But I never had any grudge against him, because he was so able in his line, and as long as my part was successful, the money with me was a secondary consideration." Edison, father of the electric industry, the recording industry, the movie industry, the modern mining industry and much more, died in 1931 at the age of 84, worth much more than the $3-million estate he left.

(Continued from page 23)

with sheer determination. Otherwise the pitfalls will put you off.

"This is why big companies have to go out and acquire smaller ones. There is a quality in starting a business that only an entrepreneur can provide. My accolades to Reynolds for what they've done since they took over Chun King. But no big company can do as good a job as the individual entrepreneur."

Expensive Is Cheap

Another trait these brilliantly successful entrepreneurs share is a belief in the importance of supplementing their own talents with those of others. They know their limitations. Self-confident though they are, they don't regard themselves as gods. "The most important thing in business," says Neison Harris, "is having people work with you, not for you." Even Lear, who has a reputation for being a lone wolf, emphasizes people. "The greatest mistake I ever made was hiring the second-best man for the job. You pay a terrible penalty for that. No matter what it costs, it's cheaper than hiring the second-best man."

"The most important thing in any business," says Max Geffen, "is attaching the right people to you. The people below you. The people next to you. And the people above you."

Sherman Fairchild waxes eloquent on the subject of getting the best people. Fairchild says that as an entrepreneur he gets as much kick out of devising new organizational tools as out of inventing such things as the aerial camera. New ways to get and keep top-notch people, for example.

"One thing I try to do is regard my executives as partners. My father used to tell me, 'Son, don't worry about how much money you're going to make. Get the right guy in and make *him* a lot of money and that's all you'll need.' I've always followed that advice."

In getting Dr. C. Lester Hogan to leave Motorola and come to Fairchild (FORBES, *Dec. 1, 1968*), Fairchild found a new way to follow his father's advice. He lent Hogan $5 million, interest free, to buy Fairchild stock. "This was a very new thing," Fairchild says, "but a very logical thing. I didn't get him on the basis of 'Look I'm going to pay you more money.' I talked with him, found out what he wanted in life. I put myself in his place. I asked what would attract him. That's when I came up with the restricted options and the interest-free loan."

Fairchild has thought a good deal about the characteristics he wants in his executives. "I look for the ability to study a situation and not be blinded by a lot of past statistics that say it can't be done. Sure it's going to be tough. If it wasn't, some dope would have done it already. The man I want thinks the thing through. He thinks what are the factors that have to be put together. You can't decide this on an accountant's report. There are too many factors that just don't show up in the figures.

"What I want is to surround myself with entrepreneurs. A foreman in a shop can be an entrepreneur. If he takes existing things and puts them together in a new way. That guy usually ends up being head of the company."

"Bah!"

Perhaps it's the generation gap, but many of the entrepreneurs FORBES interviewed professed scorn for today's younger conglomerators. Eduard Baruch says: "I wouldn't give you a dime for some of these hotshot boys who are forming conglomerates. They're financial manipulators, pure and simple." Sherman Fairchild criticizes a good deal of today's acquisition-mindedness. "Too many of these people are just not entrepreneurial. They pay through the nose for acquisitions instead of trying to put small things together into bigger, better things." Max Ries says: "They give people watered stock. Bah!"

However, at least two of these men singled out Dan Lufkin, chairman of Wall Street's Donaldson, Lufkin & Jenrette, as being a true entrepreneur of the younger school. They admire his refusal to allow New York Stock Exchange rules to prevent his firm from going public. Max Geffen calls him "the most brilliant young man I know today." Eduard Baruch also singled out Lufkin, saying: "He sees opportunities and he moves ahead."

Sherman Fairchild, perhaps because he runs bigger companies than the others, disagrees with the general idea that big companies always smother the entrepreneurial spirit. "They don't at IBM," he says. "They don't buy things outside. They start them themselves. They're their own entrepreneurs. They avoid the costly business of having to buy a going organization and product acceptance."

Max Ries has some advice for executives who work for big companies and want to preserve their entrepreneurial spirit: "Be true to yourself. Do not crawl to the president or kiss the chairman's shoes. Do whatever you think you should do and if they won't let you, then leave. That's the only way." ■

For the sake of greater profit on the part both of the larger company and of its smaller suppliers and customers —

Management Assistance for Small Business

By L. T. White

Last spring over seven million small businesses reviewed their results for the 1964 calendar year. A few reported profits in the millions of dollars, but more than one-seventh of these companies had losses.

The difference between profit and loss often lies in the ability to manage. If the successful managers could share their skills with the losers, there would be more employment, more profits, and less poverty.

Sharing Business Skills

The problem of sharing management skills poses a great challenge to those who deal with small business. Sharing skills can be profitable on both sides. An examination of the largest industrial, financial, insurance, merchandising, transportation, and utility companies shows that the leader in any industry is generally that company which is most helpful to its small business associates.

General Motors, Brown Shoe, Pillsbury, and Armstrong Cork, to name a few, are known for providing assistance to help strengthen the management skills of smaller customers. But many more large and medium sized companies could profitably share their management know-how with those who supply them or distribute their products. Where there are relatively few business "Dutch uncles," there should literally be

thousands. For, if the business community doesn't take care of its own, who will?

Reasons Why

Caring for your own applies to any business. You need not be the leader to consider providing management assistance to your business associates. All you need is the desire to improve your own business. And the cost can be kept small. In fact, one large wholesaler told me: "All it cost me was a change in attitude. I actually saved money from the day I began counseling my retailers."

The reasons why it is good business practice for top management to provide assistance to small business associates are listed here more or less in the order of importance:

- To increase sales where trade acceptance must be created.

- To protect product reputation when it requires expert instruction and service.

- To reduce operating expense where there is a high turnover of dealers.

- To expand and grow when normal outlet channels are overburdened or completely clogged.

There are two other sound reasons why it is good business practice for a larger company to offer management assistance:

(1) With such a program, the larger company can show the small retail dealer or service tradesman how to maximize profit on his limited capital

68   *HBR July–August 1965*

investment. In the long run the more profitable dealer will be a better customer for the larger company.

(2) If a small businessman sells to a large merchandiser or manufacturer, he may learn how to step up his own productive output. The large organization provides management assistance to inform him and to encourage him to expand his operation, with the assurance of a healthier profit return for both companies.

To illustrate the management assistance approach used by industry leaders, I will discuss the individual methods practiced by four large companies. Then, a little further along in this article, I will demonstrate how a relatively small company provided assistance to dealers in an industry which is characterized by many giants. This is the unique low-budget method used by the Bennett Pump Division of the John Wood Company in the oil marketing industry.

Telltale Signs

The public is often more aware of poor business practice than is the small retailer or manufacturer, who is often surprised when sales decline or payments come more and more slowly. That's because the public is quick to spot the noticeable signs which indicate improved management is needed by small manufacturers, retailers, and service tradesmen.

Notable examples of this were gathered by a team of reporters in a northern city. Working in pairs, they would walk through the business district and stop men or women shoppers. They would ask, "Can you think of some businessman who shouldn't be in business?" It was surprising how many people knew a businessman who annoyed or disappointed them and why.

Then the field workers would go to that businessman and ask his candid opinion about local business conditions. He was always willing to talk, but never willing to admit that he was part of the problem.

One member of the research team would note the telltale signs of poor management:

Anger	Idleness
Boredom	Lateness
Clutter	Loose money
Danger	Lost articles
Darkness	Rudeness
Dirt	Shouting
Excuses	Sloppiness
Extravagance	Stock deficiencies
Greed	Waste

Meanwhile, the other reporter would listen for comments which would also be indicative that the businessman could be helped by new attitudes and information. Here are common responses:

— "You can't get good employees today."

— "My competitors are crazy."

— "Taxes are killing my business."

— "Customers who owe me walk right by."

— "I'll start advertising when customers start coming."

— "Training employees is a waste of time and money. They won't stay long enough."

— "We hire relatives. They are loyal."

— "No, I won't tell how I manage. That's my secret."

— "I never want to depend on hired help or borrowed money."

Aiding Small Business

Those who counsel small businessmen are well aware of the fact that free advice and proffered criticism, no matter how constructive, are generally resented. Small proprietors get lots of both from customers, employees, suppliers, and competitors.

Proprietors' Situation

In several ways the small businessman is a headstrong adventurer. He wants to be his own boss, to do things his own way. He wants to see the results of his work. He is willing to accept full responsibility for his decisions, but he also wants his share of the rewards.

The small businessman deals constantly with people. He talks business all day long. He handles money continually — all kinds of it — pennies, nickels, dimes, quarters, and folding money. He engages in hundreds of transactions each day that must be exact, and this involves precise use of arithmetic. It entails rigid control of cash and inventory; the small businessman can't afford to drop many pennies. He is forced to struggle with record keeping and credit, which means a painstaking attention to detail that "wheelers and dealers" generally detest. In extending credit he must sometimes say *no* to the very people with whom he is trying to do business.

Many small businessmen find it difficult to

start employing others. They feel that hiring a man means taking money out of their own pockets, or even out of the mouths they must feed. For example:

◖ A woman who started a typing and duplicating business told of the first employee she hired, a typist who charged 70¢ an hour. To pay her for three hours' work, $2.10, the owner did without lunch for three days.

◖ A trucking company operator described payday as "That's the day when the help has money and I have none."

But when the businessman learns that his profit is produced by the people he employs and that, as the owner, he can grow by taking a proportionally smaller share of the income, he becomes willing to learn more about the skills of managing.

'Sensible Way'

One counselor has drawn up what he calls the "sensible way" to penetrate the defensive armor and attitudes of small businessmen. Much of their aggressive blaming of "big" labor, business, and government is really a mask for their own weaknesses, which they could correct once they admit to themselves they could use assistance in managing their little enterprises. The approach utilizes the small businessman's five senses to:

• Let him *see* his weaknesses for himself — through the means of some device, such as a scale, thermometer, mirror, tape recorder, bank statement, inventory list, sales record, balance sheet, or operating statement.

• Let him *hear* for himself — by asking his customers, employees, suppliers, creditors, and competitors how he rates in their eyes as a businessman.

• Let him *smell* trouble — by permitting him to stretch his excuses to the ridiculous. At this point he may realize, "I might be wrong, too."

• Put him in *touch* with a wider circle of businessmen — by getting him to join a civic club or trade association, attend management institutes, take part in discussions, exchange experiences, and find out how others have solved problems similar to his.

• Give him a *taste* of success — by having him meet the leaders in his field. Be prepared if he asks for information or assistance. Urge him to try

something new. Praise his efforts. Encourage him to re-try if he stumbles.

When you really come to understand your small business associate — his attitudes, needs, aspirations, and how to make him aware of them — it's time to decide on whether to make the private or direct approach, which requires a considerable outlay of time and money, or to use the missionary method of the trade association and public education. The latter low-cost alternative is within the means of any business, from ultra-small to the largest in the industry.

Potential Hazards

Whether you have a small organization servicing the needs of 5 customers, or a large company supplying 20,000, there are certain pitfalls you can avoid. For example:

A national group of dealers actually revolted in the midst of an extended manufacturer-sponsored program that the corporate executives thought was just what their dealers wanted.

In the early sessions the dealers had never been able to get a word in edgeways. The company executives talked down to them. So the dealers met privately, in advance of a scheduled session, and figured out a neat way to have their say.

When the president rose to open the next part of the program, the agenda of which included only the corporation officers and experts as speakers, one dealer got up and asked, "Mr. President, don't you feel we should start with a prayer?" The president was surprised, but he said, "Of course! Won't you lead us in prayer?"

In a loud, carrying voice, the dealer prayed for guidance for the factory men to design a better product, for better marketing and advertising. In fact, he prayed that every wrong might be righted. He continued for 50 minutes, no one daring to interrupt.

The brass still shudder when they recall that shattering experience. But it worked. They were forced to listen. They adopted many of the dealers' suggestions. Then both dealers and manufacturer did better.

The point is clear — don't arbitrarily assume that you and your staff know what's on the minds of your small business associates. They are men with minds of their own. They are independent risk-takers, while you and your staff are salaried men, a lot more secure in your positions and careers.

Small businessmen resent the word "training" because it smacks of regimentation and drilling. They hate being jammed into an organizationally conceived mold. They wish to learn, but at their own pace and choice of subject. They are skeptical of free educational events or materials.

Don't assume that the high cost of texts, manuals, films, or meetings is an indication of the media's worth. There have been cases where million-dollar training programs were complete flops. To illustrate:

One company published a handsome accounting manual for its retail dealers. It was titled *System-eering*, and it was designed in the grand Madison Avenue manner. The company gave one to every dealer free of charge.

A year later, the company executives were shocked to learn that few of the manuals had been put to use. They then did what they should have done first — made inquiries among the dealers. One dealer said, "It cost you a lot of money, so I figured it would help you most. Maybe you wanted us to keep standardized books so you could cut our discounts."

One more hazard: don't expect immediate results. Development projects are like marriage. They are for keeps. They should never be undertaken on a "let's see" basis, or considered as something you can turn on and off at your whim, like a water faucet. You are dealing with men's livelihoods. Management development is not like a sales campaign or a new product introduction.

Starting a Program

Let's assume that you are thinking of starting a development program to give management assistance to your small business associates. What department should you assign to direct the program — sales, purchasing, production, or public relations?

The answer is: none of them. The development department should be independent, and its director should be chosen from among members of the president's staff. A few of the department's general rules of operation should be to —

. . . help the small businessman help himself;

. . . offer no unrequested advice or information;

. . . create a desire on the part of small businessmen for self-improvement;

. . . respect each dealer's confidence.

In addition to these general rules of operation, the budget should be modest and the staff small; and the department should be given no authority or authorization to discuss company products, prices, personnel, or practices; nor should the department make commitments which involve the sales organization. Two field men with secretaries and a librarian can be the nucleus for the development department of a billion-dollar company.

Successful Patterns

Many major companies have used the management assistance approach. While the specific method of each company has been different, there is one common characteristic of successful programs: early recognition of the large company's dependence on its small business associates. Somebody at a top policy level in the company decided to find out for himself what the dealers' problems really were, and as a result the program has been well supported and consistent. In addition, the management assistance program has been a contributing factor in establishing the company's character and integrity. I will discuss briefly each of the methods used by four "leader" companies — General Motors, Brown Shoe, Pillsbury, and Armstrong Cork — which have contributed to the growth of both the major company and its small business associates.

General Motors Corporation. One reason for the consistent growth of General Motors through 57 years has been the corporation's practice of assisting dealers for over 40 of those years.

This is described carefully by Alfred P. Sloan, Jr. in his remarkable book, as follows:

"In those early days we along with the Industry lacked techniques that today are taken for granted. Things just seemed to happen — to us, and to the industry. The number of sales by dealers was unknown. The number of cars held by dealers was unknown. . . . Production schedules, therefore, were set with no real relationship to final demand. . . ."

"When I was chief executive officer of General Motors, I gave a large part of my attention to dealer relations, amounting at times, you might say, almost to a specialization. . . ."[1]

[1] *My Years with General Motors,* edited by John McDonald with Catharine Stevens (Garden City, New York, Doubleday & Company, Inc., 1964), p. 437, p. 279. For a review of this book see Harold Wolff, "The Great GM Mystery," *HBR* September–October 1964, p. 164.

Then Sloan performed what is known today as the "hat trick." He put it on and went out to hear people who didn't come in. He visited from five to ten dealers a day in cities throughout the country. This led to new selling agreements and to the creation of the Motors Accounting Company. Then came Motors Holding Corporation, which developed management techniques for dealers, backed them with equity capital, and produced profit sufficient to retire Motors Holding's interest so the dealers could become independent.

Later, the General Motors Dealer Council was formed so that there would be face-to-face discussions on distribution policies between a group of top corporate executives and a rotating panel of dealers. Then the Dealer Relations Board, with an impartial umpire, was set up to hear and determine appeals by dealers from decisions of the divisions.

Since 1960, the average volume of business by General Motors dealers has been 2.5 times the 1939 average. Their net worth of $2 billion is 2.7 times the 1941 figure. General Motors itself is the world's largest and most successful corporation.

Brown Shoe Company, Inc. Probably the most thorough management assistance program in existence, the Brown Shoe Company's close-working relationship with independent retailers, started in 1920 with 12 stores which were in financial difficulties. The Independent Retailers Division now serves over 900 shoe dealers with a 24-man team of counselors. These men are stationed so that they can reach an average of 27 accounts with short trips.

J. R. Johnston, Vice President and General Manager of Brown Shoe's Independent Retailers Division, has said: "Our program is designed specifically to sell ideas. We observe, we analyze, we recommend; we do not dictate to the retailer because he owns the business. We suggest. He decides."

Brown offers an 11-point management assistance program which has produced profits for the dealer who uses it. The average I.R.D. store has a net profit equal to 11.2% of sales, while the average family shoe store has a net profit of only 5.7%, according to the most recent survey.

With a store doing $100,000 annual sales, the 5.5% profit differential through management assistance "ain't hay," as the boys say. The

dealers say thanks to Brown in their own way: Brown's own sales were about $250 million in 1964.

Pillsbury Company. Standing 137th in the list of the 500 largest industrial concerns in 1964, Pillsbury has built an annual business of $446 million. Harry D. Kreiser, Jr., who is now Vice President of the Institution Food Service Division, connects this growth in part to the company's policy of assisting small bakers to be more efficient: "We like to have our bakers look to us as their idea factory and staff — since with ideas we can make them stronger."

Pillsbury's assistance to small bakers embraces the following five-point program:

1. A full-time engineer to consult on bulk material handling.

2. An industrial engineer to help reduce costs and damaged goods, and to make more effective use of storage and manufacturing space.

3. A bakery equipment program that provides the baker with modern automatic apparatus along with a plan to finance it.

4. A technical assistance program, which is the oldest of the company's advisory services. This helps the baker to establish and maintain a high level of product quality.

5. A finance program for distributors which not only furnishes credit on normal terms, but sometimes grants extended terms or offers outright working-capital loans.

In addition, Pillsbury offers assistance in market research, sales training, advertising, packaging, and public relations.

Armstrong Cork Company. Charles H. Walker, Jr., General Credit Manager of Armstrong Cork Company, encourages that company's wide practice of "sharing with our customers the company's management and business aids." He made the following statement:

"There is a phrase that you hear at Armstrong quite frequently, which is, 'partners in business.' In a true sense of the word we consider our customers to be our partners in business, for only through the continued profitable growth of our customers can we hope to attain the objective which we have set for our company.

"The founder of our company, Thomas Morton Armstrong, transmitted this characteristic to the business early, when it was small and struggling. He changed the old 'Let the buyer beware' to 'Let the buyer have faith.'"

72   *HBR July–August 1965*

The management assistance team at Armstrong Cork is headed by an assistant credit manager, and can draw on any department for a specialist to help solve customer problems. In addition, the company holds management seminars in which independent acoustical contractors study situations that involve them in setting short- and long-range objectives in planning, organizing, personnel, and control.

Armstrong Cork's placement of customer management assistance under the aegis of the credit department is wise. The company's interest is in seeing the customer solvent at all periods of his growth.

Helping an Industry

Small manufacturers, wholesalers, and trade associations will be interested in the petroleum industry's Jobber Management Institute for more than 16,000 oil jobbers. The institute's better-management program is in its twelfth year, with member interest and attendance still growing.

Direct Approach

The institute story has provoked discussion in that industry, where marketing is a prime problem.

In the fall of 1951, members of the Texas Oil Jobber Association found themselves with many problems. Since the most pressing problem was the supply of good service station employees, they asked the state's educators for help. They were surprised to hear that, as an important first step, their own management should and could be improved.

This led to the first oil jobber management institute, held in Austin in 1952. Forty-two jobbers enrolled. Because it was their own affair, one for which they recognized the need and sought a solution, they organized the program and "sold the tickets." This makes a point: management programs should be "by, of, and for" the small businessmen themselves.

What this first group learned was useful. They began at once to practice better employee-honoring methods. Employee productivity improved, station operations ran more smoothly, sales rose, expenses fell, and the jobber's life became somewhat easier.

Similar management institutes were tried by oil jobber associations in Georgia, Wisconsin, Connecticut, Arkansas, and Missouri. There were hopes expressed that management institutes would be adopted by the oil jobber associations in all states, that more and more jobbers would attend them, and that the institutes would be continued year after year.

Missionary Method

Word of these various hopes reached Arch Jordan, President of the Bennett Pump Division of the John Wood Company. The division manufactures gasoline pumps for service stations, thousands of which are operated or leased by jobbers.

First, Jordan ascertained that management institutes were good for all concerned — jobbers, dealers, and the motoring public. Then he felt they should be continued and expanded. This work would require a missionary who had nothing to sell but that idea. He would have to be free to go wherever he could be of help and have the means to do so. Then Jordan made an intuitive decision. There was no precedent, no assurance that it would work or pay. In fact, because it was a radical change, it might even prove unpopular. But Jordan's reasoning was sound. He said, "We believe books do more good than booze. We decided to find a fellow and put him on the job."

A firm of industrial psychologists found John Shields for him. Because Shields knew oil marketing, he talked the jobber's and dealer's language. His role was like that of the legendary Johnny Appleseed, who traveled throughout the early American colonies, giving people apple seeds and suggesting how to plant them and raise orchards.

Jordan made sure Shields would keep moving among jobbers and their 30 state associations. He gave him no office or secretary, and told him to do business out of his hat and away from the factory. He gave Shields an expense advance, and credit cards for telephone, air lines, railroads, auto rentals, hotels, motels, and restaurants. Because ideas are the best "stimulants," Jordan told Shields the one item that he would scrutinize in his expense accounts would be "entertainment." He told Shields to avoid mentioning the Bennett company or its pumps, except when jobbers asked, "What do you cost us?" Then he was urged to say, "Nothing. I'm Bennett Pump's visual aid for Jobber Management Institutes."

Shields went to work 12 years ago and has since traveled a million miles. He is detached from the company's sales and production operations. All of his trips and time are in the jobbers' interest.

Occasionally Jordan is asked, "What does Shields cost per year?" When this happens, he says, "If you're asking because you are thinking of providing such a disciple of good management for your industry, figure on from $25,000 up." (The Bennett Pump Division will in the future share this expense with The Guardian Light Company and several trade associations.)

Such a question and answer are interesting. They reveal whether the person making the inquiry takes the long or short view of his own managing. There are many court decisions that such measures are legally and tax-wise correct. Certainly, helping small, struggling businessmen to help themselves is ethically right. Time proves the economic wisdom of strengthening the independence of a company's small business suppliers and users. The major oil company refiners have been especially cooperative and encouraging.

Of the 31 associations, serving 39 states, which conduct annual management institutes, Shields has personally been instrumental in introducing 22. His initial contact is with the association's executive secretary. Working with the secretary, Shields then approaches the board of directors, and points out that an institute would help the membership improve management techniques and increase profits.

When the state association has decided to run a management institute, Shields works closely with the appointed committee. He often contributes suggestions for a program, arranges for cosponsorship by a university or state department of education, and sets up meeting facilities. When the committee agrees on the expected attendance, Shields helps to develop a budget and set a registration fee which will effect a complete recovery of costs for the association. Later come the problems of promoting attendance and developing the final program, and Shields also helps the association with these tasks.

In the oil marketing industry, management institutes are well into their second decade. Attendance is growing annually, and the future is bright. There are constant challenges to reach more jobbers, and to find new and better ways to help all jobbers to grow.

The management institutes for oil jobbers are one of the best examples of the approach open to many medium sized companies that want to help their smaller business associates.

Somewhat earlier, I mentioned how the public is quick to spot the telltale signs of poor business practice and how through a program of management assistance the small businessman can be helped to overcome his operating faults and improve his profit potential. Of course, no figures are available to prove the extent to which better business practice — as a direct result of a management development program — has been reflected in profit improvement.

Perhaps the most impressive evidence that this program pays is the fact that the oil jobbers have received public recognition. Last November, a special report to the petroleum industry cited the following impressive statistics of jobbers in public service: 13% are bank directors; 27% have been elected to public office; 34% are directors of other companies; and in addition 83% of the jobbers have been in business over ten years in their home communities.[2]

Conclusion

An examination of the largest industrial, financial, insurance, merchandising, transportation, and utility companies shows that the leading company in any industry is generally the one which is most helpful to its small business associates.

One executive from a large company decided to test this hypothesis through a little informal research of his own. You might say he really wanted to learn from small businessmen. So he began to invite his local butcher, florist, gift shop owner, and other small retailers — along with each individual's wife — to join him and his wife at dinner in fine restaurants. He quickly discovered that when his guests felt his respect for their point of view and realized he had no axe to grind, they were willing to talk freely.

He asked them questions such as: "What large company in your line is the most helpful to you?" "What does the company do for you?" "Do you appreciate the company's extra assistance?" "Do you think it pays the company to offer management assistance to you?"

The executive's guest would invariably name such a helpful large company very quickly. He

[2] "The Jobber and the Petroleum Industry — 1964," *The National Oil Jobber*, November 1964, p. 11.

would specify why he liked the company. He was grateful and loyal for the company's interest in him as an associate.

From this, you can see how the concept applies. The customer — whether a small retailer or service tradesman, or the public-at-large — does business with the company which is most helpful.

The potential power available through encouraging America's millions of small business proprietors should inspire every management who can help. Management skill has been advanced to a brilliant level, but the small company which possesses a high degree of such brilliance is rare. Probably less than one firm in a thousand has it. Therefore, it can be profitable, as well as wise, for the company which has such talent to share it with small businessmen who are struggling to learn, with only painful experience for the most part as their tutor.

MOST small businessmen have a high regard for the profitable results of so-called scientific management — and only wish they could use its techniques and practices in their own businesses. They have difficulty, however, in understanding exactly what scientific management is, and they are likely to be in doubt about how to apply it to their own companies. They tend to think of scientific management, in other words, as a body of doctrine that is very useful to big business but "over the head" of the little fellow.

The term, which is somewhat fashionable, connotes complicated procedures. That in itself is one mental block since the small businessman feels he is already involved in an excessively complex existence. He tries to avoid unfamiliar ideas that threaten to make his work more burdensome. On the other hand, there is always the tempting possibility that scientific management may simplify his work and improve his competitive position. Curiosity about that may even induce him to try to find out something about it, to experiment with it in his own business. . . .

The development of the inquiring mind, which in a very real way is the essence of scientific management, is itself one of the more valuable *results* of trying to apply its principles, as well as being a *motive* for investigating its possibilities. Intelligent self-criticism thus prompted enables the small businessman to obtain very definite benefits. And it is not amiss to expect that the inquiring mind will criticize some of the doctrine of scientific management in turn. The axiom that such criticism is not justified unless it is constructive seems to me to be very questionable. Can the inquiring mind be of any real value if it is asked to stop inquiring at some prescribed limit? Since the inquirer has no way of knowing ahead of time where his thinking will lead him, he must be prepared to accept any criticism — destructive or not. Otherwise his work can scarcely be called scientific.

Harry S. Freedman, "Scientific Management in Small Business"

Harvard Business Review, May 1950, p. 33.

WHAT ENTREPRENEURS LEARN FROM EXPERIENCE

by Lawrence M. Lamont

Introduction

There is an old saying that practice makes perfect. Applied to business, it means that a task can always be performed more effectively the second time it is attempted. Surprisingly, the same principle applies to technical entrepreneurship. Entrepreneurs with previous experience in founding and developing a company exhibit substantial learning when they start another business. More often than not, their experience is reflected in superior corporate performance.

The importance of prior experience becomes meaningful when one examines the self-generating nature of the entrepreneurship process.[1] The creation of a technology-based enterprise (called a "spin-off") occurs when an entrepreneur starts a business to commercialize technology transferred from his previous source of employment. As the new firm develops, it in turn becomes a source of technology and entrepreneurs for a second generation spin-off and so on. Entrepreneurial learning becomes apparent when the principal of a first generation spin-off leaves to start another

Dr. Lamont is assistant professor of marketing at the University of Colorado. He was formerly associated with Dow Corning Corporation as a technical sales representative, and subsequently as a research associate at the Institute of Science and Technology at the University of Michigan, where he was a consultant to technology-based firms in the Ann Arbor area. His research and publication activities include the fields of industrial marketing, small business management, corporate responses to consumerism, and consumer purchase behavior for durable goods.

[1] Dean C. Coddington and James F. Mahar, "The Scientific Complex—Proceed with Caution," *Harvard Business Review,* XLIII (January-February, 1965), pp. 141-44.

technology-based firm. Arnold Cooper's recent research on technical enterprise formation in the Palo Alto area summarizes the pattern:

Past entrepreneurship also generates experienced entrepreneurs. Some of these men stay with their firms as they grow. However, many of the firms are acquired and many of the founding teams break up. After the merger or after the fight with the co-founder, what does the former entrepreneur do? Often he turns to entrepreneurship again.

Eight of the 30 companies studied intensively in the Palo Alto area were founded by men who previously had been in the founding groups of other companies. One man was starting his fourth new business. Without exception these men stated that it was easier to start a company the second time, both in regard to making the decision psychologically and in knowing what was involved in launching a firm.[2]

What does the technical entrepreneur do differently when he participates in the formation of a second generation spin-off? Why does his technology-based firm typically perform in a superior manner? These questions are examined in the present article. The answers are of interest to existing and potential entrepreneurs because they can shorten the learning process and improve their chances for success. Venture capital firms, private investors, and businesses interested in acquiring technology-based companies will also find this article useful because it provides insight into the decision to invest in a small business.

My comments are based on an empirical study of a matched sample of 24 technology-based enterprises located in a major scientific complex. Twelve of the

[2] Arnold C. Cooper, "Entrepreneurial Environment," *Industrial Research,* XII (September, 1970), p. 75.

firms are first generation spin-offs founded by individuals without previous entrepreneurial experience. The balance of the sample consists of 12 second generation spin-offs founded by technical entrepreneurs who had been previously involved in the formation and management of a technology-based enterprise.

Aside from differences in the business experience of the entrepreneurs, the firms were similar in many respects. New businesses having less than $100,000 of sales were included as well as firms with annual sales of several million dollars. Both groups ranged in age between 1 and 11 years and averaged 3.5 years of business operations. The firms were also involved in similar technologies, primarily electronics and optics.

Comparative Performance

Part of the entrepreneur's ability to perform more effectively the second time is reflected in the various measures of corporate performance. Several were examined, including sales growth, profitability, and financial strength. Comparative sales performance shows that the second generation firm experiences a greater rate of sales growth. This is reflected in Table 1 where first year sales are shown for each group of firms.

Over 91 percent of the first generation firms reported sales in the range of $0-100,000 during the first complete year of operations. By comparison, 75 percent

of the second generation enterprises reported sales over $100,000 during a similar period. The differences in sales performance were not a short-run phenomenon. After each group of firms had completed an average of 3.5 years of business, 83 percent of the second generation firms reported sales over $100,000 compared to 58 percent of the first generation spin-offs.

Profitability data confirms the superior performance of the second generation firms during their latest year of business. Over 60 percent of these firms reported profitable operations, while only 25 percent of the first generation spin-offs earned profits. The second generation firms also achieved profitability earlier in their life cycle, were financially stronger and had better credit ratings as reported by a leading business information service.

What Do Entrepreneurs Learn?

During the formation of a second enterprise, the entrepreneur has an opportunity to apply his previous small business experience. Typically it is reflected in a firm having a product orientation, a higher level of capitalization and a better balance of essential business skills.

A product orientation. Technology-based firms can engage in a variety of different business activities. They include consulting, research and development, engineering, and manufacturing on a

Table 1

First Year Sales Performance

Sales	First Generation Spin-off Firms		Second Generation Spin-off Firms	
$0-100,000	11	91.7	3	25.0
Over $100,000	1	8.3	9	75.0
Total Firms	12	100.0%	12	100.0%

contract basis and the provision of proprietary products. Table 2 indicates that first generation firms were performing contract activities during their first year of business, while the second generation spin-offs were usually involved in the development and marketing of proprietary products.

What accounts for the significant variation in business orientation? Most of the difference can be attributed to the entrepreneur's previous small business experience. He has learned that contract-oriented businesses are highly unstable and that products are needed to maintain a profitable level of operations. The point is illustrated by the comments of a first generation entrepreneur. After several years of business his contract engineering firm decided to develop and market an industrial control instrument. He remarked:

> The development of products is a natural extension of our contract capability. These developments give us an opportunity to share on a continuing basis the things we have been doing for other companies on an hourly basis.

The comment illustrates another important characteristic of the technology-based enterprise. As the firms mature, their development is marked by dramatic changes in the nature of their business. Several development patterns are possible, but generally contract-oriented firms move toward a product orientation. A first generation spin-off included in the study illustrates this common pattern.

The firm began business in contract research and development performing environmental studies for the government space program. Two years after formation, two electronic measuring instruments were developed using technology transferred from the government research. In a short period, the first generation spin-off's business had changed from a research and development orientation to a product orientation.

This type of change was quite evident in the sample of firms studied. In the latest year of business operations reported, 33 percent of the first generation spin-offs had achieved a product orientation and 75 percent of the secondary spin-offs had completed the transition. Obviously, the second generation firm has a head-start on the product development.

How does the experienced entrepreneur assure a product orientation for his new firm? To form the technical base for the business he transfers technology from his previous source of employment. Usually this technology includes information related to the development and manufacture of specific products. The entrepreneur takes advantage of the product knowledge the first firm may have taken years to develop.[3] A case in point: One second generation entrepreneur interviewed developed nine products during the first year of business. Prior to starting operations he had completed the design and engineering for these products so that

[3]Victor J. Danilov, "The Spin-Off," *Industrial Research,* XI (May, 1969), p. 58.

Table 2
First Year Business Activities*

Type of Business Activity	First Generation Spin-off Firms		Second Generation Spin-off Firms	
Contract	11	91.7	5	41.7
Product	1	8.3	7	58.3
Total Firms	12	100.0%	12	100.0%

*Firms are classified as product or contract oriented on the basis of sales data and the major focus of their business.

most of the first year of operations was devoted to developing a manufacturing capability and organizing a distribution network. All of the products were improved versions of those marketed in the first business he was associated with. To a large degree, the product orientation of the entrepreneur's second firm accounts for the superior sales performance.

Adequate initial financing. The significance of financing to new technical firms is confirmed by the research of Dr. Edward B. Roberts, Associate Professor of Management, Massachusetts Institute of Technology. He notes that one of the essential characteristics of successful spin-off firms is "large initial capitalization, preferably $25,000 to $50,000."[4] However, obtaining the capital to initially finance the technology-based company is a difficult problem according to Kenneth G. Germeshausen, a first generation entrepreneur and board chairman of EG&G.

> The principal problem is the convincing of financial sources that the idea really is a good one and in obtaining the required financial support without losing control or too much of the equity.[5]

Many of the technology-based firms in the study were undercapitalized at the time of formation and throughout the early stages of development. Again, the second generation entrepreneurs' experience was worthwhile. Their firms had an average initial capitalization of $33,700 compared to the first generation spin-off's average of $19,600. Part of this difference reflects the business orientation of the second generation firms. Product oriented firms simply require higher levels of initial capitalization to finance the product development and the requirements for plant and equipment,

inventory, and labor. Much of the difference, however, is the result of the experienced entrepreneur's knowledge of sources of venture capital, his ability to make a convincing presentation to potential investors and the lower level of risk involved in a business having a tangible product

A balance of business skills. The majority of first generation spin-offs are founded by scientists and engineers having only a casual interest in the business activities required to successfully operate a business. In many firms the situation is perpetuated by hiring only technical personnel whose interests are compatible with those of the original entrepreneurs. The entrepreneur of the second generation firm usually realizes the need for help in management, production, and the other functional areas of business. When it is financially possible, he carefully selects his employees to complement the existing technical and business skills present in the firm.

As shown in Table 3, all firms reported that either a principal founder or employee had research and development or engineering experience at the time of founding. This was expected because the technical experience of the personnel is the primary basis for the firm's creation. However, when the presence of various business skills is considered, the second generation firms clearly have an advantage. They are more inclined to have production, general management, and marketing initially present in their organization.

The difference is due not only to the learning that occurs during the process of entrepreneurship, but it is also the result of a need for a broader range of business skills to successfully operate a product-oriented business. This explains the higher percentage of second generation firms reporting production experience in their business. The contrast in the percentage of firms having marketing and general management experience is a reflection of

---

[4]Edward B. Roberts, "Influences Upon Performance of New Technical Enterprises," A paper presented at the Symposium on Technical Entrepreneurship, Co-sponsored by the Krannert School of Industrial Administration, Purdue University, and the Center for Venture Management, Milwaukee, Wisconsin, October 7-8, 1970, at Purdue University.

[5]Danilov, *op. cit., p.58*

Table 3

Business Experience Present at the Time of Founding*
(Percent of Firms Reporting Each Type of Experience)

Type of Experience	First Generation Spin-off Firms		Second Generation Spin-off Firms	
Research, Development and Engineering	12	100.0%	12	100.0%
Production	1	8.3	10	83.3
General Management	1	8.3	9	75.0
Accounting or Finance	6	50.0	4	33.0
Marketing or Sales	3	25.0	7	58.3
Total Firms	12		12	

*Percentage total exceeds 100.00% because of multiple response.

the fact that first generation spin-offs are frequently weak in marketing and less concerned about the personnel and project management aspects of the business. Experienced entrepreneurs recognize the significance of marketing and management skills and are more willing to hire specialists to handle the business functions.

Taking Advantage of Experience

The fact that learning occurs in technical entrepreneurship implies that existing and potential entrepreneurs can improve their business skills by taking advantage of the experiences of successful entrepreneurs. However, understanding what entrepreneurs learn and do differently does not automatically lead to concepts that can be applied in a small business setting. In the following sections are discussed some specific ways in which a new enterprise may benefit from the previous entrepreneural experience of its founder.

Market planning. Entrepreneurs with previous small business experience are able to transfer important market knowledge to their new firms. They are usually aware of specific business opportunities and know in advance where their sales are going to come from. Without the benefit of experience, extensive market planning must be performed to focus the company's product and marketing strategy. More specifically, the plan must define market opportunities, product requirements, potential customers and competition. It also specifies the sales techniques needed to penetrate potential markets, sales goals by product and market, and a detailed marketing budget.

Most experienced entrepreneurs have completed the market planning phase when they begin operations. Even though the approach may have been informal, it helps to direct the operations and maximize the efficient use of the firm's financial and technical resources. By comparison, first time entrepreneurs usually begin business without clear corporate goals and fail to define the scope of their technical and marketing effort. Only after several unsuccessful projects does the entrepreneur begin to realize the necessity for market planning.

Financial planning. A well prepared marketing plan specifies the financial requirements of the business. Experienced entrepreneurs recognize this and carefully project working capital needs to finance the marketing program, product development, inventory, and work (products and contracts) in process. These financing needs are then matched with sources of funds including proprietary product sales and progress payments from contracts. The difference must be made up from external sources—namely profits, loans from private investors, sales of stock, lines of credit from financial institutions, and short term trade credit

The financial and market plans become the basis for a formal presentation to the financial community—including individuals, venture capital firms, SBIC's and other financial institutions. A well prepared presentation emphasizing a marketable product, financial control, and management depth usually enables the entrepreneur to obtain the financing needed to assure a successful start for the business. Experienced entrepreneurs are typically able to secure the necessary financing prior to starting business. The first generation entrepreneur is often in business a year or more before he begins to perceive the need for additional funds. The failure to prepare a financial plan usually means that the firm will be undercapitalized and highly susceptible to a cash flow crisis.

A balanced management team. First-time entrepreneurs admit that technical experience alone is not sufficient to manage and develop a new business. Weaknesses in marketing and management and inexperience in the methods of conducting business spell failure for many new firms. In putting together a management team, the experienced entrepreneur usually recognizes the importance of business experience and the need to interact with the business community. Multiple founders are typically used to provide a balance of business skills and part of the financing. Operating management is hired with emphasis on selecting individuals experienced in project and production management. The experienced entrepreneur surrounds himself with good people and delegates authority. The first generation entrepreneur too often tries to manage everything himself and is labeled as a poor manager.

Interaction with the business community is made possible by having outside members on the board of directors or an executive committee made up of corporate management and outside advisors such as a C.P.A., lawyer, venture capitalist, consultant, etc. This latter technique works well as a method of bringing outside expertise to bear on the company's problems because the committee can meet informally and with greater frequency than a board. Some venture capital firms are making the establishment of an executive committee a requirement in all firms they finance. Most entrepreneurs welcome the idea because the outside individuals provide an excellent sounding board for new ideas.

Conclusions

Learning is a property of almost all business activity. Applied to technical entrepreneurship it means that experienced entrepreneurs exhibit substantial learning when they form a second technology-based enterprise. Usually their experience is reflected in a business having a product orientation, substantial initial financing and a balance of essential business skills.

Market and financial planning are key factors in the experienced entrepreneurs' performance. Entrepreneurs should strive to begin business with a market plan that focuses the technical activity and gives the firm a head start on the required product development. Careful financial planning is also necessary. Investors are reluctant to provide capital for a business venture when the requirements are uncertain. When these tools are combined with an experienced management team, the business has a sense of direction and a high probability of success.

Stanley M. Davis

Entrepreneurial Succession

This paper examines three patterns of entrepreneurial succession in private enterprise in developing countries. The process may be thought of as the succession from entrepreneurs to executives. The findings suggest significant variation in the adaptability of each type to the development of modern organizations in which the function of management is distinct from the manager as a person.

Stanley M. Davis is assistant professor in the graduate school of business administration at Harvard University.

MEN die, but organizations generally continue to exist beyond the life of their leaders. The dilemmas of succession in leadership are usually considered a potential source of danger and conflict.[1] In large and complex organizations, managers are expected to move around as they climb the corporate hierarchy, and this expectation greatly reduces the potentially disruptive aspects.[2]

[1] Two important case studies of succession are Alvin W. Gouldner, *Patterns of Industrial Bureaucracy* (Glencoe, Ill.: Free Press, 1954), and Robert H. Guest, *Organizational Change: The Effect of Successful Leadership* (Homewood, Ill.: Irwin-Dorsey, 1962). See also A. W. Gouldner, "The Problems of Succession in Bureaucracy," in his *Studies in Leadership: Leadership and Domestic Action* (New York: Harper, 1950), pp. 644–659; R. H. Guest, Managerial Succession in Complex Organizations; and Comment by A. W. Gouldner, *American Journal of Sociology,* 68 (July 1962), 47–56.

[2] For a discussion of this point, see Bernard Levenson's statement on *anticipatory succession,* in "Bureaucratic Succession," in Amitai Etzioni (ed.), *Complex Organizations: A Sociological Reader* (New York: Holt, Rinehart, and Winston, 1961), pp. 362–375. For discussions of the relation of organizational size to succession, see Oscar Grusky, Corporate Size, Bureaucratization, and Managerial Succession, *American Journal of Sociology,* 67 (November 1961), 261–269; and Louis Kriesberg, Careers, Organization Size, and Succession, *American Journal of Sociology,* 68

ENTREPRENEURIAL SUCCESSION   403

Although the problem of succession therefore can create strains in an organization's structure, it seldom is severe enough to destroy that structure.

While an organization may seem immortal, however, it does have a beginning.[3] The first succession in leadership is crucial, because it can determine whether the organization will continue to exist beyond the life of its founders. This problem is inherent to all forms of organization, whether religious groups, educational institutions, and even nation-states.[4] Max Weber referred to it as the institutionalization of charisma.[5] Generally, the problem of succession refers to the separation of the functions of leadership from the personage of the leader. In an industrial context, this process may be thought of as the distinction between the *function* of management and the manager as a *person*.

Although the succession from one manager to another may be clearly marked, the separation of function and person does not occur at any official or specific time. In traditional business enterprises, it is particularly significant during the first transfer of leadership, and the process may take several years, if not a decade or more.

The succession from entrepreneurs to executives, as this process

(November 1962), 355–359; C. Roland Christenson, *Management Succession in Small and Growing Enterprises* (Boston: Graduate School of Business Administration, Harvard University, 1953); Donald B. Trow, Executive Succession in Small Companies, *Administrative Science Quarterly*, 6 (September 1961), 228–235. See also O. Grusky, Administrative Succession in Formal Organizations, *Social Forces*, 39 (December 1960), 105–115; also his, Managerial Succession and Organizational Effectiveness, *American Journal of Sociology*, 69 (July 1963), 21–31; and Richard O. Carlson, Succession and Performance among School Superintendents, *Administrative Science Quarterly*, 6 (September 1961), 210–226.

[3] The two case studies by Gouldner and Guest deal with succession in firmly established organizations, *Patterns of Industrial Bureaucracy* (Glencoe, Ill.: Free Press, 1954), and Robert H. Guest, *Organizational Change: The Effect of Successful Leadership* (Homewood, Ill.: Irwin-Dorsey, 1962).

[4] Seymour Martin Lipset discusses the importance of George Washington's declining to run for a third term in office as a crucial decision because it institutionalized presidential succession, which provided stability without stagnation; cf. *The First New Nation* (New York: Basic Books, 1963). See also Nicholas J. Demerath, Richard W. Stephens, and R. Robb Taylor, *Power, Presidents, and Professors* (New York: Basic Books, 1967), pp. 148–178.

[5] See H. H. Gerth and C. Wright Mills (trans. and eds.), *From Max Weber: Essays in Sociology* (New York: Oxford, 1946), pp. 262 ff.

may be called, is particularly relevant in developing economies. Because of the importance attached to the role of entrepreneurs in development,[6] their ability to resolve the succession problem in their own organizations has important consequences for the industrial growth of their country. The entrepreneur is important not only in his ability to take risks, innovate, and put together new organizations, but also in his ability to leave a successfully operating organization in which the function of management can be transmitted to other persons.

To study the problem of entrepreneurial succession, case studies were made of five family firms in Mexico, and focused interviews were obtained with twenty other Mexican entrepreneurs faced with the problem of succession. Mexico was selected as an excellent place to examine succession, because of its rapid rate of overall development in the last 25 years. The organizations varied from 50 to 1,200 employees, from ten to forty-five years old, and from labor-intensive textile companies to capital-intensive chemical companies. The research showed three recurrent patterns of conflict in organizational leadership, and found significant variation in the adaptability of each type to new organizational requirements. Before considering the patterns of conflict, however, it is important to understand the place of the family firm in the general process of industrial development.

FAMILY FIRM AND INDUSTRIALIZATION

The extended family is generally the most basic and stable unit of social organization in traditional society. It is the locus of all economic, political, social, and religious life. It provides companionship and protection, a common set of values, and highly

[6] The literature on entrepreneurs is too extensive to be catalogued here. Some of the earlier important statements on the role of entrepreneurs in economic development can be found in Arthur Cole (ed.), *Change and the Entrepreneur* (Cambridge: Harvard University, 1949). The journal, *Explorations in Entrepreneurial History*, is largely devoted to this subject; some of the most important articles from it may also be found in Hugh G. Aitken (ed.), *Explorations in Enterprise* (Cambridge: Harvard University, 1965). See also Joseph A. Schumpeter, *Capitalism, Socialism, and Democracy* (New York: Harper, 1942), and *The Theory of Economic Development* (Cambridge: Harvard University, 1951). Schumpeter's stress on entrepreneurship, rather than on the entrepreneur, reflects the importance of the separation of the function from the person.

proscribed means of fulfilling them. Early forms of commercial and industrial activity therefore represent an extension of the family system rather than a break with it. The intimate connection between family and business is considered natural and compatible, and with industrialization, the larger village community accommodates itself to the presence of a factory.[7] Writing of the agrarian heritage of the Puerto Rican businessman, for example, Thomas C. Cochran states:

The family-centered pattern was undoubtedly weakening among those who worked for wages in the larger industrial centers, but our evidence indicates that among the business elite it survived in an altered form. Close relatives were turned to for assistance in managing business properties. In this way, the extended family moved from a social system based on agriculture to a system of economic control based on the family firm.[8]

During early development, moreover, the control of the family firm is usually complete; investment rights, coincide with financial and managerial control.[9] Although the general trend of development shows a growing separation between ownership and management, the basic family foundation remains.[10]

The compatibility of family and business institutions, and of village life with factory life, requires social values in harmony with traditional economic activity. For an organization to survive for any length of time, this overlap of values of the family and the firm must occur at all levels of the social structure. In order for the small family firm to survive rapid industrial growth, the large corporation must continue to maintain strong family values. In other words, both the small family firm and the large corpora-

[7] For two studies of this process of accommodation, see A. F. A. Husain, *Human and Social Impact of Technological Change in Pakistan* (Dacca, Pakistan: Oxford University, 1956); and Manning Nash, *Machine Age Maya, The Industrialization of a Guatemalan Community* (Glencoe, Ill.: Free Press, 1958).

[8] Thomas C. Cochran, *The Puerto Rican Businessman* (Philadelphia: University of Pennsylvania, 1959), p. 118.

[9] Wilbert Moore uses this threefold scheme to describe the growth of the corporation and professional management in *Industrial Relations and the Social Order* (New York: Macmillan, 1951), pp. 41–64.

[10] W. Paul Strassmann, "The Industrialist," in J. Johnson (ed.), *Continuity and Change in Latin America* (Stanford: University of California, 1964), p. 168.

tion must follow these values, or else the former must ultimately succumb to the competitive power of the larger corporation. Such a family pattern survived in France, and David Landes described the typical French business in 1950 as, "family structured in a way that has generally been associated with precapitalist economies . . . the justification of survival lies not in the ability to make a profit, but in the correct performance of a social function."[11]

The family firm, then, is a positive impetus to entrepreneurial activity in early periods of modernization, which harmonizes with traditional patterns. It has also survived where goals and organization of large businesses maintain the characteristics of the modest family firm, and where social function takes precedence over economic profit. When a national ideology favors rapid economic development, however, this pattern is not likely to survive; traditional family-firm values of enterprise stability and perpetuity clash with new economic goals of sustained investment and expansion. The more competition invades the marketplace, the more vulnerable the traditional structures and the values associated with them become.[12] Under such conditions, the family firm must adapt to the requirements of modern industrial enterprise or ultimately face extinction. It cannot survive continuous and rapid industrial growth in its present traditional form. Or, by corollary, to the extent that this traditional form does perpetuate itself, industrial development will be impeded.

[11] David Landes, "Business and the Modern Businessman in France," in E. Earle (ed.), *Modern France* (Princeton: Princeton University, 1951), pp. 336, 348. In the same volume, see John E. Sawyer, "Strains in the Social Structure of Modern France," pp. 293–312. Also, see D. S. Landes, French Entrepreneurship and Industrial Growth in the Nineteenth Century, *The Journal of Economic History*, 9 (May 1949), 45–61; D. S. Landes, Observations on France: Economy, Society, and Polity, *World Politics*, 9 (April 1957), 329–350; J. E. Sawyer, "The Entrepreneur and the Social Order, France and the United States," in William Miller (ed.), *Men in Business* (Cambridge: Harvard University, 1952); and Charles Kindleberger, *Economic Growth in France and Britain, 1851–1950* (Cambridge: Harvard University, 1964), particularly chs. v, vi.

[12] Marion Levy speaks on this point in "Some Sources of the Vulnerability of the Structures of Relatively Non-industrialized Societies to Those of Highly Industrialized Societies," in B. Hoselitz (ed.), *The Progress of Underdeveloped Areas* (Chicago: University of Chicago, 1952), pp. 113–125.

Industrial trends in developing countries have in fact shown a reduction of both family ownership and family management. Moreover, the firms that have remained under family control and have flourished have been those that were able to adapt to the changing industrial requirements. Some of the adaptations have been providing employment on the basis of competence rather than family connection, employing non-related personnel at managerial levels and delegating authority to them, adapting technological innovations, specifying jobs, and maximizing profits. Changes such as these are likely to conflict with traditional organization and goals, which make little or no distinction between family and business, or between manager and management.

SUCCESSION

When Emerson said that an institution is the lengthening shadow of one man, he aptly described the intimate relation between the business firm and the person who heads it. A shadow is a fleeting thing, however, and if the firm is to persist beyond the lifetime of its founder, the leadership of the firm must pass from one generation to the next. Within a family firm, this pattern is obviously the succession of father to son, but only in theory do the two cast the same shadow. Typically, the father started his small business with a little capital, struggled, built it up through experience, and then sent his son to receive a formal education. The difference between experience and education often reflects different personalities, operating by different methods, and pursuing different goals. The task of management also differs. The founding father in one family firm said: "I had to work hard, but the management was easy"; while his son said, "I don't have to work too hard, but the management is much more difficult."

The separation of the managerial function from the individual is seldom a simple task of passing the authority from father to son. When the son enters the firm, he typically shares authority with his father, beginning in a slightly subordinate position and gradually assuming all responsibility. Several patterns repeatedly occur during this transitional period of shared authority among the two generations in the family firm. These patterns, of course, are abstractions of general tendencies; nevertheless, the evidence suggests that certain commonalities predominate, and it is these common aspects which are emphasized here.[13]

Pattern One: Strong Father and Weak Son

The first is the pattern of strong father and weak son. Here is the pioneer man of business who fought his way to the top. His case is a paradigm of all the clichés: sheer drive, stamina, judgment, risk, courage, and luck. He is typically proud of where he has "gotten" and is well aware of his importance, both in his family, his firm, and perhaps even in his community and society. He has a personal dynamism about him, knows every inch of his business, every man in his firm, and every trick in the book.

He runs his family and his business with the same iron hand, and his word is law. He is respected and often loved by his workers, and he is the epitome of a stern but benevolent *patrón* to them. Many of his workers have been with him for many years; they are loyal to him, would not want to work for anyone else, and will carry out almost any order—because it comes from him. Indeed, his relationship with his workers often *seems* more idyllic than his contact with his son. For the distinctions of class, status, and power between this *padre de familia* and his workers are clear and delimiting, while the distinction between father and son is not.

The fatal flaw in such a "man of iron" is that he cannot transmit his strength to his son. Often he only transmits the opposite: the father is all that the son is not. In terms of power, if the father rules like a tyrant, his son is often incapable of making and enforcing his own decisions. In terms of prestige, if the father considers social standing and refinement irrelevant to running a business, then his son is likely to emphasize prestige and gracious living to the exclusion of a concern with running the family business. Or, in less extreme cases, the father may

[13] Although the family firm seldom involves only one father and one son, these patterns do provide the outline for succession of a numerically more complex form. When more than one son is involved, it is usually the oldest who is most closely bound to the pattern, because of primogeniture. When more than one father is involved (say two brothers), then both may exhibit the same characteristics, or one may trigger one pattern of succession and the other set a second in process.

consider such factors necessary but not sufficient qualifications for administering the family's interests, whereas his son will rely on their sufficiency. Finally, in terms of wealth, where the father wants to make money, the son wants to spend it; he is the first family playboy.

The major focus of conflict between this father–son pattern is in authority and responsibility. The father has made all the major decisions and taken all responsibility for them. He is the sole authority, and all employees and workers know this. Consequently, his son lacks any real power, has never become capable of successfully wielding what power he does have, and is not likely to make any appreciable gains in power in the foreseeable future. The father simply cannot let go of his command; he cannot retire himself. While outwardly he makes a display of pride in the way his son is taking over the business, the son makes none of the real decisions and is nothing but windowdressing.

Despite the father's overt pride in his son, he seems more to be taking covert pride in his own abilities. In fact, the son may even represent a threat of displacement to the father, which only drives him further toward centralizing his control. When the son returns with a degree in business administration, engineering, or the like, he often has new ideas. Each time the son tries to act on his own, however, he is either bridled or crushed by his father. With the father's attitude that only he knows what is best, the son does not have an opportunity to exercise his initiative as he waits to receive his authority within the firm. This father–son relationship is a psychic struggle between generations and has an intense undercurrent of conflict.

The virulence of this relationship in Mexican life makes it especially relevant to patterns of organization within the family firm. Psychologists of the Mexican personality have considered this a reflection of the psychological and historical relation between father and son, with its roots in the family structure during the Colonial period. In this setting, which observers feel has influenced present-day family relations, the all-powerful Spanish father and the powerless Indian mother have produced a *mestizo* (hybrid) son who must endlessly search for his own identity. As an adolescent he is caught in the dilemma of wanting to imitate the manliness and freedom of his father, whom he loves but fears, and wanting to denigrate his mother, whom he loves but looks down upon because she is female, Indian, and weak. In consequence, his adult life is an endless search for his masculinity, that heroic and unreal power which he either lacks or feels that he lacks.[14]

Pattern Two: Conservative Father and Progressive Son

The second pattern that predominates in father–son relations in the family firms is less psychological. The differences in personality between father and son, and their consequences for the organization are more a function of age. In this pattern of conservative father and progressive son, the typical father is also a hard-driving man who began with nothing and gradually built up a solid and successful business. The unstable days and severe market fluctuations following the Revolution are still vivid in his mind, and he is no longer the young man of the early post-revolutionary days. He is tired of fighting and struggling; he wants to enjoy some of the fruits of his labor in his old age. By now he is a grandfather and he would like to devote himself more to his growing family. He has fulfilled his goal as far as the business is concerned.

In this second pattern, the son receives a formal education, often in the United States or in Europe, and returns to the family business full of "new ideas," but he is held back. The father, here, is willing to give more control to his son, but he still serves as overseer to all major decisions. He is very reluctant to make the major decisions that the son would like to make, and to any radically new suggestion he will say, "We knew nothing when we started, but we have made out all right, so why should we change? We've always done it this way." The contrast, here, is not so much between a traditional father and a modern son as

[14] For a fuller treatment of this theme, some of the better works are: Octavio Paz, *The Labyrinth of Solitude* (New York: Grove Press, 1961); Samuel Ramos, *El perfil del hombre y la cultura de méxico* (Mexico D. F.: Espasa-Calpe Argentina, 1951); Francisco González Pineda, *El mexicano: psicología de su destructividad* (Mexico D. F.: Editorial Pax, 1961); Santiago Ramírez, *El mexicano: psicología de sus motivaciones* (3rd ed.; Mexico D. F.: Editorial Pax, 1961).

ENTREPRENEURIAL SUCCESSION   411

it is a father who was modern for his time, but has become conservative with age.

The immediate focus of conflict between father and son in this second pattern often involves issues which develop as a result of the son's higher education. The son brings back many ideas about products and procedures, some of which can be imitated directly while others can be adapted to local requirements. The more general focus of conflict is in the area of the firm's change and growth, for technological adaptations seem more readily acceptable than administrative ones.[15] In this pattern, the son is given both authority and responsibility, but his mandate is to maintain the status quo. For the father, to continue the success of the firm is to follow in the same path; for the son, the same path in the future means failure. For the son, the family firm is a restraint as long as he is not free to build his own successful organization. He wants to do more than manage the family firm, but he is held back by respect for and obligation to his father. "I was offered a number of jobs," said one son, "but finally, after talking to my father, I decided that I couldn't abandon him and therefore I went into the family business."

In the first pattern, it appears to be the son who becomes the hanger-on in the management structure; in the second pattern it is the father who begins to get in the way of the son. For the son in the first pattern, the firm provides financial success, although the emotional relations may be difficult; whereas for the son in the second pattern the emotional problems are manageable, but the financial future worries him as long as he is not allowed to carry out expansion of the firm.

The fathers also differ in their personalities, in their family relations, and in their management goals and actions. In the extreme formulation of the first pattern, the father expresses the lone, aggressive, and invulnerable figure portrayed as the *macho,* the embodiment of masculinity, and summed up in the word power.[16] In the second pattern, however, the father is less tense

[15] This phenomenon has been given considerable attention in the past by anthropologists. It began with William F. Ogburn's notion of *cultural lag* in his book, *Social Change* (New York: Viking Press, 1922).

[16] Octavio Paz, *op. cit.,* p. 81.

and explosive; he is more willing to rely on his son as he begins to relax and withdraw. The first fears retirement and the second sees in it the fulfillment of his career. In the first pattern, the transfer of power will take the form of a contest in which, if the son rises to the struggle, leadership must be wrested away. In the second pattern, succession is a slow process of waiting out the natural change in generations.

The immigrant family is an important subcase of this second pattern, where the father in a family firm has migrated from another country, particularly to a different culture and one where he is of a minority group. The overriding value of such immigrant families is to "stick together," and family comes before business. Conflict is likely to arise when the second generation, which does not have the direct immigrant experience, begins to see the family enterprise as "just a business." Because of the insulation of the family, the son generally accepts the responsibility of taking over the firm, but begins to resist the restrictions involved in the transfer. He is less involved in the family experience. This pattern is especially characteristic of refugee families.[17]

Pattern Three: Branches of the Family

In addition to the conflict between father and son, conflict also occurs between various branches of a family. This third pattern may, therefore, be found in family firms where the first or second patterns are also present. The family branch groupings are highly correlated with the managerial division of labor, and are particularly related to the distinction between technical and administrative responsibilities. Where two brothers are involved, one will take charge of production while the other will concentrate on relations with the community. In time, and depending upon the closeness of the family and the size of the firm, these positions

[17] This runs somewhat counter to the interpretation offered by Strassmann that the immigrant father, as an outsider, has less to lose and is therefore more radical an innovator than his more assimilated son, who in turn becomes more conservative because of his greater stake in the existing social structure. Cf. *Continuity and Change, op. cit.*, pp. 164–166. See also, Louis Kriesberg, Entrepreneurs in Latin America and the Role of Cultural and Situational Processes, *International Social Science Journal*, 15 (1963). See also, Luis Bresser Pereira, Origenes Étnicas e Sociais do Empresário Paulista, *Revista de Administração de Empresas*, Vol. 2, No. 11 (1964), 83–106.

will be available for inheritance and succession among the younger generation. Each member of the founding generation is usually entitled to bring in at least one son to replace him in his position. If two brothers have started a business, with one having technical responsibilities and the other administrative responsibilities, then the succession of sons will parallel this distinction.

The closer the family relationship among the first generation, the less formal are the relations between family lines and organizational inheritance. When two brothers direct a firm, for example, the domain of one is still more open to his nephew than when two brothers-in-law or two cousins head a firm. Also, the smaller the firm, the less marked are these distinctions. Another variation in inheritance and succession is that the least educated and/or least ambitious of the sons more frequently assumes the technical responsibilities.

The division between in-plant (technical) and out-plant (administrative) management is important within the family firm, because of the prestige of the office within the enterprise. In Mexico, administrative personnel, at comparable levels, have more prestige than the technical personnel. The branch of the family in administration therefore has greater prestige; that is, the dominant family branch tends to go into administration rather than in the technical direction.

Although the distinction between technical and administrative roles is based upon the functional necessities of an organization, the separation of family groupings is not such a rational separation. The family firm, at least in its origins, is intimately linked to family values as well as business values. The connection between organizational roles and family groupings suffuses the requirements of the former with the values of the latter. Tension between two branches of a family, for example, may be reflected in the conflict between the technical and administrative tasks. Conversely, the different perspectives and requirements of the technical and administrative roles may cause dissension among family members. Conflict normally arising from differences between one set of roles is heightened by its confluence with the differentiation of roles from the other setting.

On the other hand, when neither the conflict between generations nor the conflict arising from family divisions along functional or nuclear lines is severe enough to destroy the family-firm
bond, the overlapping of conflict may, in fact, prevent any one
conflict from becoming so severe as to cause a complete rupture.[18]
Ultimately, the decision must be made in each family firm between family relations and profit.

SUCCESSION AND THE FUTURE OF FAMILY FIRMS

At this point it is appropriate to ask what the patterns indicate
about administrative change in industrial enterprises in developing economies. Because the traditional family firm is incompatible with rapid industrial advances, either the goals and organization of the family firm must change to meet the new industrial
requirements,[19] or else the family firm will be superseded by the
share-holding, executive-managed, corporate enterprise.[20]

To understand the direction of organizational development in
a country, one must understand the typical family firm, the social
relationships, and how these are affecting the development of the
enterprise. Unless longitudinal studies are made of the same firm
through time, it is difficult to make definitive statements about
the future of an enterprise, but some hypotheses are possible.

The pattern characterized by the strong father and weak son
seems likely to fail. The father is incapable of preparing anyone
else to replace him, therefore the son is not apt to be prepared
for the task of directing the enterprise. Although Harbison and
Myers were not distinguishing between family patterns, they sum
up this type, when they state:

The one-man ruler delegates too little, does too much himself, and
thus has little time for effective organization building or for creative
thinking. As a consequence, this type of management is likely to be
defensive, enervated, and static. It breathes only at the top and when

[18] For an elaboration of this point, see Lewis Coser, *The Functions of Social
Conflict* (New York: Free Press, 1956).

[19] Typical in Japan, and exemplified in Latin America by DiTella of Argentina,
and until recently by Ford in the United States.

[20] The typical United States pattern. For recent and rapid changes in England
toward the same pattern, see Anthony Sampson, *Anatomy of Britain Today* (London:
Hodder and Stougton, 1965), pts. ii, iii.

ENTREPRENEURIAL SUCCESSION   415

the top disappears, the organization either collapses or must be completely rebuilt.[21]

The only question is the disposal of the firm, and two courses seem predictable. The weak son may attempt to direct the enterprise himself, in which case the enterprise is likely to fail; from Louis XIV to Louis XV within the family firm. The failure is predictable in the transition from the first to the second generation, but it is in the change from second to third generation that failure often occurs.[22]

The other alternative is public sale of the business. If the sale is made in time, the enterprise may be made profitable again. In the past three years since the field work was conducted, this has been a frequent solution. The buyer is often a foreign company, which retains the firm's original and already established name for advertising and public relations. Sometimes the buyer is a young native-born entrepreneur, who sees a financial opportunity in putting an ailing firm on its feet. A third possibility is that the government itself will take over the firm, which is especially likely to occur when the financial prospects are not very good, but the organization cannot be allowed to fail for social or political reasons. Each of these means the introduction of outside capital and management. Whether the business fails or grows, it will not remain within a traditional family form, and the distinction between managers and management will be instituted.

[21] Frederick Harbison and Charles Myers, *Management in the Industrial World* (New York: McGraw-Hill, 1959), p. 41.

[22] Observers report that the succession from second to third generation is the crisis period in the European family firm. Despite a few exceptions, most of the Mexican private enterprises are still owned and managed by the founding fathers, and the developing patterns of conflict, succession, and hence survival, with which we have dealt involve the change from first to second generation. It is therefore difficult to say which succession of generations is the more critical in the Mexican family firm. The change to third generation, however, is critical because of an overabundance of heirs. Unlike Europe, the Mexican birth rate, average family size, and extended family values create a critical proportion of sons and relatives pressing for privileged positions by the time of the first succession. And where crisis in the family firm is concentrated on how to maintain financial and managerial control, the patterns of succession have more relevance than the number of generations. This, of course, is conjectural until the succession to the third generation can be observed. See David Granick, *The European Executive* (New York: Doubleday, 1962), pp. 303–320.

In the pattern of conservative father and progressive son, the danger is that the son might get bored waiting. The father basically trusts his son and recognizes the need for transmitting authority to him; the son respects his father and does not push too hard. As the reins gradually change hands, so too does the entire character of the organization; the chances are good that such an enterprise can adapt to necessary change and still maintain the family trademark.

Such family firms can benefit from industrial growth and in turn contribute to it, to the extent that the transfer process gives the son an increasing freedom to institute expansion and change. If a family member is incapable of handling his job, then a school chum with the necessary training is brought in to replace him. If outside technical advice is required, then that too will be brought in. The firm will remain within the family, not because it resists outside influences, but because it incorporates them into its changing framework. In this second pattern, (as with the German family), "The good of the family enterprise is more likely to take precedence over the preferences of the individual family members."[23]

The future of the third pattern is related to the strength of conflict that develops between the various family factions and to the weight which expressive sentiments between relatives carry. The two are conversely related and have opposite effects on both the family and the firm. The deeper the internal strife, the more likely it is that one group will buy the other out and, in general, this will be advantageous for the firm.

Despite differences about how the family business should be operated, personal relations among relatives often take precedence over maximum profit. With this mixed pattern of social and business relationships, the firm can survive only as long as the market for its product is expanding more rapidly than its competitors can meet that demand. When family factions divide a firm, therefore, the change may be either in the direction of modernization within the family framework or into the nonfamily executive management enterprise. Bringing about entrepreneurial succession is essential for survival in a competitive market.

[23] Granick, *ibid.*, p. 313.

Harry Levinson

Conflicts that Plague the Family Business

*Discord between father and son and other
rivalries among relatives can paralyze
the organization unless they are confronted*

Foreword

The job of operating a family-owned company is often grievously complicated by friction arising from rivalries involving a father and his son, brothers, or other family members who hold positions in the business, or at least derive income from it. Unless the principals face up to their feelings of hostility, the author says, the business will suffer and may even die. He offers some advice on how relatives can learn to live with their peculiar situation. But he concludes that the only real solution is to move toward professional management.

Mr. Levinson is the Thomas Henry Carroll Ford Foundation Distinguished Visiting Professor of Business Administration, Harvard Business School, and is President of the Levinson Institute. He is the author of many previous HBR articles, including "On Being a Middle-Aged Manager" (July-August 1969) and "Management by Whose Objectives?" (July-August 1970). His latest books are *Executive Stress* (Harper & Row, Publishers, Inc., 1970) and *Organizational Diagnosis*, which is to be published next summer by the Harvard University Press.

In U.S. business, the most successful executives are often men who have built their own companies. Ironically, their very success frequently brings to them and members of their families personal problems of an intensity rarely encountered by professional managers. And these problems make family businesses possibly the most difficult to operate.[1]

It is obvious common sense that when managerial decisions are influenced by feelings about and responsibilities toward relatives in the business, when nepotism exerts a negative influence, and when a company is run more to honor a family tradition than for its own needs and purposes, there is likely to be trouble.

However, the problems of family businesses go considerably deeper than these issues. In this article I shall examine some of the more difficult underlying psychological elements in operating these businesses and suggest some ways of coping with them.

They start with the founder

The difficulties of the family business begin with the founder. Usually he is an entrepreneur for whom the business has at least three important meanings:

1. The entrepreneur characteristically has unresolved conflicts with his father, research evi-

---

1. For two thoughtful views of the subject, see Robert G. Donnelley, "The Family Business," HBR July-August 1964, p. 93; and Seymour Tilles, "Survival Strategies for Family Firms," *European Business*, April 1970, p. 9.

dence indicates. He is therefore uncomfortable when being supervised, and starts his own business both to outdo his father and to escape the authority and rivalry of more powerful figures.[2]

2. An entrepreneur's business is simultaneously his "baby" and his "mistress." Those who work with him and for him are characteristically his instruments in the process of shaping the organization.

If any among them aspires to be other than a device for the founder—that is, if he wants to acquire power himself—he is soon likely to find himself on the outside looking in. This is the reason why so many organizations decline when their founders age or die.

3. For the entrepreneur, the business is essentially an extension of himself, a medium for his personal gratification and achievement above all. And if he is concerned about what happens to his business after he passes on, that concern usually takes the form of thinking of the kind of monument he will leave behind.

The fundamental psychological conflict in family businesses is rivalry, compounded by feelings of guilt, when more than one family member is involved. The rivalry may be felt by the founder —even though no relatives are in the business— when he unconsciously senses (justifiably or not) that subordinates are threatening to remove him from his center of power. Consider this actual case:

□ An entrepreneur, whose organization makes scientific equipment and bears his name, has built a sizable enterprise in international markets. He has said that he wants his company to be noted all over the world for contributing to society.

He has attracted many young men with the promise of rapid promotions, but he guarantees their failure by giving them assignments and then turning them loose without adequate organizational support. He intrudes into the young men's decision making, but he counterbalances this behavior with paternalistic devices. (His company has more benefits than any other I have known.)

This technique makes his subordinates angry at him for what he has done, then angry at themselves for being hostile to such a kind man. Ultimately, it makes them feel utterly inadequate. He can get people to take responsibility and move up into executive positions, but his behavior has made certain that he will never have a rival.

The conflicts created by rivalries among family members—between fathers and sons, among brothers, and between executives and other relatives—have a chronically abrasive effect on the principals. Those family members in the business must face up to the impact that these relationships exert and must learn to deal with them, not only for their own emotional health but for the welfare of the business.

I shall consider in turn the father-son rivalry, the brother-brother rivalry, and other family relationships.

Father-son rivalry

As I have indicated, for the founder the business is an instrument, an extension of himself. So he has great difficulty giving up his baby, his mistress, his instrument, his source of social power, or whatever else the business may mean to him. Characteristically, he has great difficulty delegating authority and he also refuses to retire despite repeated promises to do so.

This behavior has certain implications for father-son relationships. While he consciously wishes to pass his business on to his son and also wants him to attain his place in the sun, unconsciously the father feels that to yield the business would be to lose his masculinity.

At the same time, and also unconsciously, he needs to continue to demonstrate his own competence. That is, he must constantly reassure himself that he alone is competent to make "his" organization succeed. Unconsciously the father does not want his son to win, take away his combination baby and mistress, and displace him from his summit position.

These conflicting emotions cause the father to behave inexplicably in a contradictory manner, leading those close to him to think that while on the one hand he wants the business to succeed, on the other hand he is determined to make it fail.

The son's feelings of rivalry are a reflection of his father's. The son naturally seeks increasing responsibility commensurate with his growing maturity, and the freedom to act responsibly on his own. But he is frustrated by his father's intrusions, his broken promises of retirement, and his self-aggrandizement.

The son resents being kept in an infantile

2. See Orvis F. Collins, David G. Moore, and Darab B. Unwalla, *The Enterprising Man* (East Lansing, Michigan State University Bureau of Business Research, 1964).

Harvard Business Review: March-April 1971

role—always the little boy in his father's eyes—with the accompanying contempt, condescension, and lack of confidence that in such a situation frequently characterize the father's attitude. He resents, too, remaining dependent on his father for his income level and, as often, for

title, office, promotion, and the other usual perquisites of an executive. The father's erratic and unpredictable behavior in these matters makes this dependency more unpalatable.

I have observed a number of such men who, even as company presidents, are still being victimized by their fathers who remain chairmen of the board and chief executive officers.

'Why don't you let me grow up?'

Characteristically, fathers and sons, particularly the latter, are terribly torn by these conflicts; the father looks on the son as ungrateful and unappreciative, and the son feels both hostile to his father and guilty for his hostility.

The father bears the feeling that the son never will be man enough to run the business, but he tries to hide that feeling from his son. The son yearns for his chance to run it and waits impatiently but still loyally in the wings—often for years beyond the age when others in nonfamily organizations normally take executive responsibility—for his place on the stage.

If the pressures become so severe for him that he thinks of leaving, he feels disloyal but at the same time fears losing the opportunity that would be his if he could only wait a little longer. He defers his anticipated gratification and pleasure, but, with each postponement, his anger, disappointment, frustration, and tension mount. Here is a typical situation I know of:

□ Matthew Anderson, a man who founded a reclaimed-metals business, has two sons. John, the elder, is his logical successor, but Anderson has given him little freedom to act independently, pointing out that, despite limited education, he (the father) has built the business and in-

tuitively knows more about how to make it successful.

Though he has told John that he wants him to be a partner, he treats John more like a flunky than an executive, let alone a successor. He pays the elder son a small salary, always with the excuse that he should not expect more because someday he will inherit the business. He grants minimal raises sporadically, never recognizing John's need to support his family in a style fitting his position in the company.

When John once protested and demanded both more responsibility and more income, his father gave Henry, the second son, a vice presidential title and a higher income. When Henry asked for greater freedom and responsibility, Anderson turned back to John and made him president (in name only). The father, as chairman of the board and chief executive officer, continued to second-guess John, excluded Henry from conferences (which of course increased John's feelings of guilt), and told John that Henry was "no good" and could not run the business.

Later, when John sought to develop new aspects of the business to avoid the fluctuations of the metals market, his father vetoed these ideas, saying, "This is what we know, and this is what we are going to do." He failed to see the possible destructive effects of market cycles on fixed overhead costs and the potential inroads of plastics and other cheaper materials on the reclaimed-metals business.

The upshot was that profits declined and the business became more vulnerable to both domestic and foreign (particularly Japanese) competition. When John argued with his father about this, he got the response: "What do you know? You're still green. I went through the Depression." Once again Anderson turned to Henry —making the black sheep white, and vice versa.

Angered, John decided to quite the business, but his mother said, "You can't leave your father; he needs you." Anderson accused him of being ungrateful, but he also offered to retire, as he had promised to do several times before.

Despite his pain, John could not free himself from his father. (Only an ingrate would desert his father, he told himself.) Also John knew that if he departed, he could not go into competition with his father, because that would destroy him. But John shrank from entering an unfamiliar business.

Nevertheless, from time to time John has explored other opportunities while remaining in the business. But each time his father has undercut him. For instance, John once wanted to borrow money for a venture, but Anderson told the bankers that his son was not responsible.

Now, when John is middle-aged, he and his father are still battling. In effect John is asking, "Why don't you let me grow up?" and his father is answering, "I'm the only man around here. You must stay here and be my boy."

'He's destroying the business'

The son also has intense rivalry feelings, of course. These, too, can result in fierce competition with his father and hostile rejection of him, or abject dependence on him. Sometimes the competition can lead to a manipulative alignment with the mother against him. Consider this actual case:

□ Bill Margate, a recent business school graduate, knew that he would go into his father's electronic components business. But he decided that first he should get experience elsewhere, so he spent four years with a large manufacturing company. From his education and experience, he became aware of how unsophisticated his father was about running the business and set about showing the senior Margate how a business should be professionally managed.

Margate can do no right in Bill's eyes, at least not according to the books which he has read but which his father has never heard of. Bill frequently criticizes his father, showing him how ignorant he is. When Margate calls his son "green," Bill retorts, "I've forgotten more about managing a business than you'll ever know."

Bill's mother is also involved in the business; she has been at her husband's side for many years, though their relationship is less than the best. Mrs. Margate dotes on her son and complains to him about her husband, and she encourages Bill in his attacks on his father. When Bill undertook several ventures that floundered, she excused the failures as being caused by his father's interference.

But whenever the father-son battle reaches a peak, Mrs. Margate shifts allegiance and stands behind her husband. So the senior Margate has an ally when the chips are down, at the price of a constant beating until he gets to that point.

The struggle for the business has remained a stand-off. But as the elder Margate has grown older, his son's attacks have begun to tell on him. Bill has urged him to take long Florida vacations, but Margate refuses because he fears what would happen when his back is turned. For the same reason, he does not permit Bill to sign checks for the company.

Now Margate has become senile, and Bill's criticism of him continues, even in public. "He's destroying the business," Bill will say.

However, Bill cannot act appropriately to remove his father (even though he is now incompetent) because of his guilt feelings about his incessant attacks. That would destroy his father, literally, and he cannot bring himself to do it.

'The old man really built it'

The problem for the son becomes especially acute when and if he does take over. Often the father has become obsolete in his managerial conceptions. The organization may have grown beyond one man's capacity to control it effectively. That man may have been a star whose imagination, creativity, or drive are almost impossible to duplicate. He may also have been a charismatic figure with whom employees and even the public identified.

Whatever the combination of factors, the son is likely to have to take over an organization with many weaknesses hidden behind the powerful facade of the departed leader. For these reasons many businesses, at the end of their founders' tenure, fall apart, are pirated, or are merged into another organization.

The Ford Motor Company, at the demise of Henry Ford, was a case in point; a completely new management had to be brought in. Henry Ford II was faced with the uncomfortable task of having to regenerate a company that appeared to have the potential for continued success, but which, according to some, could easily have gone bankrupt.

While the son is acting to repair the organizational weaknesses left by his father, he is subject to the criticism of those persons who, envious of his position, are waiting for him to stumble. They "know" that he is not as good as his father. If he does less well than his father, regardless of whether there are unfavorable economic conditions or other causes, he is subject to the charge of having thrown away an opportunity that others could have capitalized on.

The scion cannot win. If he takes over a successful enterprise, and even if he makes it much more successful than anyone could have imagined, nevertheless the onlookers stimulate his feelings of inadequacy. They say, "What did you expect? After all, look what he started with." To illustrate:

Harvard Business Review: March-April 1971

□ Tom Schlesinger, the president of a restaurant chain, inherited the business after his father had built a profitable regional network of outlets with a widely known name—a model for the industry.

Tom has expanded it into nearly a national operation. He has done this with astute methods of finance that allow great flexibility, and with effective control methods that maintain meal quality and at the same time minimize waste. By any standards he has made an important contribution to the business.

But those who remember his father cannot see what Tom has done because the aura of his father still remains. They tend to minimize Tom's contribution with such observations as, "Well, you know, the old man really built that business."

Tom cannot change the attitude of those who knew his father, and he feels it is important to keep lauding his father's accomplishments in order to present a solid family image to employees, customers, and the community. But he is frustrated because he has no way of getting the world to see how well he has done.

Brother-brother rivalry

The father-son rivalry is matched in intensity by the brother-brother rivalry. Their competition may be exacerbated by the father if he tries to play the sons off against each other or has decided that one should wear his mantle, as I showed previously. (In my experience, the greatest difficulties of this kind occur when there are only two brothers in the organization.)

The problem is further complicated if their mother and their wives are also directly or indirectly involved in the business. Mothers have their favorites—regardless of what they say—and each wife, of course, has a stake in her husband's position. He can become a foil for his wife's fantasies and ambition.

The rivalry between brothers for their father's approval, which began in childhood, continues into adult life. It can reach such an intensity that it colors every management decision and magnifies the jockeying for power that goes on in all organizations. Consider this situation:

□ Arthur, five years older than his sibling, is president, and Warren is an operating vice president, of the medium-sized retailing organization which they inherited. To anyone who cares to listen, each maintains that he can get along very well without the other.

Arthur insists that Warren is not smart, not as good a businessman as he; that his judgment is bad; and that even if given the chance, he would be unable to manage the business.

Warren asserts that when the two were growing up, Arthur considered him to be a competitor, but for his part, he (Warren) did not care to compete because he was younger and smaller. Warren says that he cannot understand why his older brother has always acted as if they were rivals, and adds, "I just want a chance to do my thing. If he'd only let me alone with responsibility! But he acts as if the world would fall apart if I had that chance."

Every staff meeting and meeting of the board (which includes nonfamily members) becomes a battle between the brothers. Associates, employees, and friends back off because they decline to take sides. The operation of the organization has been turned into a continuous family conflict.

The elder . . .

Ordinarily, the elder brother succeeds his father. But this custom reaffirms the belief of the younger brother (or brothers) that the oldest is indeed the favorite. In any event, the older brother often has a condescending attitude toward the younger. In their earliest years the older is larger, physically stronger, more competent, and more knowledgeable than the younger merely because of the difference in age, as in the case I just cited.

Only in rare instances does the younger broth-

er have the opportunity to match the skills, competence, and experience of the elder until they reach adulthood. By that time the nature of this relationship is so well established that the older brother has difficulty regarding the younger one as adequate and competent.

Moreover, the eldest child is earlier and longer in contact with the parents, and their control efforts fall more heavily on him. Consequently, older children tend to develop stronger consciences, drive themselves harder, expect more of themselves, and control themselves more rigidly than younger ones. Being already, therefore, a harsh judge of himself, the eldest is likely to be an even harsher judge of his younger siblings.

. . . and the younger

The younger brother attempts to compensate for the effects of this childhood relationship and his older brother's efforts to control him by trying to carve out a place in the business that is his own. This he guards with great zeal, keeping the older brother out so he can demonstrate to himself, his brother, and others that he is indeed competent and has his own piece of the action for which he is independently responsible.

If the brothers own equal shares in the organization and both are members of the board, as is frequently the case, the problems are compounded. On the board they can argue policy from equally strong positions. However, when they return to operations in which one is subordinate to the other, the subordinate one, usually the junior brother, finds it extremely difficult to think of himself in a subservient role.

The younger one usually is unable to surmount this problem in their mutual relationship. He tends to be less confident than his brother and considers himself to be at a permanent disadvantage, always overcontrolled, always unheeded. Since the older brother views the younger one as being less able, he becomes involved in self-fulfilling prophecies. Distrusting his younger brother, he is likely to overcontrol him, give him less opportunity for freedom and responsibility—which in turn make for maturity and growth—and likely to reject all signs of the younger brother's increasing competence.

If for some reason the younger brother displaces the older one, and particularly if the latter becomes subordinate to him, the younger brother is faced with feelings of guilt for having attacked the elder and usurped what so often is accepted as the senior brother's rightful role.

Intrafamily friction

The problems of the father and brothers extend to other relatives when they, too, become involved in the business. In some families it is expected that all who wish to join the company will have places there. This can have devastating effects, particularly if the jobs are sinecures.

The chief executive of a family business naturally feels a heavy responsibility for the family fortunes. If he does not produce a profit, the effect on what he considers to be his image in the financial markets may mean less to him than the income reduction which members of his family will suffer. So he is vulnerable to backbiting from persons whom he knows only too well and whom he cannot dismiss as faceless. Consider this case:

☐ Three brothers started a knitting business. Only one of the brothers had sons, and only one of the those sons stayed in the business; he eventually became president. The stock is held by the family. Two widowed aunts, his mother, his female cousins (one of whom was already widowed), and his brother, a practicing architect, depend on the business for significant income.

When business is off, the women complain. If the president wants to buy more equipment, they resist. If they hear complaints from employees or merchant friends, they make these complaints known at family gatherings. The president is never free from the vixens who are constantly criticizing and second-guessing him.

Perhaps more critical for the health of the business are the factional divisions that spring up in the organization as associates and subordinates choose the family members with whom they want to be identified. (Often, however, those who take sides discover that in a crisis the family unites against "outsiders," including their partisans, who are then viewed as trying to divide the family.)

If the nonfamily employees or board members decide not to become involved in a family fight and withdraw from relations with its members until the conflict is resolved, the work of the organization may be paralyzed. Worse yet, the dispute may eventually embroil the entire organization, resulting in conflicts at the

Harvard Business Review: March-April 1971

lowest levels, as employees try to cope with the quarrels thrust on them.

Now the business has become a battleground that produces casualties but no peace. Such internecine warfare constitutes a tremendous barrier to communication and frustrates adequate planning and rational decision making.

A business in which numerous members of the family of varying ages and relationships are involved often becomes painfully disrupted around issues of empires and succession. Its units tend to become family-member territories and therefore poorly integrated organizationally, if at all.

As for succession, the dominant or patriarchal leader may fully expect to pass on the mantle of leadership to other, elder relatives in their turn. He may even promise them leadership roles, particularly if he has had to develop a coalition to support his position.

But for both realistic and irrational reasons he may well come to feel that none of the family members is capable of filling the role. He cannot very well disclose his decision, however, without stirring conflict, and he cannot bring in outside managers without betraying his relatives or reneging on his promises. On the other hand, he fears what would happen if he died without having designated a successor.

He may decide that the only way out is to sell the business (at least each relative will then get his fair share). But that solution is costly—it signifies not only the loss of the business as a means of employment, but also the betrayal of a tradition and, inevitably, the dissolution of close family ties that have been maintained through the medium of the business.

Facing up to it

What can be done about these problems?

Most entrepreneurial fathers seem unable to resolve their dilemma themselves. They tend to be rigid and righteous, finding it difficult to understand that there is another, equally valid point of view which they can accept without becoming weaklings. Well-meaning outsiders who try to help the father see the effects of his behavior and think seriously about succession usually find themselves rejected. Then they lose whatever beneficial influence they may have had on him.

Several approaches have worked well. In some instances, sons have told their fathers that they recognize how important it is to the father to run his own business, but it is just as important for them to have the opportunity to "do their own thing." They then establish small new ventures either under the corporate umbrella or outside it, without deserting their father.

In a variant of this approach, a father who heads a retail operation opened a store in a different community for each of his sons. They do their buying together, with appropriate variations for each community, and maintain a common name and format, but each son runs his own operation while the father continues to run his.

In still another situation, the father merged his company into a larger one. Each of his two sons then became president of a subsidiary, and the father started a new venture while serving as a policy guide to his sons.

The son's role

Whether such alternatives can work depends in part on how the son conducts himself. He must be honest with himself and consider his paternal relationship candidly. He must take steps like these:

□ He must ask himself why he chose to go into the family business. Most sons will say it is because of the opportunity and the feelings of guilt if they had not done so. Often, however, the basic reason is that a powerful father has helped make his son dependent on him, and so his son is reluctant to strike out on his own.

He rationalizes his reluctance on the basis of opportunity and guilt. Struggling with his own dependency, he is more likely to continue to fight his father in the business because he is still trying to escape his father's control.

□ Having examined this issue, and recognizing whatever validity it may have for him, the son must realize how often his own feelings of rivalry and anger get in his way. The more intense the rivalry, the more determinedly he seeks to push his father from his throne and the more aggressively the latter must defend himself. The son must therefore refrain from attack.

□ He must quietly and with dignity, as a mature man, apprise his father of the realities—that he needs an area of freedom and an independent medium to develop skills and responsibilities. He can do so within the company framework or, if that is not feasible, outside it. In his own self-interest, as well as the company's, he must be certain that he gets the opportunity.

☐ He must not allow himself to be played off against his brother, and he must not allow his guilt to be manipulated. By the same token, he himself must not become involved with others in manipulation.

☐ He must honestly recognize and respect his father's achievement and competence. To build a business is no mean task, and usually the father still has useful skills and knowledge. Furthermore, the son should recognize the powerful psychological meaning of the business to his father and not expect him to be rational about his relationship to it.

If the son is still unable to make choices about what he wants to do, then, despite his pain and his father's reluctance to seek help, he himself must do so. Only he can take the initiative to relieve his anguish. Here is an example of how a group of sons has taken the initiative:

In Boston, a group calling itself SOB's (Sons of the Boss) has been formed to encourage men in that position to talk over common problems and share solutions. After educating themselves about the psychological dimensions of their situation, the group will make it a practice from time to time to invite their fathers as a group to discuss their problems openly. Then fathers and sons will get together separately.

This procedure may enable fathers and sons to realize that their particular problems are not unique to themselves, and to obtain support from those in a similar predicament.

Another approach for a son would be to ask his father to read this article and then discuss it privately with a neutral third party of their choice, to develop a perspective on their feelings and behavior. Having done so, a father is then in a better position to talk with his son, in the presence of the third party.

The third person must use his good offices to subdue recrimination. At the same time he must foster the father's expression of his fears over losing control, being unneeded, and suffering rejection, as well as the son's concerns about being overcontrolled, infantilized, and exploited.

If meeting with the third party fails to help, the next step is consultation with a psychologist or psychiatrist. There are rare instances, usually when conflict becomes severe, in which father and son are willing to go to a professional together or separately. In such cases it is often possible for the father to begin to make com-

promises, learn to understand his and his son's motivations, and work out with him newly defined, more compatible roles. Usually, however, such an effort requires continued supportive work by the professional and strong desire on the part of both men to resolve their differences.

If all these measures fail, those who work with patriarchs must learn to tolerate their situation until the opportunity arises for a change.

Fraternal spirit

With respect to the brother-brother conflict, it is important for brothers to see that in their relationship they recapitulate ancient rivalries, and to perceive clearly the psychological posture each assumes toward the other. Once they understand these two issues, they must talk together about them. They should try to discuss freely the fears, worries, anger, and disappointments caused by each other. They should also be able to talk about their affection for each other.

Since there is love and hate in all relationships, theirs cannot, by definition, be pure. They should not feel guilty about their anger with each other, but they do need to talk it out. Having done that, they then must consider how they can divide the tasks in the organization so that each will have a chance to acquire and demonstrate competence and work in a complementary relationship with the other.

A brother cannot easily be subordinate at one level and equal on another. If a brother is an operating executive subordinate to the other, he gets into difficulty when he tries to be an equal on the board of directors. If more than one brother is on the board, then only one, as a rule, should be an operating executive. Of course, such rules are unnecessary if the brothers work well together.

If the brothers still cannot resolve their conflicts, then it becomes necessary to seek professional aid. If that does not help, they should consider being in separate organizations. In such a case, the big problem is the guilt feelings which the departing brother is likely to have for deserting the other and the family business.

Toward professional management

Where there are multiple and complex family relationships and obligations in a company, and particularly problems about succession, the best

Harvard Business Review: March-April 1971

solution is a transcendent one. The family members should form a trust, taking all the relatives out of business operations while enabling them to continue to act in concert as a family.

The trust could allot financial support to every member who desires it to develop new business ventures on behalf of the family, thus providing a business interest that replaces the previous operating activity. This also helps maintain family cohesion and preserve the family's leadership role in the community.

In general, the wisest course for any business, family or nonfamily, is to move to professional management as quickly as possible. Every business must define its overriding purpose for being, from which it derives its objectives. Within this planning framework, the business must have a system for appraising the degree to which it and its components are achieving the goals that have been set.

All organizations need to rear subordinates in a systematic manner, thus creating the basic condition for their own regeneration. I know of no family business capable of sustaining regeneration over the long term solely through the medium of its own family members.

Where there is conflict, or inadequately rationalized territories, members of the family should move up and out of operations as quickly as possible into policy positions. Such movement recognizes the reality of ownership but does not confuse ownership with management.

It also opens the opportunity for professionally trained managers to succeed to major operating roles, instead of having to go to other organizations as soon as they are ready for major responsibility. The more competitive the business situation, the more imperative such a succession pattern is.

More than others, the family members need to have their own outside activities from which they can derive gratification equal to what they can obtain in the company. Otherwise they will be unable to let go and will continue to be barriers to others. Moreover, they will make it

difficult to recruit and develop young persons with leadership potential who, as they mature, will see the inevitable barriers.

A number of family businesses have handled these issues wisely and have become highly professional in their management. The Dayton-Hudson Corporation and E.I. du Pont de Nemours are examples. Family members in both organizations must compete for advancement on the same terms as nonfamily managers. This practice is reinforced, at least at Dayton-Hudson, by a thorough performance appraisal system which includes appraisal of the chairman and president by a committee of the board.

Concluding note

It is very difficult to cope with the problems of the family business. That does not mean, however, that one should merely endure them. There is no point in stewing in anger and guilt, since chronic irritation is only self-flagellation. It solves no problems; it only increases anger and hostility and paves the way for explosion, recrimination, and impaired relations.

The family member can do something about such problems, as he can with any other. If reasonable steps to solve the problems do not work and he continues to feel bound to the organization, his problem is largely psychological. To free himself to make choices about what he wants to do, he must talk his feelings out with his rival in the organization, which is best done in the presence of a neutral third person. Sometimes professional help is necessary.

This will reduce sufficiently the intensity of the emotions generated by the problem, so that he can see possible alternatives more clearly and make choices more freely. That is better than the years of agitation that usually accompany such problems, unless of course the rival needs to expiate his guilt by continuing to punish himself. In that case, it is his problem and not necessarily that of the family business.

You love the daylight: do you think your father does not?

Euripides, 485-406 B.C.
Alcestis

CHAPTER 8
THE ENTREPRENEUR'S PHILOSOPHY

What is it that a man does that causes him to be labeled an entrepreneur? What factors are indicative of entrepreneurial potential? Leiberstein[1] provides some insight in noting: "The usual characteristics attributed to entrepreneurs involve gap filling as one of their essential underlying qualities. For example, it may be thought desirable that entrepreneurs possess at least some of the capacities to: search and discover economic opportunities, evaluate economic opportunities, marshal the financial resources necessary for the enterprise, make timebinding arrangements, take ultimate responsibility for management, be the ultimate uncertainty and/or risk bearer, provide and be responsible for the motivational system within the firm, search and discover new economic information, translate new information into new markets, techniques, and goods, and provide leadership for the work group . . . the entrepreneur has to possess what might be called an "input-completing" capacity. If six inputs are needed to bring to fruition a firm that produces a marketable product, it does no good to be able to marshal easily five of them. The gap-filling and the "input-completing" capacities are the unique characteristics of the entrepreneur."

By understanding the role and characteristics of an entrepreneur, some authors believe that undeveloped countries that are capital and resource rich can be economically improved by finding and training certain selected individuals to act in entrepreneurial ways. Aside from this internationally based advantage, knowing who entrepreneurs are, why they are, and what roles they play is of prime interest during the prospective entrepreneur's personal analysis of his own qualifications, and in the selection of personnel for corporate based new business ventures.

The brief article "The Entrepreneur's Quiz" was developed by myself over an eight-year period. In working with several hundred entrepreneurs, I have developed a simple 15 question quiz to determine if you are an entrepreneur or a hired hand. The quiz is an outgrowth of "Fun 'n' Guts — the entrepreneur's philosophy," a book I published in 1973 with Addison-Wesley of Reading, Mass. Why not try it and see how you score, the answers and grading sheet are also enclosed. Good luck to you. Remember, the entrepreneur's philosophy is "Fun 'n' Guts."

Mr. Lefkoe, Gardner Jones, and Sabor Awad each offer insight into the crucial legal and accounting issues of managing a small business. Each of these articles deals with maximum use of accounting information. A good manager knows intuitively that numbers are the language of management. An appreciation of the issues involved in this field is fundamental to success.

As a balance, Mr. Joseph Martellaro, discusses "The Survival of Small Business." Insight is offered as to why many small businesses fail. Not the least of which is the reality that they are undercapitalized. Taken together these three articles present valuable input into the risks and rewards of starting, financing, and managing a technical firm.

Finally, Mr. Andrew Brimmer offers insight into a specialized but current area of small business — BLACK CAPITALISM. He indicates why it hasn't worked as well as anticipated and he offers several positive suggestions for change.

As stated throughout the entrepreneur's handbook, the small business affected by changing technological and competitive environments must implement compensatory changes if it is to retain its market position. The required strategy for overcoming difficulties may overburden the small company's availability of capital — both from internal operations and external credit arrangements. Instead of merging to acquire the supplementary capital resources, as the Fillon article in the last section suggested, the company could raise the funds through a public offering of its stock. Gerald Sears in "Public Offerings for Smaller Companies" considers the advantage of going public and offers some suggestions on selecting the underwriter and preparing the offering brochure.

If the marketing of the company's stock is successful, the firm can expect future financing to be easier, less time consuming, and less costly. Borrowing capacity will be increased as a result of the firm's improved financial condition and increased lender's confidence. The firm's fair market value will be established for use in any future acquisition, merger or selling negotiations.

As Sears emphasizes, many of the potential advantages from going public will depend on the selection of a competent underwriter, experienced and familiar with the issuer's industry, to develop and implement an effective stock offering strategy.

A successful public offering, however, will depend on the occurrence of several factors. First, the firm should have a growth rate attractively higher than the average for the industry — the stock will reflect this intrinsic growth value and will be priced by the investors accordingly, resulting in a rapid placement and high P/E ratio. Secondly, the entrepreneur/owner in his new role must be able to communicate effectively with the financial community and stockholders. The last factor Sears considers necessary for a successful public offering is that the competitive position of the firm must not be impaired by revealing profit margin and similar information required for preparing the prospectus. A public offering may not be the best alternative, however, if the company has low growth, is managed by a strongly autonomous entrepreneur and is dependent on a few nonproprietary products for a monopolistic market position.

It seemed appropriate to me to conclude "The Entrepreneur's Handbook" with an article on going public. In my experience this is the silent but powerful dream of many entrepreneurs. When the business is started, all too many men are already focusing on going public. A closing note seems in order here. It is taken from page 21 of my book "Fun 'n' Guts — the entrepreneur's philosophy" from the section entitled "A Word About Motivation."

Most successful small companies are founded by someone with an idea and a dream. Making money and accumulating wealth are usually the by-product of accomplishing some nobler goal. You need an idea or a dream to provide the push for success.

In any case, good luck to all of you because we all know we all need and deserve it.

[1] Leibenstein, Harvey, "Entrepreneurship and Development," American Economic Review, May, 1968, p. 74.

Checklist for Going into Business

BEFORE YOU START

How about YOU?

Are you the kind of person who can get a business started and make it go? (Before you answer this question, use the worksheet on pages 4 and 5.)   ———

Think about *why* you want to own your own business. Do you want to badly enough to keep you working long hours without knowing how much money you'll end up with?   ———

Have you worked in a business like the one you want to start?   ———

Have you worked for someone else as a foreman or manager?   ———

Have you had any business training in school?   ———

Have you saved any money?   ———

How about the money?

Do you know how much money you will need to get your business started? (Use worksheets 2 and 3 on pages 6 and 12 to figure this out.)   ———

Have you counted up how much money of your own you can put into the business?   ———

Do you know how much credit you can get from your suppliers—the people you will buy from?   ———

Do you know where you can borrow the rest of the money you need to start your business?   ———

Have you figured out what net income per year you expect to get from the business? Count your salary and your profit on the money you put into the business.   ———

Can you live on less than this so that you can use some of it to help your business grow?   ———

Have you talked to a banker about your plans?   ———

2

How about a partner

If you need a partner with money or know-how that you don't have, do you know someone who will fit—someone you can get along with?   _____

Do you know the good and bad points about going it alone, having a partner, and incorporating your business?   _____

Have you talked to a lawyer about it?   _____

How about your customers?

Do most businesses in your community seem to be doing well?   _____

Have you tried to find out whether stores like the one you want to open are doing well in your community and in the rest of the country?   _____

Do you know what kind of people will want to buy what you plan to sell?   _____

Do people like that live in the area where you want to open your store?   _____

Do they need a store like yours?   _____

If not, have you thought about opening a different kind of store or going to another neighborhood?   _____

First printed September 1961

Revised August 1970

Reprinted March 1971

Reprinted June 1971

Reprinted January 1972

WORKSHEET NO. 1

Under each question, check the answer that says what you feel or comes closest to it. Be honest with yourself.

Are you a self-starter?

☐ I do things on my own. Nobody has to tell me to get going.

☐ If someone gets me started, I keep going all right.

☐ Easy does it, man. I don't put myself out until I have to.

How do you feel about other people?

☐ I like people. I can get along with just about anybody.

☐ I have plenty of friends—I don't need anyone else.

☐ Most people bug me.

Can you lead others?

☐ I can get most people to go along when I start something.

☐ I can give the orders if someone tells me what we should do.

☐ I let someone else get things moving. Then I go along if I feel like it.

Can you take responsibility?

☐ I like to take charge of things and see them through.

☐ I'll take over if I have to, but I'd rather let someone else be responsible.

☐ There's always some eager beaver around wanting to show how smart he is. I say let him.

How good an organizer are you?

☐ I like to have a plan before I start. I'm usually the one to get things lined up when the gang wants to do something.

☐ I do all right unless things get too goofed up. Then I cop out.

☐ You get all set and then something comes along and blows the whole bag. So I just take things as they come.

How good a worker are you?

☐ I can keep going as long as I need to. I don't mind working hard for something I want.

☐ I'll work hard for a while, but when I've had enough, that's it, man!

☐ I can't see that hard work gets you anywhere.

Can you make decisions?

☐ I can make up my mind in a hurry if I have to. It usually turns out O.K., too.

☐ I can if I have plenty of time. If I have to make up my mind fast, I think later I should have decided the other way.

☐ I don't like to be the one who has to decide things. I'd probably blow it.

Can people trust what you say?

☐ You bet they can. I don't say things I don't mean.

☐ I try to be on the level most of the time, but sometimes I just say what's easiest.

☐ What's the sweat if the other fellow doesn't know the difference?

Can you stick with it?

☐ If I make up my mind to do something, I don't let *anything* stop me.

☐ I usually finish what I start—if it doesn't get fouled up.

☐ If it doesn't go right away, I turn off. Why beat your brains out?

How good is your health?

☐ Man, I *never* run down!

☐ I have enough energy for most things I want to do.

☐ I run out of juice sooner than most of my friends seem to.

Now count the checks you made.

How many checks are there beside the *first* answer to each question?   ____

How many checks are there beside the *second* answer to each question?   ____

How many checks are there beside the *third* answer to each question?   ____

If most of your checks are beside the first answers, you probably have what it takes to run a business. If not, you're likely to have more trouble than you can handle by yourself. Better find a partner who is strong on the points you're weak on. If many checks are beside the third answer, not even a good partner will be able to shore you up.

Now go back and answer the first question on page 2.

WORKSHEET NO. 2			
ESTIMATED MONTHLY EXPENSES			
Item	Your estimate of monthly expenses based on sales of $ _____ per year	Your estimate of how much cash you need to start your business (See column 3.)	What to put in column 2 (These figures are typical for one kind of business. you will have to decide how many months to allow for in your business.)
	Column 1	Column 2	Column 3
Salary of owner-manager	$	$	2 times column 1
All other salaries and wages			3 times column 1
Rent			3 times column 1
Advertising			3 times column 1
Delivery expense			3 times column 1
Supplies			3 times column 1
Telephone and telegraph			3 times column 1
Other utilities			3 times column 1
Insurance			Payment required by insurance company
Taxes, including Social Security			4 times column 1
Interest			3 times column 1
Maintenance			3 times column 1
Legal and other professional fees			3 times column 1
Miscellaneous			3 times column 1
STARTING COSTS YOU ONLY HAVE TO PAY ONCE			Leave column 2 blank
Fixtures and equipment			Fill in worksheet 3 on page 12 and put the total here
Decorating and remodeling			Talk it over with a contractor
Installation of fixtures and equipment			Talk to suppliers from who you buy these
Starting inventory			Suppliers will probably help you estimate this
Deposits with public utilities			Find out from utilities companies
Legal and other professional fees			Lawyer, accountant, and so on
Licenses and permits			Find out from city offices what you have to have
Advertising and promotion for opening			Estimate what you'll use
Accounts receivable			What you need to buy more stock until credit customers pay
Cash			For unexpected expenses or losses, special purchases, etc.
Other			Make a separate list and enter total
TOTAL ESTIMATED CASH YOU NEED TO START WITH		$	Add up all the numbers in column 2

GETTING STARTED

Your building

Have you found a good building for your store?   _____

Will you have enough room when your business gets bigger?   _____

Can you fix the building the way you want it without spending too much money?   _____

Can people get to it easily from parking spaces, bus stops, or their homes?   _____

Have you had a lawyer check the lease and zoning?   _____

Equipment and supplies

Do you know just what equipment and supplies you need and how much they will cost? (Worksheet 3 and the lists you made for it should show this.)   _____

Can you save some money by buying secondhand equipment?   _____

Your merchandise

Have you decided what things you will sell?   _____

Do you know how much or how many of each you will buy to open your store with?   _____

Have you found suppliers who will sell you what you need at a good price?   _____

Have you compared the prices and credit terms of different suppliers?   _____

Your records

Have you planned a system of records that will keep track of your income and expenses, what you owe other people, and what other people owe you?   _____

Have you worked out a way to keep track of your inventory so that you will always have enough on hand for your customers but not more than you can sell?   _____

Have you figured out how to keep your payroll records and take care of tax reports and payments?   _____

Do you know what financial statements you should prepare? ＿＿＿＿

Do you know how to use these financial statements? ＿＿＿＿

Do you know an accountant who will help you with your records and financial statements? ＿＿＿＿

Your store and the law

Do you know what licenses and permits you need? ＿＿＿＿

Do you know what business laws you have to obey? ＿＿＿＿

Do you know a lawyer you can go to for advice and for help with legal papers? ＿＿＿＿

Protecting your store

Have you made plans for protecting your store against thefts of all kinds—shoplifting, robbery, burglary, employee stealing? ＿＿＿＿

Have you talked with an insurance agent about what kinds of insurance you need? ＿＿＿＿

Buying a business someone else has started

Have you made a list of what you like and don't like about buying a business someone else has started? ＿＿＿＿

Are you sure you know the real reason why the owner wants to sell his business? ＿＿＿＿

Have you compared the cost of buying the business with the cost of starting a new business? ＿＿＿＿

Is the stock up to date and in good condition? ＿＿＿＿

Is the building in good condition? ＿＿＿＿

Will the owner of the building transfer the lease to you? ＿＿＿＿

Have you talked with other businessmen in the area to see what they think of the business? ＿＿＿＿

Have you talked with the company's suppliers? ＿＿＿＿

Have you talked with a lawyer about it? ＿＿＿＿

9

MAKING IT GO

Advertising

Have you decided how you will advertise? (Newspapers—posters—handbills—radio—by mail?)   ____

Do you know where to get help with your ads?   ____

Have you watched what other stores do to get people to buy?   ____

The prices you charge

Do you know how to figure what you should charge for each item you sell?   ____

Do you know what other stores like yours charge?   ____

Buying

Do you have a plan for finding out what your customers want?   ____

Will your plan for keeping track of your inventory tell you when it is time to order more and how much to order?   ____

Do you plan to buy most of your stock from a few suppliers rather than a little from many, so that those you buy from will want to help you succeed?   ____

Selling

Have you decided whether you will have salesclerks or self-service?   ____

Do you know how to get customers to buy?   ____

Have you thought about why you like to buy from some salesmen while others turn you off?   ____

Your employees

If you need to hire someone to help you, do you know where to look?   ____

Do you know what kind of person you need?   ____

Do you know how much to pay?   ____

Do you have a plan for training your employees?   ____

10

Credit for your customers

Have you decided whether to let your customers buy on credit? ____

Do you know the good and bad points about joining a credit-card plan? ____

Can you tell a deadbeat from a good credit customer? ____

A FEW EXTRA QUESTIONS

Have you figured out whether you could make more money working for someone else? ____

Does your family go along with your plan to start a business of your own? ____

Do you know where to find out about new ideas and new products? ____

Do you have a work plan for yourself and your employees? ____

Have you gone to the nearest Small Business Administration office for help with your plans? ____

If you have answered all these questions carefully, you've done some hard work and serious thinking. That's good. But you have probably found some things you still need to know more about or do something about.

Do all you can for yourself, but don't hesitate to ask for help from people who can tell you what you need to know. Remember, running a business takes guts! You've got to be able to decide what you need and then go after it.

Good luck!

☆ GPO : 1972—O—456-705

WORKSHEET NO. 3

LIST OF FURNITURE, FIXTURES, AND EQUIPMENT

Leave out or add items to suit your business. Use separate sheets to list exactly what you need for each of the items below.	If you plan to pay cash in full, enter the full amount below and in the last column.	If you are going to pay by installments, fill out the colunms below. Enter in the last column your downpayment plus at least one installment.		Estimate of the cash you need for furniture, fixtures, and equipment
		Price	Downpayment	Amount of each installment	
Counters	$	$	$	$	$
Storage shelves, cabinets					
Display stands, shelves, tables					
Cash register					
Safe					
Window display fixtures					
Special lighting					
Outside sign					
Delivery equipment if needed					
TOTAL FURNITURE, FIXTURES, AND EQUIPMENT (Enter this figure also in worksheet 2 under "Starting Costs You Only Have To Pay Once," page 7.)					$

Andrew F. Brimmer: The Trouble with Black Capitalism

Whether a Negro businessman can be expected to succeed doing business almost entirely in an all-black community depends primarily on the scale and nature of his business activity.

At one extreme—consisting primarily of small-scale neighborhood retailing and the provision of personal services—the likelihood of success for at least a few businessmen seems fairly high. At the opposite extreme —in manufacturing, construction, transportation and wholesale trade— there appears to be virtually no possibility of operating a viable enterprise whose output is sold only in the Negro market.

Between these extremes, the prospect of success seems to diminish rapidly as the scale and technical sophistication of the enterprise increase.

These conclusions follow a careful analysis of capital and managerial requirements, costs and efficiency, and market conditions affecting operations of profit-making enterprises in the United States today. Unfortunately, these objective considerations are frequently obscured by the pursuit of goals (sometimes sentimental, sometimes political) which have little to do with the marketplace.

Historically, racial discrimination and segregation in this country produced effects quite similar to those associated with a protective tariff in foreign trade: Two markets emerged.

The market for goods (with the exception of housing) was generally open to all consumers, including Negroes. However, the other market— that for services—was circumscribed severely as far as Negroes were concerned. Because Negroes had little access to many establishments serving the general public such as barber and beauty shops and hotels and restaurants, Negro businessmen historically concentrated on meetings these needs with their own shops, hotels and cafes.

Thus, it is not accidental that the vast majority of self-employed Negro businessmen is found in a few lines of activity. In 1960 (the latest date for which comprehensive census data are available), about one third of the 46,400 Negro men and women in business for themselves provided personal services or operated eating and drinking places. This proportion was about double that for all self-employed businessmen and women.

In contrast, the proportion of Negro businessmen in lines such as manufacturing, construction and wholesale trade was well below the

From *Nation's Business*, Vol. 57, No. 5. © (May 1969), pp. 78–79.

340   The Future

national average. Even within the retail trade field, which accounted for nearly three fifths of self-employed Negro businessmen compared with one half of all self-employed businessmen in the country at large, black store owners were especially scarce in lines such as hardware and building materials, furniture and home furnishings, apparel and motor vehicles and accessories. All of these latter categories traditionally served Negro customers on approximately the same basis as other customers.

Impact of Desegregation

With the progress of desegregation the considerable protection which segregation provided for Negro businessmen has been eroded substantially. Thus, in virtually every large city (especially in the East and Midwest), hotels and better class restaurants which previously catered exclusively to Negroes have encountered hard times. Many have closed their doors. While the opening of new motels and specialty eating and drinking places in predominantly Negro areas has compensated in part for the losses, the migration of Negro customers to facilities catering to the public generally is striking.

The adverse impact of these developments on Negro businessmen concentrating in those activities formerly protected by segregation is also striking. This can be seen most clearly in the income trends among non-white men during the 1960's.

Between 1959 and 1967, mean income of all self-employed nonwhite males rose by roughly 114 per cent to about $7,200; among all self-employed white men, the rise was only 44 per cent to approximately $8,500. In sharp contrast, income gains for self-employed retail merchants were much smaller for both groups (39 per cent to about $7,400 for whites and 28 per cent to about $4,500 for nonwhites).

Expressed differently, in 1959, average incomes of both white and nonwhite retail merchants were well above the average incomes of all employed men (13 per cent above all whites for white retailers and 28 per cent above all nonwhites for nonwhite retailers). By 1967, however, the averages for self-employed retail merchants showed smaller rises and were below the averages for all employed men—9 per cent below all whites for white retailers and 12 per cent below all nonwhites for nonwhite retailers.

Black Capitalist Prospects

It is against these currents that many black capitalist enterprises are launched. Yet, profitable operation of many of these ventures, especially those started on the assumption that a segregated market can be restored, is by no means assured. A careful examination of the scale of operations and the size of markets necessary for an efficient, profitable business suggests that black-owned firms face severe obstacles if their activities are confined to the Negro market. In industries such as construction, manufacturing, transportation and communications, and wholesale trade, the most efficient activities seem to center in medium-to-large enterprises that require substantial capital investment and cater to markets considerably larger than can be found in local black communities.

Even in retail trade, where Negro businessmen have the greatest experience, the task of building larger units to serve the Negro market exclusively remains formidable. For example, in numerous cities, efforts are made to establish shopping centers in ghetto areas, with supermarket food stores being key units in most developments.

The experience with these projects has been mixed. In general, it seems that the initial community response has been fairly good. Before very long, however, the rate of growth typically has slackened, and in some instances it has actually declined.

At least two factors contribute: The potential demand in the local area assumed to be the outlet's natural market frequently has turned out to be less than projected, and the competition from other stores, especially from units of large chain organizations, has been more intense than anticipated. Secondly, to cover higher operating and other costs, many black-owned supermarkets have had to post prices 10 to 15 per cent above those prevailing at chain store outlets.

Aside from these adverse factors on the demand side, some new ventures have received special assistance from wholesale food distributors in stocking inventories and acquisition of buildings. The lag in sales has squeezed their cash flow and made it difficult to meet these commitments. The situation has been aggravated by high labor costs per unit of sales.

In manufacturing the outlook is even less promising—if factory production is to be sold mainly in the Negro market.

Although it may not be widely appreciated, a sizable number of Negro businessmen at one time were operating manufacturing enterprises. Their activities were focused mainly on production of cosmetics which were sold primarily through Negro barber and beauty shops and by door-to-door salesmen. However, little more than a decade ago, major cosmetic firms producing for the national market "discovered" the Negro market and began to turn out products specially designed for Negro consumers. Under the impact of this competition, most of the small-scale Negro-owned factories could not survive.

More recently, large apparel manufacturers have started producing "African motif" garments, and nationwide food processing companies may soon bring out "soul food" lines. Both areas have seen the emergence of Negro-owned firms in the last few years.

342   The Future

So black businessmen should not count on nationally oriented manufacturing firms leaving the Negro market to Negro entrepreneurs. Besides,
one should not expect Negro consumers to persist in paying higher prices
to subsidize high-cost local retailing establishments that show little prospect of achieving the economies of scale that would enable them to survive
in the long run.

Instead, one should conclude that the only really promising path to
equal opportunity for Negroes in business as in other aspects of economic
activity lies in full participation in an integrated, national economy. It cannot be found in a backwater of separatism and segregation.

To travel this more promising path will require the best efforts of all
of us—black and white—in both the public and private sectors.

Joseph A. Martellaro: The Survival of Small Business

That competition is inherently self-destructive is a common allegation. This contention is often based on an economic philosophy of competitive determinism which holds that the elimination of small enterprises is inevitable in several areas of business activity because small organizations —oftentimes incapable of matching the financial, productive, and advertising resources of the large firms—will eventually be either absorbed or driven into bankruptcy.

A typical example of *firm* absorption may be drawn from the TV and electrical appliance industry. In 1950 Crosley—by action of its parent firm, AVCO—took over the Bendix Home Appliance Corporation, a pioneer-producer of automatic washers. Six years later, AVCO sold its Crosley and Bendix holdings to the Philco Corporation. In turn and in 1961, the Ford Motor Company acquired the Philco Corporation.

In the case of *firm obliteration,* keen competition leads to the demise of one or two weak sisters, an event which initiates a long run, bumping process of *marginal elimination,* for no sooner is one marginal firm forced out of business than another company is relegated to marginal status and duly feels the competitive pinch of its stronger commercial adversaries. The liquidation process involves enterprises which, with varying degrees

From *Marquette Business Review,* Vol. XI, No. 1 (Spring 1967), pp. 1–10. Reprinted with permission.

of success, have been around for some time. In no small way, the American automobile industry has been characterized by *marginal elimination* for the last four decades.

To further substantiate the claim that competition is being stifled, the argument is frequently advanced that the development of modern technology has required, in many cases, capital outlays which are relatively high in cost in comparison to investment or bygone days. In a number of instances, these costly capital expenditures bar—or at least seriously impede—the entry of new firms into various areas of manufacturing and retailing. It is sometimes said that the pioneer-spirited entrepreneur who is able to parlay a handful of resources into a mountain of assets is rapidly disappearing on the American commercial scene.

Economic Concentration Today

At this point we might well ask: Has competition actually declined in the United States in recent decades, and if so, to what extent? Here authoritative findings seem to differ. In separate studies, Professors George J. Stigler and G. Warren Nutter think not.[1] On the other hand, another study holds that competition has declined during the current century.[2] When he spoke before the Subcommittee on Antitrust and Monopoly on July 1, 1964, Dr. Gardiner C. Means historically traced corporate growth from the Civil War.[3] He pointed out that little concentration existed in American manufacturing just prior to the Civil War since most production was performed by many small, local plants. Furthermore, whatever concentration did exist at that time was negligible.

However, by 1929, the American economy had drastically changed, for not only had the corporation become a principal form of business organization but, along with this development, manufacturing concentration had become quite evident. Dr. Means went on to say that the trend of concentration continued to increase from 1929 to 1962; moreover, during this interval, the 100 largest corporations increased their control of the net capital assets of all manfacturing corporations from 44 per cent to 58 per cent.[4]

---

[1] George J. Stigler, "Competition in the United States," *Five Lectures* on Economic *Problems,* New York, Macmillan, 1950, pp. 45–65. G. Warren Nutter, *The Extent of Enterprise Monopoly in the United States* 1899–1939, Chicago, University of Chicago Press, 1951.

[2] Arthur R. Burns, *The Decline of Competition,* New York, McGraw-Hill, 1936.

[3] *Economic Concentration,* Hearings Before the Subcommittee on Antitrust and Monopoly of the Committee on the Judiciary, United States Senate, Part 1, Washington, U.S. Government Printing Office, 1964, p. 9.

[4] *Ibid.,* p. 18.

Economic concentration in manufacturing can be measured in still another way, the extent of sellers' concentration. In 1954, the share of total sales tallied by the four leading producers in various industries ranged from three per cent in the case of concrete blocks to 99 per cent in the case of primary aluminum.[5] A comparison of 434 manufacturing industries reveals the proportion of sales assumed by the four largest firms in each of the manufacturing industries during the year 1954.[6] In 141 industries, 32.5 per cent of all those considered, the four largest sellers accounted for *at least* 50 per cent of the shipments. In 298 industries, or 68.7 per cent of the aggregate, the four largest manufactories accounted for 25 per cent or more of the sales. These findings clearly indicate a high degree of seller concentration in the American manufacturing industries.

Dr. John Blair, Chief Economist for the Subcommittee on Antitrust and Monopoly, presented some recent figures which also indicate the trend of concentration in American manufacturing.[7] On the basis of value added, he showed that in 1962 the 200 largest companies accounted for 40 per cent of manufacturing—a conspicuous increase over 1947 when the then "200 group" accounted for 30 per cent. Dr. Blair further indicated that the 50 largest firms increased their relative share from 17 per cent in 1947 to 24 per cent in 1962.

Economic concentration in big business *per se* is not within the scope of this paper; however, the implications of that power are relative, for the effects of economic concentration upon small business should not be overlooked. Many small concerns, upstream and downstream, serve as tributaries to the giant organizations. And although some may convincingly argue that this interdependence is but the inevitable consequence of the high degree of specialization in our modern, mature economy, others may as logically and persuasively argue that such economic ties can—with certain exceptions—place the small firms in a position of dependence and in some cases even subjugation.

Expansion and growth of big business and its concomitant power are not limited to the confines of a given industry, for in recent years conglomerate diversification has come into common practice among large concerns. Often a small but economically healthy firm becomes an additional piece in the quilt of diversification of some major concern. By directly and indirectly taking advantage of the resources (legal, accounting,

---

[5] Ralph L. Nelson, *Concentration in the Manufacturing Industries of the United States,* New Haven, Yale University Press, 1963, pp. 4–5.

[6] Joe S. Bain, *Industrial Organization,* New York, John Wiley and Sons, 1959, pp. 119–120.

[7] *Economic Concentration,* Hearings Before the Subcommittee on Antitrust and Monopoly of the Committee on the Judiciary, United States Senate, Part 1, Washington, U.S. Government Printing Office, 1964, pp. 80–81.

financial, purchasing, technical, etc.) of its parent organization, the new member of the corporate clan gains economies which it heretofore did not enjoy. These newly acquired economies can give the firm a distinct advantage over its competitors who continue to operate as independent entities.

Newcomers into an area of competition are usually a healthy sign. However, small-and-medium-sized firms sometimes find that a newly-founded competitor is affiliated with or owned by some concern already gigantic in some other commercial area. Of 402 fire and casualty insurance companies, *Moody's Bank and Financial Manual, 1964,* lists Allstate Insurance as the third largest on the basis of resources—this despite the fact that Allstate was founded only some three decades ago, in 1931. Moreover, the giant retail chain has extended itself into other business areas, e.g. savings and loan associations, automobile financing and chemical coating. Quite recently, steps have been taken by Allstate Enterprises, a Sears Roebuck subsidiary, to enter the securities business.

The aim here is not to disparage our large business organizations, for they not only concomitantly evolved with the growth and development of our economy over the last 100 years, but also, in many ways, they are necessary to and compatible with what our economic system has come to be. Our large enterprises have contributed magnificently to our economic growth, to a higher standard of living, and to our defense needs during periods of emergency. Furthermore, especially since the conclusion of World War II, many of our giant concerns—though primarily profit motivated (as they should be)—have readily recognized and willingly accepted their social responsibilities, and also, in several ways, they have contributed to postwar economic stability. The intention here is merely to indicate that, oftentimes, the almost incessant growth of large enterprises adversely affects a good many small concerns.

Business Failures

Table 1 indicates the incidence of business failures in the United States during the period of 1955-1964. Included are mining and manufacturing, wholesale, retail, construction, and commercial service firms. Some interesting observations may be made from the table. Until 1962, the incidence of failures was, for the most part, consistently climbing. Although comfort may be derived from the downturn in casualties after reaching a peak in

---

[8] In addition, *Moody's* lists Allstate Insurance Company's assets on December 31, 1963, as $1,070,146,986, p. 1557.

1961, the general trend of total failure liabilities has been upward, a 195 per cent increase during the ten-year period considered.[9] This sharp rise in total failure liabilities can only by viewed with apprehensiveness.

Table 1. Business Failures in the United States, 1955–1964

Year	Number of Failures	Total Failure Liabilities	Failure Rate*	Average Liability per Failure
1964	13,501	$1,329,223,000	53	98,454
1963	14,374	1,352,593,000	56	94,100
1962	15,782	1,213,601,000	61	76,898
1961	17,075	1,090,123,000	64	63,843
1960	15,445	938,630,000	57	60,772
1959	14,053	692,808,000	52	49,300
1958	14,964	728,258,000	56	48,667
1957	13,739	615,293,000	52	44,784
1956	12,686	562,697,000	48	44,356
1955	10,696	449,380,000	42	40,968

Per 10,000 listed concerns.
Source: *The Failure Record through 1964*, prepared by Dun and Bradstreet, Inc., New York, 1965, p. 3.

Although in 1964 total liabilities have fallen by about $23.4 million, the average liability per failure has continued to rise steadily, the average liability in 1964 more than doubled that of 1955. A part of this increment is probably attributable to the mounting operating costs experienced by many firms and to the inflation which occurred during the ten-year period. However, it may also indicate that, in the process of *marginal elimination,* increasingly larger firms have been falling victims to bankruptcy.

During 1964, the highest incidence of failures in manufacturing industries was in furniture, leather and shoes, electric machinery, transportation equipment, and apparel.[10] Failure rates per 10,000 operating concerns numbered 194, 166, 164, 144, and 107 respectively. In retailing the highest casualties occurred in toys and hobby crafts, furniture and furnishings, and children's wear.[11] In the same order, "fold-ups" numbered 147, 86, and 80 per 10,000 operating units.

The distribution of business failures according to the size of liability is shown in Table 2. Again a ten-year period is considered. Without exception, in any given year at least 46.6 per cent of the failures involved firms with liabilities of less than $25,000. In addition, where the percentage of casualties after 1961 took a definite downturn in the first two categories,

[9] Although inflation is a contributory factor here, it is not of sufficient magnitude to seriously detract from the value of the data.

[10] *The Failure Record through 1964,* prepared by Dun and Bradstreet, Inc., New York, 1965, p. 6.

[11] *Ibid.,* p. 6.

Table 2. Distribution of Business Failures According
to Liability, 1955–1964

Year	Under $5,000		$5,000–$25,000		$25,000–$100,000		$100,000–$1 Million		Over $1 Million	
	No.	Per Cent	No.	Per Cent	No.	Per Cent	No.	Per Cent	No.	Per Cent
1964	1,093	8.1	5,202	38.5	5,051	37.4	2,003	14.9	152	1.1
1963	1,296	9.0	5,781	40.2	5,115	35.6	2,031	14.1	151	1.1
1962	1,647	10.4	6,700	42.5	5,425	34.4	1,876	11.9	134	0.8
1961	1,903	11.1	7,378	43.2	5,725	33.5	1,973	11.6	96	0.6
1960	1,688	10.9	6,884	44.6	5,078	32.9	1,703	11.0	92	0.6
1959	1,841	13.1	6,664	47.4	4,202	29.9	1,284	9.1	62	0.5
1958	2,028	13.5	7,015	46.9	4,456	29.8	1,408	9.4	57	0.4
1957	2,001	14.6	6,699	48.8	3,847	28.0	1,147	8.3	45	0.3
1956	2,032	16.0	6,152	48.4	3,431	27.1	1,022	8.1	49	0.4
1955	1,785	16.3	5,412	49.3	2,916	26.6	820	7.5	36	0.3

Source: *The Failure Record through 1964*, prepared by Dun and Bradstreet (New York, 1965), p. 7.

the proportion of failures discernibly and steadily increased in the remaining three classes through the entire ten-year span. On the whole, the proportion of obituaries tended to be alarmingly high in the first three classes when viewed *in toto,* ranging from a high of 92.2 per cent of the population in 1955 to a low of 84 per cent in 1964.

Of the 13,051 firms which failed in 1964, 34.9 per cent had been in business for less than 3 years, 56 per cent under 5 years, and 77.5 per cent not over ten years.[12] According to Dun and Bradstreet, the greatest single cause of the failures (45.5 per cent) was inadequate sales.[13] This despite an increase of GNP from $397.5 billion in 1955 to $628.7 billion in 1964. More specifically, the underlying causes of low sales volume were incompetence, managerial inexperience, and a deficiency of "occupational savvy."[13]

Drawing the two preceding paragraphs together, the evidence therein seems to signify that a good many small businesses must manage—some way or other—to weather the adversities encountered and the costly misjudgments committed during the first five years of operation, which appears to be the most critical period of survival. And because the limited resources of the small firm often account for the underlying causes of its demise, it is doubtful that a small enterprise can alleviate its predicament only through its own efforts. Later in this paper several possible devices of relief and assistance to small firms will be viewed, self-help and external measures of assistance which might well help small enterprises make a break through this vicious circle.

---

[12] *The Failure Record through 1964,* prepared by Dun and Bradstreet, New York, 1965, p. 11.

[13] *Ibid.,* pp. 12–13.

348   The Future

Discount Retailing

Much of the pressure on small concerns comes from the very competitive national chains of discount houses. Their supermarket approaches to merchandising a myriad of consumer items plus the consumer mobility of our motorized society have made these discount operations a resounding success. Where service-after-sales is of primary importance to a consumer —as examples, in the purchase of powered lawn equipment, electrical appliances, office machines, and television sets—the small independent dealer has been fairly successful in holding his clientele by arguing that service (during and after the warranty period) as a highly personal and important aspect of those types of merchandising.

Until recently, many discount houses marketed their goods only on a cash basis. As a result, those consumers who were unable to pay cash for their purchases were willing to pay list or near-list at the small retailer in order to take advantage of credit terms. But even this has changed, for many discount houses have now made deferred payment plans available, mostly in the form of revolving charge accounts. This action on the part of numerous discount houses aggravates the dilemma of the small merchandisers.

In the past, small retailers sought sanctuary from large merchandisers through "fair trade" laws. Two congressional acts to maintain "fair trade" —the Miller-Tydings Act of 1937 and the McGuire Act of 1952—ultimately ended in failure. The latest attempt to revive "fair trade" legislation came in the form of the Quality Stabilization Act. Undoubtedly the recent keen competition brought to bear on small merchandisers by the discount houses in part accounts for the pressure placed on Congress to legalize price-fixing. However, this recent effort to legislate "fair trade" has apparently ended in failure since the proposed bill was tabled by the Commerce Committee of the Senate on June 9, 1964. This is probably for the best, for past "fair trade" acts have proven to be palliatives rather than remedies.

Self-Help Measures

Prior to considering some of the ways that small enterprises might be helped through external means, let us survey a few things which small businesses can do to help themselves.

Regardless of size, management plays a vital role in any firm, for the competency of a firm's managerial staff not infrequently spells the difference between success and failure. The management problem of small enterprises can be broadly classified as follows: *recruitment, training,* and *retention.*

Small organizations find it difficult to recruit promising and experienced management, for they find it difficult to match the salaries offered by large companies. Moreover, applicants often feel uncertain about joining a small concern because they have real or imagined doubts as to the stability of the firm. Then too, job-seeking candidates commonly believe that the best opportunities for promotion are with the large enterprises; and they especially look askance at small family businesses where they feel the opportunity for vertical mobility in the managerial ranks is highly unlikely.

Although the number of graduates leaving our collegiate business schools has been constantly growing in recent years, the aggregate demand for business graduates overwhelmingly exceeds the aggregate supply. This situation—though a desirable and healthy one—tends to compound the procurement problems of a good many small businesses. Obviously, small firms should recruit college graduates in management whenever possible, but there are other alternatives.

Small firms might do well to concentrate their efforts—as some already do—on enlisting promising local residents who hold high school diplomas and individuals who have terminated their college training prior to graduation. In addition, persons who have completed home study business courses can be tapped.

Given these possibilities, there arises the problem of training. Certainly, a good deal of training can be done on the job, but this approach has serious limitations. Frequently, the owner of a small enterprise is already burdened with a multitude of daily tasks, and he can afford little time to effectively teach an employee. Moreover, all capable managers are not good teachers. In those localities where adult educational classes are sponsored by the community school system, colleges, and universities, the employer can send his trainees to night school. As has been done in a number of localities, small enterprises, in cooperation with the educational institution, can design curriculums which fulfill their needs.

If an adult educational program is not available in the community, a number of small enterprises can establish a cooperative school of management, each firm sharing the costs. Part time faculty can be recruited from the large firms and colleges within a reasonable distance.

Still another avenue is open to small firms. A number of our universities offer correspondence courses in business. These offerings combined with any core program instituted could well provide a trainee with the necessary knowledge to work effectively as a member of management in a small firm.

Upon completing his training and gaining experience at his place of employment, there is always the possibility that the individual will move on to greener pastures. For that matter, this problem exists with big business. However, small enterprises can do certain things which will make it less likely that a member of management terminate his association. Often the managerial staffs are insufficient in numbers, and one or two members of the cadre are loaded with diverse duties. Purchasing, accounting, sales, finance, and credit are all specialties and should be treated as such. The inevitable consequence of too many duties and responsibilities placed upon a few individuals is long hours and costly mistakes and consequently dissatisfaction in the working relationship of employer and employee. Small enterprises when training management should meticulously take care that the trainee specialize in one or, at most, two areas.

Perhaps more so in the small firm than the large, recognition is essential to motivation. However, an employee is most impressed when his good works are recognized in some tangible form. The small entrepreneur can accomplish this in no better way than to formulate a sensible plan of profit-sharing with his managerial staff. And as the firm continues to grow, opportunity to share in ownership of the firm goes a long way in retaining key personnel.

External Assistance

From the conclusion of the Civil War up to the immediate postwar years of World War I, the United States became a world economic power. This catapultation, in no small way, is often attributed to the free enterprise system. However, despite the overall efficacy and strength of the free enterprise system, the mechanism was characterized by certain structural weaknesses which became most evident during the Great Depression. Since then, we have legislated a good deal of public policy which has overcome a number of these structural weaknesses. A large share of this public policy has, in effect, promoted the economic welfare of our citizenry and provided greater stability to the economy. On the whole, we are far better off because of those remedial measures.

But American tradition favors an economy which is based on the incentive system, i.e., a competitive system which applies the stick to the indolent and the incompetent and which rewards the industrious and efficient. At least in theory, most Americans tenaciously subscribe to this Darwinistic ratiocination in economics. As a result, in acting to assure personal and collective security to the citizenry while simultaneously extolling the merits of the incentive system, there has evolved during the postwar years a social intellect characterized by ambivalence. This social mentality induces us, consciously or unconsciously, to shun small business in favor of "big business," which is more compatible to an environment where security has become increasingly important.

The economic subordination of the small firm has been a social and economic cost incurred in the achievement of collective, and highly desirable, long run objectives in our economic society. Clearly, public policy that is aimed at maintaining or improving the economic well-being of society-at-large *is most highly desirable;* yet, in our eagerness to attain collective welfare, much harm has been inflicted upon those who, not only in theory but also in practice, adhere to the spirit and principles of the incentive system. And although they may not be in the majority, they do constitute at least a respectable minority. The entrepreneurs of small-and-medium-sized businesses (individual proprietorships, partnerships, and owners of closed corporations), for the most part, fall in this category. There are several things we can do to create a business environment which permits small-and-medium-sized productive units to survive alongside their bigger counterparts.

Several reasons can be advanced as to why small business should be maintained as an integral part of our economy. First, frictionless accessibility to our markets by buyers and sellers exemplifies our democratic traditions—economic, cultural, and political. Second, the commercial world has often been a means of vertical mobility for individuals short on formal education but long on innate ability and intelligence. Third, innovations are not infrequently introduced by the smaller concerns in industry. Fourth, individuals with the potential to become good administrators have an opportunity to do so on their own. In large organizations, people who possess the necessary leadership qualities to become capable managers can go unnoticed.[14] Fifth, certain productive activities can be best performed by firms of limited size. Sixth, given the opportunity, acorns do grow to become mighty oaks as we have witnessed in the case of many American firms.

At least three principal revisions might be made in our present public policy so that policy would continue to promote the general welfare yet mitigate the hardship it places on small entrepreneurs. These suggestions to be made here would apply to firms established for less than five years for, as indicated above, the first five years of operation appears to be a critical period.[15]

The first suggestion deals with Social Security. Current regulations call for each employee to contribute 4.2 per cent of his yearly wages up to $6,600, while the employer adds an equal amount for each of his employees. Small concerns can find the Social Security tax a real financial burden. Especially during the first few years in business, the tax can make the difference between *staying in or getting out of business.* The additional rate increases anticipated for the not-too-distant future will be an additional burden to small entrepreneurs. Furthermore, the possibility exists that the taxable limit per employee can be raised again as was done very recently when the maximum was hiked from $4,800 to $6,600. Newly

---

[14] Theodore Houser, *Big Business and Human Values,* New York, McGraw-Hill, 1957, p. 16.

[15] Transfers of ownership, alterations in firm names or location, changes in product name, product diversification, etc. would not be recognized as the establishment of a new firm.

established firms employing, say 25 or fewer persons and who do not exceed $1 million of business yearly, could be exempted from paying the employer's share of tax for five years. After five years—assuming the firm did not exceed the employee and monetary sales limits—the firm would commence to contribute an amount lower than the going rate, perhaps 1 per cent. In all instances, the full contributory rate would be charged to the employees of the firm so that at no time would they be barred from claiming benefits if needed.

The small businessman often finds that contributions to the unemployment compensation fund are a distressing drain on his resources. This is particularly true of productive units which specialize in services which require a high ratio of manpower to capital. Under the present law, an employing unit incurs a liability to pay into the fund if the firm has engaged four or more individuals for twenty weeks during a single calendar year. The federal rate is 3.35 per cent of the annual total wages paid, and the entire tax is paid by the employer.[16] Here again, employers, who hire 25 or fewer persons and who do less than $1 million of trade annually, might be exempted from the tax for a five-year period. An individual who becomes unemployed by such a firm should not be denied unemployment compensation benefits should he find it necessary to apply for them.

Third, relief in the form of federal income tax could be provided during the critical five-year interval. New firms might be taxed on a special scale, a proportional-progressive income tax. Taxable income would be divided into a number of categories; however, the ranges of each class would be quite wide. A single tax rate would be applicable to any amount in a given category with rates starting conservatively in the lowest income bracket and, of course, constantly increasing in each successive bracket. However, in no case would the rate equal that which is charged on comparable income under our present income tax law. At the conclusion of the five-year period, a firm would lose its special tax status and would assume full tax liability under the prevailing progressive income tax law. Such public policy could apply, let us again say, to all individual proprietorships, partnerships, and corporations employing no more than 25 employees and with sales not exceeding $1,000,000.

Conclusion

Since 1955, the incidence of failures among small businesses on all levels—retailing, wholesaling, and manufacturing—has been alarmingly high. A number of factors account for this: the concentration of "big

---

[16] State rates, which are creditable toward the federal rate, vary. Moreover, merit ratings are given to employers with good employment records.

business," the inability of firms with limited financial resources to make high capital outlays, the deficiency of working capital, diversification by large concerns, and discount selling on the retail level. Moreover, certain public policy designed to make our economic system work better and to promote the general welfare tends to discriminate against the small entrepreneur. Public policy which works adversely to the interests of small productive units should be modified. This is especially true of our social security regulations, unemployment compensation requirements, and our federal income tax schedules, which place onerous requirements on small firms. The federal income tax law should be revised to extend special rates to newly established firms of limited size. These recommendations, which certainly do not exhaust the realm of possibilities, are neither means of providing small enterprises with direct subsidies (the emphasis here is on exemptions and special income tax treatment), nor are they intended to place such enterprises in a position of privilege.

The criteria in the determination of those firms which would qualify for exemptions, i. e., concerns which employ fewer than 25 persons, and which do not exceed a yearly sales volume of $1 million, are proposed as mere possibilities. Only an intensive study by tax experts and economists could result in realistic considerations. The five-year exemption period has not been chosen arbitrarily, for reliable data do indicate that these formative years are the crucial ones for small business organizations. And because managerial incompetence and inexperience were prime underlying causes for business failures, such an exemption period would allow the small manager time to gain sufficient experience. Too often, individuals become engaged in commercial activities for which they are ill-prepared. Under those circumstances, enthusiasm and incentive, regardless of how intense, may not be enough. Besides allowing the novice in small business time to gain experience, the exemption period would provide the opportunity to adjust and to gain strength through self-help measures—some such measures are considered in this article.

The author readily acknowledges that a case can be presented in opposition to the above recommendations to provide exemptions and special tax treatment for our small enterprises. As an example, one can argue that the adoption of such measures would shift the burden upon other sectors of our economic society. This might be the case, but the marginal social benefits derived from such policy could well exceed the marginal costs incurred. Such revisions in public policy would contribute to the preservation of what many people consider an integral sector of our free enterprise system. If we think that small business is worth having, then solutions must be sought to effect a more reasonable balance in the competitive capabilities between big and small business in a dynamic economy in which small enterprises are apparently finding it increasingly difficult to survive. The writer hopes that this article stimulates additional thinking along those lines.

HOW TO OBTAIN THE GREATEST

BENEFIT FROM YOUR CPA

By M. R. Lefkoe

Today's CPA has a lot more to offer the businessman than a certification required by some outside agency. The modern CPA is a professional financial advisor whose function is to help corporate management increase profits, not just to audit them.

IF YOU are a typical business executive, you regularly retain an independent public accounting firm, usually a firm of certified public accountants. CPAs are, of course, accountants who have passed a rigid examination testifying to their professional experience and ability.

One of the primary purposes for which you generally hire a CPA firm is to audit your books annually. The audit is designed to provide you with an objective review of your financial statements and to insure that they have been prepared in accordance with generally accepted accounting principles.

If you think, however, that the audit is essentially all that your CPA firm has to offer you are mistaken. The expert services provided by CPAs, above and beyond their professional opinions on financial statements and tax work, fall into two essential classifications which are not always easy to separate: advice arising as a by-product of the audit itself and separate engagements specifically designed as management consulting work.

Concerning suggestions arising as a by-product of the audit, a large national CPA firm has commented: "While our principle function in auditing is to examine and report upon financial statements, it is the aim of our firm in each engagement to render the fullest professional service. An intimate knowledge of clients' financial problems, gained through our auditing services, places us in a position to offer constructive suggestions and advice that enable clients to improve accounting procedures, to effect operational economies, and in some cases to strengthen financial structure."

The "constructive suggestions and advice" are made possible by the thoroughness of the usual audit. The following brief summary of the steps taken in a typical audit indicates how deeply your auditor delves into the workings of your business—and how it is often possible for him to see problem areas or areas for improvement of which you may not have been aware.

It should be noted that CPAs generally take a somewhat different approach in auditing small companies (sales up to about $5 million) as compared to larger companies. Most smaller firms do not have an accounting executive (financial vice president, controller, etc.) to act as an adviser to management. Thus, an auditor almost automatically assumes more of an advisory capacity in such a firm, as compared to a larger company which has executives who perform a specific financial function.

Nevertheless, there are many things that a CPA will do in the course of an audit which will be the same for both large and small companies. For example, an auditor will generally check a company's fiscal year to see if it is the most advantageous for purposes of presenting the most liquid position if significant seasonal fluctuations exist in the business. The CPA would suggest that the fiscal year end when inventories are lowest, and cash highest. Another suggestion frequently made by an auditor before he even begins his audit pertains to the use of available industry information. Quite often industry trade associations compile a great deal of financial and operating statistics which can be extremely valuable to the management of a company operating in a particular industry.

Following a consideration of general issues such as these, the auditor studies the firm's financial statements for indications of unusual accounting or auditing problems and for signs of important changes or trends in the business. Signs of important trends or changes in the business, if any, will show up when the auditor compares the current year's balance sheet and income statement with those of previous years.

Industry Comparisons

An indication of the type of trend which an auditor might notice and bring to the attention of management is a situation where plant and equipment assets as a percent of total assets are growing faster or slower than the average for the industry. If faster, it could be a case of overexpansion; if slower, the company might be losing a competitive cost advantage to other companies which are modernizing their plant and equipment at a faster rate.

These matters, as well as any problems expected to arise, are discussed in conferences with the company's executives. Before work on an audit starts, an inspection trip of the plant is usually made with company representatives in order to learn more about its operations and facilities.

The initial review is helpful in determining the areas needing special attention (as described above) and in outlining a general program for the audit. The extent to which various audit tests are applied, however, depends upon the auditor's judgment of the company's internal control and accounting system—whether its accounting procedures and the arrangement of duties within its organization lend weight to the reliability of the accounting records and provide adequate safeguards over the company's assets.

It should be noted, parenthetically, that this review of a company's internal control and accounting system—a standard part of any audit—is itself often worth the price of the whole audit. Not only do effective measures of internal control greatly lessen the opportunity to perpetrate and conceal a fraud, but the nature of the financial information available to management and the time it takes for management to receive the data depends largely on the nature of the internal accounting system.

The company's accounting system and procedures are studied and members of its accounting staff are observed while carrying out their various

M. R. Lefkoe is a professional writer whose articles have appeared in the Wall Street Journal, Fortune, Barron's Financial Analysts Journal, *and many others. He also has held positions with several leading investment and security analyst firms.*

functions. The nature of their records and duties is discussed with them and a review of their work on a sampling basis for selected periods is made.

These initial tests may lead to a conclusion that the system effectively minimizes the possibilities of error or misrepresentation, in which case the auditor may not need to apply the tests of documents and records to more than a relatively small portion of the transactions. In many companies, however, there are at least some aspects in which the system is not entirely effective. In the case of smaller companies, the size of the business often precludes arrangements of duties that would be economical and, at the same time, provide satisfactory internal control. In these situations more extensive tests are made than would have sufficed if there were more effective internal control.

Outside Evidence

Regardless of the effectiveness of a company's internal control system, its underlying records must be confirmed by additional means, often by obtaining outside evidence.

Accounts receivable are usually checked by a letter from the auditor to a selected number of firms who are listed as owing money to the company. The letter shows the amount of money listed in the books and requests the firm to confirm it or state where the discrepancy lies.

Such communications, which are always made with the client's authorization, are not limited to customers. Creditors, suppliers, bankers, etc. are contacted to confirm the amounts shown in the client firm's books. Answers to the auditor's letters may reveal discrepancies requiring explanation and reconcilement.

Actual count of assets such as securities and cash establish whether the amounts shown in the accounts are, in fact, on hand. Furthermore, because the auditor's certificate indicates that the financial statements are being fairly presented, all contingent liabilities of consequence must be noted. Thus, the auditor consults with his client's attorneys in order to gain a clear understanding of any legal matter affecting the accounts, such as pending suits which might be a contingent liability to be noted in the financial statements.

Tests of purchase, production, and sales records can establish tentatively the adequacy of the client's accounting system for recording the various activities that affect the final inventory balance. An auditor can be fully satisfied concerning the final balance, however, only through additional procedures. These include, for example, obtaining evidence as to the existence of inventory, considering its condition, and determining the weight to be given (as appropriate) to original costs and to current market prices.

Before rendering his report at the conclusion of an audit, the auditor reviews the financial statements with his client's executive officials, especially as to clarity and adequacy of disclosure. He discusses with them the implications of significant data, and considers with them the form and content of the statement.

It is usually at this meeting, if not before, that any problems found by the CPA are discussed with management. The following case histories clearly show how profitable suggestions arise as a by-product of the audit.

Case History #1

Because reviewing insurance coverage is a normal auditing procedure, executives of a manufacturing firm recently had reason to thank their CPA that a plant fire loss was not as great as it might have been. Some weeks before the fire the CPA had helped his client make a re-evaluation of inventory. As a consequence, he had suggested to company officials that they contact their insurance broker and arrange for increased coverage. The broker readily agreed and the new coverage was in force at the time of the fire.

Case History #2

In the course of a recent audit, a CPA reviewing a manufacturing company's inventory costs found that markups on the spare parts it produced varied greatly. Investigation showed that the foreman in charge of each of the company's different divisions (plastic, steel, rubber, etc.) had sole authority to establish the markups on the products manufactured by his division, without review by the sales manager. As a result, some spare parts were being overpriced (and not selling as well as possible), while other spare parts were being underpriced (with an obvious effect on profits).

After being informed of this fact by their CPA, top management instituted a new policy of having all prices reviewed by the sales manager before

being passed along to the company's salesmen.

Case History #3

Executives of a manufacturing company mentioned to their auditor that his opinion would be submitted to a bank along with the company's application for a loan. Remembering that all the company's plant and equipment was owned outright, the auditor suggested that management consider raising the necessary money through a mortgage rather than an unsecured bank loan. The company's management followed through with the CPA's suggestion and was able to borrow the needed money at a lower interest rate than it had expected to pay.

*   *   *

Tax planning is a somewhat less direct by-product of the audit in that it doesn't occur during the audit itself, but rather, is made possible by the audit.

As the partner of one CPA firm explains: "As a result of his audit, the CPA has a unique opportunity to help the businessman discover tax-saving opportunities. He has a constant 'weather-eye' out for items in the accounts which have a tax effect on the business. His intimate knowledge of the operation, plus his specialized knowledge of the tax laws enable the CPA to offer the businessman constructive tax-saving suggestions—and he will.

"Long-range tax planning is possible because many seemingly routine business transactions can be handled in alternative ways for tax purposes. The CPA can make certain that such items are treated in the most advantageous way. . .

"In sum, the CPA can provide . . . ideas for improving his client's business in many of its facets. The ideas are by-products of the annual audit. From the examinations and analytical techniques then applied comes a wealth of information and knowledge about the business. This background, combined with the CPA's experience in business, broadly puts him in a position to act not only at audit time, but at any time during the year to offer constructive advice based upon the best available facts."

It should now be clear that many services which could well be called "mangement consulting"—such as: a certain amount of tax planning, preparation of financial data, various types of money-saving suggestions and recommendations, advice on matters of accounting treatment—are done in the course of, or arise as a by-product of, the regular audit. This type of advice represents "traditional" management consulting by CPAs.

Management Services

But many CPAs are willing and able to provide much more in the way of management consulting (called "management services" by the CPA profession) as a result of their thorough knowledge of the client company obtained during the audit and also their general business experience.

Any given CPA will offer only services for which he has experience and ability. As a result, not every CPA or CPA firm will offer every type of management consulting service, but almost every service conceivable is offered by some CPA.

The scope of the assignment given a CPA will depend on what a company wants, and what the CPA can do effectively. In principle, a consulting engagement might cover any one or combination of the following types of services: fact-gathering, analysis, recommendations, assistance in putting the recommendations into effect.

As an indication of how deeply some CPA firms are engaged in management

services, it is interesting to note that most of the large, national accounting firms have separate management services divisions—some of which have as many personnel as the largest management consulting firms. This type of work is not limited to large firms, however, for many local CPA firms also offer a wide range of services.

One of the most obvious types of management services develops out of the CPA's audit ability: an evaluation of companies which are prospective merger candidates. Each company involved in merger negotiations must obtain a detailed financial analysis of the other company. A CPA is the natural person to call upon for such an analysis.

A committee of the American Institute of Certified Public Accountants has compiled a list of various management services which have been performed by CPAs. Some of the areas covered include: general management, accounting costs and budgeting, industrial management, organization and personnel, data processing, marketing and operations research.

The following short case history is illustrative of management consulting assignments performed by CPAs.

A CPA firm was asked by a company, whose specialty was delivering packages for other companies, to calculate the best places to locate substations where merchandise would be transferred from large vans to small delivery trucks for delivery to homes. The problem involved more than geographic positioning of substations. It also involved the range of packages, their value, weight, size and, in some cases, their perishableness. It entailed considering the cost of vans, labor, loading equipment, buildings, etc. It had to take into account time delays in transferring packages, traffic conditions, breakage, logical route areas for the drivers, and many other factors. All of them had to be weighed as to their relative importance. Through Operations Research —which is the application of scientific techniques to business problems—a solution was reached which gave the optimum locations for the substations.

CPAs are no longer, if they ever really were, qualified *soley* as adutiors. Your independent certified public accountant is, in fact, an outside expert whose function is to provide you with a wide range of professional management services. But in order to take full advantage of everything he has to offer, you must know what services he can perform—and let him know how he can be of help to you.

If your auditor finds anything during the audit which he thinks you, as a company executive, should be aware of, he usually will tell you. But his comments often will be limited to a statement of what he sees as a problem or a potential problem; the solution might take a considerable length of time to work out and is usually considered a separate assignment.

You should be aware that a CPA will *usually* mention things which he thinks are being handled wrong or which could be handled better—but not always. There are several reasons for this.

To begin with, your CPA might not always know about your company's future plans. You might, for example, be planning to purchase equipment during the forthcoming year which, if the potential tax liability were taken into consideration, should be leased instead. If your auditor knew of your plans, he probably would tell you that a careful analysis should be made of the tax implications of each potential course of action. If he does not know of your plans, he cannot be expected to raise the issue with you.

Professional Men

There is another, perhaps more significant, reason why your auditor might not tell you about every single thing he has observed in your company which potentially could be changed or improved. CPAs—like attorneys and physicians—are professional men. Their code of ethics prohibits them from advertising their services, and often makes them hesitant in "pushing" themselves. They do not want to be in the position of "selling" you on hiring them to perform extra services. Thus, your auditor might casually mention a potential problem area or procedure which could be improved, but not stress it too much. You, in turn, might feel that his casualness implies that what he is telling you is not of great importance.

Because your knowledge of your company's future activities is greater than your auditor's, and because your CPA is a professional man, you will be able to derive a much greater benefit from your auditor if you ask him questions. He will be in a better position to know what you consider important and he will feel much freer in suggesting additional research or analysis if you explicitly ask him questions designed to elicit from him everything he has observed during the course of his audit. You, are of course, under no obligation to hire him or any other CPA to perform the additional services.

In addition, you should discuss your problems with him throughout the year, not only when he arrives to do the annual audit. Let him know that you are aware of—and interested in—the extensive professional services he has to offer. Consult him whenever a major business decision has to be made. If he has suggestions or thinks additional analysis should be made, he will let you know; if he thinks that another specialist should be consulted, he will refer you to the right person. Let him know that you are always open to and interested in his suggestions regarding areas for further study.

You might be surprised at the improvement in your profit and loss statement if you do—and it won't be merely in terms of its appearance.

ENTREPRENEUR VERSUS ORGANIZATION

By Auren Uris

"Should I start my own business, or take a job with General Motors?" (Or any one of the more than four million corporations that dot the American business landscape.) Clutching his new sheepskin or a recent inheritance, many an ambitious, success-minded young man confronts this basic question. The two alternatives are decidedly different in terms of working climate, opportunities, and demands on the individual. They are *so* different, in fact, that the man who goes into business for himself when he really has the makings of an organization man is almost bound to fail; and the man who might perform brilliantly as an entrepreneur often suffers the throes of a fish out of water as a member of a corporate team.

Business ownership has always occupied a special place in the American dream. Aside from the lure of personal profit unlimited, as measured against company-wide wage levels or a figure that will pass the scrutiny of a board of directors, it strongly appeals to the American emphasis on "independence" and "being one's own boss." The individualistic frontier spirit likes to feel he is the master of his own fate, accounting to no man — save the tax collector. A business of one's own also gives a man a chance to prove himself in a special way. The thought is, "If I run my own show, and have ability, initiative, and a bit of luck, I can prove my worth by means of a favorable balance sheet." And, of course, reap commensurate rewards.

Fortune magazine polled employees of a number of corporations on the question, "Would you like to go into business for yourself?" Approximately 50 per cent answered "Yes." Yet the fact is, there are many more people who don't go into business for themselves than who actually do, despite *Fortune's* fifty-fifty response. What considerations separate the entrepreneurs from the organization men? Seldom is the choice made by chance. Both situational and personality factors, it seems, nudge an individual into the one road rather than the other.

SITUATIONAL FACTORS THAT FAVOR THE "OWN BUSINESS' CHOICE

In the case of Owen K. Murphy, it was the novelty of an idea that suggested a new business. Here the situation has two facets: first, it's often difficult, even risky to try to interest an established business in a new product or service. The risk lies in the possibility of having the idea "adapted." If it's not protected by patent, the inventor may have no practical recourse from an idea-hungry and unethical management. Second, a new idea, if it's commercially viable, suggests the possibility of a fortune to be made. Then why not make it for one's self?

Another situational factor becomes obvious when viewing the employment field in general. Some individuals may discover at a certain point that they are practically unemployable. They are forced to go into business for themselves because no one will hire them. Typical is a marketing manager who functioned as a capable executive until he had a severe nervous breakdown. After a year's stay in a mental hospital, he was pronounced cured and set out to resume his profession. Then began a series of grim disappointments. Whenever his interlude at the mental institution became known by a potential employer, the prospect of landing a job vanished. Finally he decided to try to cover up the detrimental episode. He was told by an employer that he was hired — pending a check of references and a pre-employment investigation. Subsequently his secret was discovered by the employer's investigating agency and he was turned down. "I had no recourse," said the executive bitterly. "It was either go into business for myself or starve."

Similarly, men may be considered unhirable because of health reasons, criminal record, unsatisfactory past performance for other employers — they may find that the only solution is to go into a business of their own, or to buy part ownership of an existing company.

Occasionally an executive who has acquired experience in a large company in some specialized area — it may be engineering, production, finance, research and development — may leave to start his own consulting business.

From time to time, one hears of a successful enterprise that grew from a hobby. In one case, a woman started designing clothes for friends. She had a flair for design, and enjoyed the activity as an escape from housewifely duties. Demand for her clothes soon outgrew her circle of immediate friends, and she eventually started her own custom dress shop. Similar interests and development of capabilities have led to the founding of antique shops, bakeshops, food-specialty plants. And, of course, on the masculine side, superior mechanical or manual skills have been the basis of starting up service stations, machine shops, and contracting firms.

One final reason should not be overlooked; the need for more money, or the desire to augment an unsatisfactory income. Feeling this prod, the individual looks for a business that can be operated in his spare time, with little capital investment. The mail-order business is one that has lured many would-be entrepreneurs. Home landscaping, where the man with a power lawnmower and a few hand tools can satisfy his enterprising spirit and at the same time be paid for easing the strain on the homeowner's back, is another. Ingenuity and imagination from time to time add other low-investment enterprises to the list.

SITUATIONAL FACTORS THAT FAVOR THE ORGANIZATION MAN

It was suggested earlier that for some people, the choice between self-employment and taking a job is a career crossroad which is consciously confronted at one time or another. This is true. But many individuals make the choice without a second thought. They are so preconditioned — usually by family or social contacts — that only one alternative is even considered. For instance, family or community tradition often makes the employee road a foregone conclusion. "My family has always had its sons go to work for local industry," explains a Newark resident who reached the vice-presidential level in a plastics plant.

Interest in a specific type of endeavor is another motivation that may steer a man into company employment. If he has an interest in automobiles, it's natural to try to land a job with Ford, American Motors, and so on. The man who is fascinated by computers and their future potential will head for IBM, Remington Rand, or any of the dozens of computer organizations that have sprung up in recent years.

Jim Connaughton, now the president of the Wheelabrator Corporation (not a company that he founded, but one that hired him as president) is a good example of a highly successful business-man whose technical and managerial abilities are most valuable within the framework of a complex, already existing company. Connaughton is a production man who can examine the inner workings of almost any heavy production industry and then reorganize the setup to make it more efficient and more profitable than it was before. Working for a series of different companies as a "trouble shooter," Connaughton made a name for himself as a man with a great knowledge of technical production methods, engineering, financial structure and management techniques. Eventually he was asked by Wheelabrator to become their chief executive. Upon accepting the position, Connaughton was given over a year to familiarize himself with every aspect of the company's activities before he was formally designated president. Because of his knowledge of the fundamentals and his great ability to adapt to new organizations, he was able to assume full control in only four months. Talents like Jim Connaughton's seem tailor-made for

the corporate structure.

A negative factor has forced the choice, however, for some organization men. "My brother opened a small lumberyard and building supply shop in a Chicago suburb," says a top executive of a food products company. "I saw his struggles to make it pay, and believe me, it was painful. After three years, he had to fold. Working for somebody else looked like heaven, compared to that."

PERSONAL DIFFERENCES BETWEEN BUSINESS OWNER AND COMPANY EXECUTIVE

The most obvious trait of the man who starts his own business is usually his desire to "be the boss," or "be his own boss," as the feeling is often expressed. But there's more to it than that. Psychological studies tend to show marked differences between the man who rises to the top through a company hierarchy, and one who makes it on his own. One such study, by Orvis F. Collins and David G. Moore, entitled *The Enterprising Man*, focused on a sample of over a hundred small manufacturers in the Michigan area. The "typical" small-business owner emerged from the study as follows:

He's less likely to be native born." In the matter of national background, the authors found that 20 percent of the group was foreign-born, 35 per cent more were U.S.-born with foreign-born fathers. These figures are particularly interesting when compared to the average business leader — that is, big-company executive. Of the latter group, only 5 percent were foreign-born and 20 percent were U.S.-born of foreign-born fathers.

"*He's no Joe College.*" Only about 20 percent of the small-businessmen were college graduates. A separate study of big-business executives showed a 57 percent figure. Thirty-six percent of the small-businessmen had not graduated from high school, as compared to 13 percent of big-business leaders.

"*He tends to be a rebel.*" The study indicates that interpersonal ties, such as those with an older man who is a teacher or mentor, tend to be short-lived. Say the authors, "The entrepreneur learns that he can live neither within the restrictions of large organizations nor within the restrictions of protege-sponsor relations. Instead, he rebels."

"*He's self-made — and it hasn't been an easy job.*" The old Horatio Alger idea that anyone can succeed in business simply by trying is badly damaged in the Michigan study: "For most entrepreneurs, success in business was preceded by a long period of training and trial, often marked by periods of broken dreams and bankruptcy. It is in this crucible of experience that the entrepreneur develops his skills and learns his trade."

"*He's a driven man.*" It's in the area of motivation that the study is particularly revealing. Our small-business entrepreneur is the antithesis of the organization man. He doesn't stay in an established company because he can't stand the atmosphere. The authors conclude: "The small businessmen are often driven men who have deliberately placed themselves in "open" positions because they would rather face the impersonal forces of the economy than cope with interpersonal relations that they find in the established organization."

"He's creative." The authors conclude that the enterprising men they studied have made a definite contribution to society: "They found an outlet for their creativity by making out of an undifferentiated mass of circumstance a creation uniquely their own: a business firm."

In drawing conclusions from the Collins-Moore study, two limitations must be remembered: the businessmen studied were all from the Michigan area. A study from a different geographical area might very well turn out differently. Also, in getting the group together, no distinction was made as to the capability or degree of success being achieved.

WHAT PRICE DIPLOMA?

The Enterprising Man makes interesting generalizations about the educational backgrounds of the entrepreneur as compared to the company executive. The entrepreneur is best off when his education or training enables him to operate as a kind of one-man army in an open field. The theoretical outlook and rigidities that sometimes result from education, or overeducation, would hamper the entrepreneur in his flexibility and ability to buck the established order of things that is often his trademark. That's why a man who's to go it alone is best educated by being thrust upon his own at an early age. He learns to survive by his wits. He learns about life by living it. He learns about people by dealing with them, often in pressure situations. His ability to deal with people on a realistic basis is strengthened, because he builds a structure of relationships outside established organizations. There are no rules, and perhaps no genteel traditions that guide or limit what can be done.

By contrast, the company executives in the higher corporate echelons generally have sophisticated technical training — in engineering, finance, or a combination of disciplines. A study by Dr. Mabel Newcomer and *Scientific American* found that 38 percent of a group of one thousand top executives either had degrees in engineering and the natural sciences or the equivalent in on-the-job experience. The study shows, further, that the proportion of top executives with degrees in science or engineering jumped from 7 percent in 1900 to 20 per cent in 1950. The 38 percent figure, a 1964 finding, confirms the long-range trend.

SHAPE OF THE UNIVERSE

The "models" of the world in which the businessman and the executive operate are quite different. Although each is dominant in his particular sphere, the "hill" of which each is "king" has different aspects. The enterprising man, by and large, builds his own world. He sees it not as a hierarchy, a pyramid with himself at the top, but rather as a kind of open market place, an activity of exchange and transaction, one that he put together by trading and making deals. Surprisingly, he doesn't see himself as a leader of men, but rather as a key figure in a network composed of buyers, sellers, arrangers, promoters, people to call on for help, people whose skills and capabilities are to be used to further his objectives. In comparison, the executive who makes it to the top of a corporate pyramid sees the world of business as an entirely different kind of place. First, he has achieved his success by rising through an established social and authority structure. He has had subordinates and superiors. To some extent, the successful paid manager has learned how to exploit both — not necessarily in a selfish or destructive way, but for the "good of the team" — for the sake of efficiency and company profit.

The self-employed entrepreneur sitting on top of the self-made mountain enjoys a very different kind of status from the pyramid climber. Being an owner endows him with a sense of feudal nobility. Elevator men, waiters, secretaries, subordinates react to him with a certain deference unconsciously engendered by the man's own bearing and attitude. He can actually behave as he pleases, for he's untrammeled by any big-company public relations policy that requires its top executives to act with democratic and even humble mien. On the other hand, the top executive in a corporation well knows he is not a free spirit. Even the president has a boss. It may be a board of directors or a group of stockholders. And this means, he dare not exercise power willfully, nor behave like "the king." The corporate image always comes first.

THE RISKS AND REWARDS

The entrepreneur and the company executives also operate with different feelings toward the vehicle of their success. To the executive, "the company" is an organization of which he is an important member, and towards which he feels loyalty and dedication. The entrepreneur's identification with *"his* company" is much closer, and stronger. The degree of ego-involvement can be tremendous. Certainly, it's often enough to keep him working long hours, seven days a week, to keep the business alive and growing.

The hazards of the entrepreneur are usually more threatening. The number of failures of corporations, given as 13,514 in 1965 by Dunn and

Bradstreet, remind the entrepreneur all too vividly, of the fate that awaits a single major slip or error in judgment. A verbatim statement by an entrepreneur — in this case, the proprietor of a small retail shop — gives a view, perhaps exaggerated, but at any rate colorful, of the basic outlook of the entrepreneur versus the company executive:

Big-shot executives hand me a laugh. They're like big-game hunters operating in a zoo. Where's the risk? Look what I'm up against. It rains, or the temperature drops too far, and wham, my cash register is paralyzed, and Mama cooks old shoes. I gotta buy and sell and be my own mule. A big-business guy, he's got everything going for him. He's got secretaries and think machines and experts to hold his hand when he gets scared or lonely. When my business goes bad, I gotta worry about bread on the table. He only has to worry about how to make it good to the stockholders or to the bank.

In the final analysis, the business owner is playing for big stakes. If he loses, he may be set back to the starting line — no cash, no prospects, no business. The fate of the company executive, in case of failure, is far less devastating. He may simply get "kicked upstairs." True, he is taken out of a position of authority, but he's often given a well-paying sinecure. And if his fall from grace is sufficiently serious to warrant firing — well, there's always the chance of a job in another company, possibly a competitor's, where he may well be welcomed with open arms, because of his experience in the enemy camp.

EXECUTIVE SELF SELECTION IN SMALL BUSINESSES

By Louis L. Allen

No book about personnel management, to my knowledge, devotes any significant amount of space to the selection of people for small business ownership. Unlike the giant firm which has recruiting and selection experts to screen the wheat from the chaff, the small business firm, which comprises the most common economic unit in our business systems, cannot afford to employ a personnel manager. The end result is that in the 4.5 million businesses in this country, the vast majority of which are small, the vast majority of the top managers have been through a rather unsystematic personnel selection process in terms of conventional personnel theory. More than that, there's something very special about the selection of the owners:

They Have Selected Themselves

Study a dozen texts in employment and selection, and you'll find none have a chapter or even a paragraph to cover the problem of the man who must screen himself for top management in his own small firm.

In this article I propose to fill this gap in the literature — not completely, but in a few key ingredients that have impressed me as essential in your own self selection process if you're toying with the idea of starting your own business.

Please note that these observations are subjective and aren't based on any of the newest findings of behavioral research. I am essentially a banker. My bank is a rather specialized kind, a SBIC (Small Business Investment Company) which is limited to making loans to people who have selected themselves to be owners, presidents or managers of small firms, and also seek some financial backing. As I face self-selected top managers across my desk, or visit them in their plants or offices, I become more and more impressed with the fact that this self-selection process if far more important to the success or failure of the company the man is starting than the monetary aspects of our negotiations.

What's proposed here isn't a complete guide to self-selection — or self-elimination — for top management of the small firm. I'll stick to being a banker, and let the professors write such a book. When they do, however, I'd like to suggest a few key points which they should include that have impressed me as germinal in the top management self-selection process.

Perhaps, if you are going into small business, or have been thinking about it, you can't await

the complete guide. If this is the case, perhaps this stop-gap article will help.

GUIDE NUMBER ONE

About 18 months ago, in the course of one day, I had an appointment with two different groups. One group consisted of three engineers from a national electronics firm who wanted to start a business of their own. The other group comprised an engineer with an electro-mechanical background and a CPA who wanted to start their small business. The story of what happened to these groups illustrates the point which this article will attempt to make, i.e., a small businessman's success will be measured in direct proportion to the sacrifices he will be willing to make in order that his small business succeeds.

The three engineers sat across my table and outlined their background. Each was making over $35,000 a year, married and had several children. Their program was to start a business of their own in a line of products directly related to the work they were doing for their present employer. Their program was beautifully presented in an impressive binding with five-year forecasts and a complete analysis of all the salient facts. Naturally, I was quite impressed. They needed $350,000 and when I asked the question "how much can you come up with as a group?" the spokesman for them said "just a minimal amount, perhaps $25,000." I next asked them what salaries they were willing to work for and explained that it was certainly no crime in this day and age to be poor. I also said I was not impressed with the savings that they were able to accumulate, so, I naturally assumed all they had to put into this business was their time, and thus, I was interested in the charges they would levy for their efforts. After a brief consultation between them, the consensus was that they might be able to reduce their salaries to $25,000 apiece. At that point, it was completely obvious they had no idea what self selection into a small business meant, and they were completely unprepared for what lay ahead, in spite of the fact that their brochure is still one of the most complete that I have ever seen.

The other group I talked to that day was just two men, the engineer and the accountant. And, like the first group, this second group started off by telling me that the engineer was now making $18,000 a year and that the CPA had a practice which he and his wife ran in which they had gross draw of $15,000 after expenses. Their first statement was that they had, jointly, been able to save $15,000 and that this amount was completely committed to the program. Furthermore, the engineer went into some detail with me to show how it would be possible to keep his family together and meet minimum expenses on $8,500 a year, a reduction in pay of $9,500 from the $18,000 he was currently earning.

Also, the CPA stated flatly that he was willing to give up two days a week of his own time and a day a week of his wife's time, to work directly for the company at no charge. This group then presented me with a program of projected sales and income which was broken down in such a way that the investment could be made step by step with a review at each period. This program showed an ultimate need of $200,000 from the investor. The profit potential as outlined by the second group was roughly similar to that of the first although the product line was technically different.

I recommended to my loan committee that we make an investment in the second group and, of course, we gave a complete turn-down to the three engineers in the first group. Eighteen months later the situation is this: the first group of engineers found investors to put up the $350,000, and when that turned out to be insufficient got another $150,000 from the same investors. The company that they formed is bankrupt, and all of the invested capital has been lost. Ostensibly, it was salary costs that ate them up. Actually, they had selected people (themselves) who wouldn't pay a present price for future success.

The second group now has a sales volume running at an average of $45,000 a month, and their profit is just a little better than 27% on sales before depreciation and taxes. The president of the second group is now drawing $12,000 a year salary, and the accountant, although he is no longer associated with the company because of a new situation that presented itself, has been paid a fair price for the original cash investment which he made. It is the contention of the writer that given a half decent idea for a needed product or service, the first essential in a small business is selection of the man or men who are running the business. I have never seen a small businessman go broke if he was willing to make the necessary sacrifices. On the other hand, nearly every small business failure which I have seen is a direct result of a lack of willingness to make the appropriate sacrifices on the part of one or more of the principles.

A few well known ideas: "bread cast upon the waters" or perhaps "ask not what your business can do for you, but . . ." apply in the early years and formative periods. This does not mean to say that great personal sacrifices always have to accompany the successful growth of a small business because sometimes good fortune and other events work towards the situation in which the progress is made without the attending sacrifices. Nor will self-sacrifice replace a hopeless product or service nobody wants. Hence, the first guide is:

BE WILLING TO PAY THE PRICE

I would like to touch just briefly on several of the other important areas of personal sacrifices which seem to me fundamental in terms of the commitment that man must make before he goes out on his own.

One area requiring major sacrifice is well documented by a conversation I had several weeks ago. A gentleman who was very highly recommended came into my office. In his opening remarks he said the following. "I like the idea of forming my own sales representative organization." There are two things that are basically wrong with this statement, and they are among *the most common of the mistakes* I have observed on the part of self-selected small businessmen. The first mistake is that a man, and particularly a small businessman, cannot afford the luxury of indulging himself in an avocation that he "likes." If you pick yourself for top man in your own firm because you think in so doing you'll avoid the menial or unpleasant jobs, your selection is weak. The world is full of very capable individuals who are doing an excellent job at their assigned tasks. Therefore, my first comment to this young man was that he spend some time learning what he must do to make his business succeed and then forcing himself to learn to like it. Hopefully, he might prove competent as a salesman, but the proof was needed. He selected himself as head of his own sales organization because he disliked his recent job.

The second major fallacy with his opening remark is somewhat similar. No one who has taken the trouble to look into the problems and the attendant sacrifices which have to be made by small businessmen, could possibly say that "he would like to be a small businessman," that is, unless he is a glutton for punishment. The reason why a man selects himself to head his own small business is because he *must* do it. The American dream is made up of such urges. The drives which force him to do this are as old as capitalism itself. A man may have complete security as somebody else's employee where he is fed, clothed, housed, where his medical needs are taken care of, but he has fewer prerogatives of his own. On the other hand, the individual who wishes to accept the responsibility for providing his own security has complete freedom of choice in selecting the means for providing the security he wishes. Thus, in return for abdicating his individual prerogatives, one individual may choose the security which some rather facetiously have termed being in jail, while the other individual may choose to be hungry or cold or sick or any combination of these conditions merely for the privilege of determining his own future.

Thinking that "owning my own business is all rosy" is an illusion.

GUIDE NUMBER TWO

Some time ago, I was asked to appear as a guest lecturer at a well-known graduate school of business administration and to talk there to the class which was dealing particulary with the problems of small business. By way of some material for preparation, I presented the students with the following situation:

FIGURE I

Assume you are thinking of purchasing control of a manufacturing concern. In descending order of importance, rank the following results of your investigation:

1. The plant and equipment are old and need attention.
2. After deducting the purchase price, you have left what you consider to be barely adequate funds to supplement working capital.
3. The existing management you will inherit is old in age but has many years' experience in this field.
4. You, personally, have less than three years actual working experience in this industry.
5. The company's product or products meet the needs of a broad class of customers, and well-established distribution methods exist in this industry.

Based on these assumptions, would you go ahead or not?

An amazing compilation of answers were given to this simple question. Not one of the 198 students ranked first in importance Item No. 4 which had to do with personal working experience in the industry being reviewed. To the writer this was a shock. There is no more important aspect of self-selection for small business ownership than facing sacrifices which a man must make, especially spending his personal time learning completely about an industry before making the commitment to get into it on his own. In the writer's experience, over half of the small businessmen who have failed have had a real blank in their own personal experience in the business which they were trying to run.

Don't choose yourself as a candidate to run your own business if you don't know that business extremely well.

Let's look back at the situation described in the first few paragraphs of this article. One of the first things that a self-selected small businessman needs is money. Yet, it is this writer's firm conviction that a worthwhile program presented by a man who knows his business is *capable of being adequately financed.* If his small business venture is to have any chance for success, he must couple his own time and effort with cash; by time, I mean up to 15 hours a day, 7 days a week, for as long as it takes the company to cross the first major plateau where it is established in the eyes of its customers. If your self-selection system shows you to be a confirmed 9 to 5 type, better stay out of small business.

There are always a great many reasons why small businessmen say they need money. In the writer's experience, the infusion of money never cures a problem of poor self-selection, and this has lead the writer to come to the conclusion that money cannot be the main problem.

GUIDE NUMBER THREE

Can you accept personal inconvenience?

Some areas in which the small businessman is frequently unwilling to make the necessary sacrifices are: (1) he could not reduce his living standards and had to draw a larger salary than the company could afford; (2) he could not control himself in his desire to acquire more machinery or other fixed investment than he needed and could get by without, provided he was willing to sacrifice some effort and be willing to accept, possibly, a product that does not have the same quality as could be made on more expensive equipment; (3) He was unwilling to live where his business had the best chance of success; or (4) he insists upon hiring people to do jobs he should be doing himself.

PERSONAL SUCCESSES

A man I had known and liked for nearly 10 years stopped in to see me several months ago and said that he desperately needed some financing for his business. Upon examination he indeed appeared to have a cash problem. When he came in, he brought his papers, and the facts showed that he had been drawing some $3,500 a month salary out of his business because that was the amount required to continue the living standard which he and his wife had adopted while this man had been employed in a very large national concern in a top executive post. My friend had left his business in order to go into business for himself, and he had done quite well at the start. A cash problem? On the surface it seemed so, but it was more than money.

I was much distressed to have to tell my friend that before I could help him, he would have to reduce his draw to not more than $1,500 a month. This was a very unacceptable proposition to him, and he left in somewhat of a huff. Several weeks later he came back saying that he had found that other bankers with whom he had talked had adopted an attitude like mine, and since he was going to have to cut back on his living standards, he would prefer to do it with an old friend rather than with a stranger, and would I still do it? The answer was "yes." My friend then did the following things. He sold his house, which was a beautiful place and was on the cover of a magazine, and moved into a small modest home which he rented. He put the proceeds of the sale into his business. He let his maid go. And in other ways he reduced his requirements so he could keep his family going on the $1,500 a month. Very happily his business continued to prosper, and with the adequate cash produced by a new self-perception, the future of his business looks very bright indeed. Was it the cash alone that tipped the scale? Hardly, it was the eased pressure and determination to place his long run goals ahead of immediate income.

One of the first prospects who came into my bank for financing was a man in the millwork and woodworking business. He was doing a considerable volume and seemed to be making a profit, yet he was continually pressed for cash. The situation was sufficiently interesting to warrant a visit to his plant which I made very shortly thereafter. Having once been in the sawmill and logging business myself, I can state without fear of contradiction, that this man had the most beautifully equipped shop I had ever seen. I admired his plant immensely. Here was his problem, he could not control himself in the acquisition of machinery. This man eventually ended up in bankruptcy, and his machinery account which had a book value of over $600,000 was sold at auction for $92,000.

A different problem was presented to me by a young engineer who had started a company in a very specialized product line with which he was completely familar. His initial success was very encouraging, and on the strength of this good history he decided to expand into other lines. To do this, it was necessary for him to hire other engineers. The problem that he faced when he came to talk to me was that in order to keep his expanded product line from becoming technologically superannuated, he had to hire more and more engineering talent. And this direct payroll expansion had to be incurred substantially in advance of any product sales and profits which might accrue. After he had outlined the problem to me, he said with a half smile on his face that what he really wanted to do was to continue his program of deficit financing. Quite obviously, this type of a program was zero incentive for an investor, and my bank declined the risk. One of his problems was that so long as his product line was one which he personally could develop, he could keep himself in the forefront of the technology. In his zeal for technical achievement, he lost sight of his business goals. When he hired other engineers, these men could not provide the same drive in their areas and had little concern for where the money would come from. When I suggested that he start making a profit soon, even if it meant

deferring some technical schemes which intrigued him, he left in a cold mood.

CONCLUSION

In this article I have tried to suggest a few key points which those thinking of starting their own business might well consider. They are based, of course, only on my own personal experiences and observations as a banker. Take them for what they are worth, and realize that when thinking of starting your own business, you are really selecting yourself to be a top executive. In summary, remember: (1) there is nothing to be obtained without paying the price; (2) self select only experienced men to start new enterprise; and (3) ask yourself whether you can accept personal inconvenience? If you're with me up to here, maybe my bank, or somebody else's, will be more willing to consider you as a good loan prospect.

THE FOUNDING OF
TECHNOLOGICALLY-BASED FIRMS©

Arnold C. Cooper
Professor
Krannert Graduate School of Industrial Administration
Purdue University

PREFACE

It is indeed a great pleasure for The Center for Venture Management to publish and make available this study and thus add to the growing literature on technical entrepreneurship. It is only when we understand the well-springs of enterprise will we, as a Nation fully understand the essence of free enterprise. At its core, free enterprise relies on the motives and actions of a single individual or small group of individuals acting in concert to bring about the formation of a new firm. This study delves into the background and work experiences of a group of highly trained persons who then went about the business of forming a new, high-technology enterprise.

We take this opportunity to thank Dr. Cooper for his efforts in completing this study, which was the first major research activity undertaken by the newly formed Center for Venture Management. And we hope that this study will be read and used by scholars of enterprise and induce them too, to undertake further research into this fascinating field.

John L. Komives

The Center For Venture Management Milwaukee / Wisconsin / 1971

ACKNOWLEDGEMENTS

Many people have contributed to this effort. Among the foremost are the founders of the new, technologically-based firms on the San Francisco Peninsula. Because this work is based upon empirical data, gathered primarily in interviews, the assistance of these very busy men was essential. Without their willing cooperation, this research could not have been done.

Dr. John Komives and The Center For Venture Management provided vital support and encouragement. During the summer of 1969, The Center supported this work and enabled me to spend the summer in Palo Alto gathering data. Subsequently, Dr. Komives urged me to write this monograph for publication by The Center For Venture Management.

During the academic year, 1967-1968, while a visiting professor at Stanford University, I became deeply interested in the process by which new, technologically-based firms are founded. The deans and faculty of The Graduate School of Business at Stanford extended many kindnesses to me during that year, as well as during the summer of 1969 when I returned to pursue this research further.

My colleagues, Associate Dean Rene P. Manes and Professor Robert W. Johnson reviewed the manuscript and made helpful comments, as did Dr. Komives of The Center For Venture Management. My appreciation is also extended to Dean John S. Day for his continuing support.

Typing was done y Mrs. Rebecca Phillippo, Miss Evelyn Swartz, and particularly by Mrs. Elizabeth Tisley.

TABLE OF CONTENTS

CHAPTER I

Introduction

In certain parts of our country, such as Boston, Palo Alto, and Los Angeles, large numbers of new, technologically-based firms have come into being in recent years. Business Week calls these firms "Xeroids" (Xerox plus Polaroid). Investors search for future "Xeroids," while regional development commissions dream of creating local versions of Boston's Route #128.

Many of these firms have been responsible for significant techno-logical innovations. For instance, consider three companies formed in 1957: Digital Equipment, Raychem Corporation, and Fairchild Semi-conductor (a division of Fairchild Camera and Instrument). Digital Equipment pioneered in developing small computers; Raychem played a leading role in the development of irradiated plastics; Fairchild was a leader in the then infant semiconductor industry. By 1969, the sales of these firms were $87 million, $45 million, and $150 million respectively. The remarkable records of these three firms are by no means typical; many other new companies have enjoyed only modest success or have met with failure. Nevertheless, new, technologically-based firms (NTBF's), considered as a group, have had a significant economic and tech-nological impact. They complement our existing industry by con-stituting hundreds of additional centers of innovation and ini-tiative, searching for opportunities to match developing techno-logies and market needs. In fact, the "Panel on Invention and Innovation," convened by the Secretary of Commerce and made up principally of representatives of large firms, concluded:

> "Independent inventors and small firms are responsible for an important part of our inventive process, a larger percentage than their relatively small investment in R & D would suggest."[1]

Some individual engineers and technical managers function ef-fectively in the large company environment; others do not. When new and small firms exist, there are alternatives for career ful-fillment, and individuals can seek out those environments where they will be most fulfilled and productive.

From the standpoint of regional economic development, NTBF's are often viewed as highly desirable. They make pleasant neigh-bors, producing relatively little noise and pollution. They often employ substantial percentages of highly paid scientists and en-gineers. Since these are corporate headquarters, their profes-sional employees are likely to be more committed to the commu-nity, thinking in terms of a lifetime involvement, rather than a two-year stay before the next move.

It is unlikely that any single company or management group can always be right in "betting" on future markets and technologies. However, a region whose growth and stability are tied to many independent centers of decision-making may be better able to respond flexibly in a rapidly changing environment. In relation

1

---

[1]Technological Innovation: Its Environment and Management. Washington, D. C.: U. S. Government Printing Office, 1967, p. 17.

to this, a Stanford Research Institute study of the development of "research complexes" concluded:

> "All of the evidence in this series of studies suggests that attracting corporation divisions does not provide the most effective or desirable path to development. On the contrary, establishment of a number of small and medium size technical companies is the most effective way to provide for the development of a complex."[2]

In their efforts to develop technologically-based industry, communities have often competed to attract branch laboratories or plants of national firms. In many instances, the efforts have met with frustration and the industrial parks are still empty. Sometimes a single large defense contractor has been attracted, but subsequent heavy community dependence upon the fluctuating fortunes of a dominant firm has proved to be a mixed blessing.

In contrast to all of the effort to attract firms from elsewhere, relatively little attention has been devoted to encouraging the birth and growth of new local firms. In part, this may be due to lack of understanding about how new firms are brought forth and nurtured.

The importance of new, technologically-based firms suggests that we need to learn more about how they come into being. This study is concerned with adding to our understanding about the birth of these firms. It develops a basis of factual data and a conceptual framework for understanding technical entrepreneurship. A number of major questions relating to entrepreneurship are considered:

1. What are the factors bearing upon the birth of NTBF's?

2. To what extent do entrepreneurs move to other geographical areas when founding their firms?

3. To what extent are NTBF's related in terms of technology and markets to the established organizations which the founders leave?

4. What motivates the founders?

5. In what ways do the established firms in an area influence entrepreneurship?

6. In an area of active entrepreneurship what are the spin-off rates from established organizations? Are there substantial variations?

7. Do average spin-off rates vary by type or size of established organization?

8. What factors bear upon differences in regional rates of technical entrepreneurship?

9. How does past entrepreneurship influence future entrepreneurship?

10. What are the roles of local sources of venture capital,

2

[2]K. Draheim, R. Howell, and A. Shapero, The Development of a Potential R & D Complex, Menlo Park, California: Stanford Research Institute, July, 1966, p. 9.

of universities, and of living conditions in influencing entrepreneurship?

11. In an entrepreneurially active area, what are the annual birth-rates of new firms? What are the survival rates of these firms?

These questions have implications for many groups, including executives of the established organizations from which entrepreneurs spin off, engineers or technical managers who envisage becoming entrepreneurs some day, and those concerned with regional economic development.

A word of warning. This is not a definitive and exhaustive study of all of the complex processes influencing technical entrepreneurship. This research is of limited scope, concentrating on certain aspects of the total process. It is an introductory study; most of the questions considered here have not been the subject of much previous research. Within these limitations, the objective here is to add to our understanding of entrepreneurship in general and technical entrepreneurship in particular.

CHAPTER II

Definitions Used And The Nature of The Research

What is a new, technologically-based firm? It is not easy to say when a firm comes into being, nor is it always easy to determine whether a particular company is "new." In an area of active entrepreneurship, there are companies and dreams of companies in many different stages of development. Some would-be entrepreneurs have developed plans to varying degrees of completeness, while continuing with their present jobs. Others, on a part-time basis, are designing products in their garages or doing consulting. Some have left their previous jobs and are devoting all of their time to trying to get new firms started. One will hear that "John Jones has quit Fairchild and is trying to raise capital for a new firm." Sometimes the company will "surface" a few weeks later with a newspaper announcement describing the founding group and the initial business address. In other instances, never publicized at the time, the aspiring founder meets with frustration and begins consulting or takes another job to support his family.

A hard-to-classify situation, for example, was a new semiconductor firm which virtually failed with its initial founders. New managers (or entrepreneurs?) came on the scene, bringing with them additional capital. Building upon the shell of what they found, they succeeded in getting the company off the ground. Under such circumstances, when was the company founded, or is one talking about the founding of two different firms?

Who are the founders of a new firm? In many instances, one or more men clearly occupy this role. In other situations, deciding who are the founders is difficult because key men make varying degrees of commitment or join the new firm at different stages of its development. For instance, one part-time business became a full-time venture with considerable promise after an outside investor gave not only funds, but also advice, encouragement, and assistance in raising money from others; yet, he limited his own involvement to a part-time commitment. Some founding groups will describe themselves as made up of "early founders" and "late founders." In one new firm, the "early founder" made a full-time commitment in April, concentrating on product development; he was joined in October by the "late founder," whose major contributions were to be in management and marketing.

The variety of situations described above demonstrates that definitions in this field must be somewhat arbitrary, and that some firms defy neat classification.

In this study, when a member of top management (usually the president) of the new firm was contacted, he was asked whom he considered to be the founders. If the men named had made a full-time commitment, they were counted as founders.

In regard to firms studied, this research concentrates solely upon businesses which had reached a stage of development in which

4

the full-time efforts of the founders were required; no "part-time" ventures were studied. The date-of-founding was defined as the time when at least one manager or scientist began to devote full-time to the business. If the prospective founder was initially unsuccessful in raising capital or putting together an entrepreneurial group and then intermittently pursued such efforts while consulting, the date-of-founding was counted as that time when a viable firm was finally launched. In the case of a business which was substantially boosted or revived by a second wave of founders, it was rather arbitrarily decided to count it as only one firm, with the focus being upon the "first" set of founders and the "first" founding date.

A technologically-based firm is defined as a company which emphasizes research and development or which places major emphasis on exploiting new technical knowledge. The typical firm studied had a "product" which was technical hardware or technical studies. Explicitly excluded from the study were firms offering only management consulting, computer software, or wholesaling and selling services. Also omitted were "sponsored spin-offs," in which a parent firm voluntarily established and held stock in a newly formed company intended to perform some of the business of the sponsoring firm.

THE RESEARCH

The research was conducted primarily in one of the nation's centers of technical entrepreneurship – the San Francisco Peninsula area around Palo Alto, California. The boundaries of the region studied are indicated on the map in Exhibit II-1. The study concentrated upon companies founded during the decade of the 1960's, specifically those founded between January 1, 1960, and July 1, 1969. Because of the industrial make-up of the Palo Alto area, these were principally firms operating in or associated with the electronics industry.

The first phase of the research involved intensive structured interviews with 30 entrepreneurs. The typical interview lasted about two hours and focused upon the events and decisions associated with the founding of the firm.

In the second phase, an attempt was made to gather summary data, chiefly through telephone interviews, relating to the founding of all of the NTBF's started on the San Francisco Peninsula since 1960. In total, data were gathered on the founding of about 220 additional new firms, bringing the total studied to approximately 250; this included a number of companies no longer in existence. As nearly as can be determined, these data represent most of the companies of this type started in the area since 1960, and may be regarded as a census of the population.

A third step involved interviews with executives from established organizations. Data were gathered about spin-offs from their firms and about internal factors which may have encouraged or discouraged entrepreneurship. The focus was upon those major organizations from which many entrepreneurs have come, or upon unique

5

Exhibit II-I

GEOGRAPHICAL AREA STUDIED

New firms studied were within the
region bounded by dotted line

types of organizations such as universities and non-profit research organizations.

The companies studied do not represent a statistical sample of the population of NTBF's; they do represent an attempted census of the total population of these firms. When the research was started, the population of new firms which had been founded during the 1960's was not known, although there were knowledgeable observers who knew of many foundings. One product of this research is the development of a list of firms which were started – an itemization of the members of the population. Many of the companies studied no longer exist as independent firms, having since been discontinued or merged.

The initial approach to identifying NTBF's was to rely upon three sources: present and past membership of the Western Electronic Manufacturers Association, announcements in the business section of The Palo Alto Times, and present and past listings in the yellow pages of the telephone directories of the various cities in the region. These data were culled to eliminate firms founded before 1960, divisions of existing firms, or other companies not meeting the criteria described above. In most instances, a senior executive of the firm was contacted, either through telephone or personal interview. After information was gathered about the founding of that firm, the executive was then asked about spin-offs from his company or about spin-offs from the company for which he had previously worked. The process was continued, with each new firm mentioned being investigated, and with each new executive contacted being asked about other spin-offs. In some instances with firms long discontinued, it was possible to obtain only partial information, such as name of firm and probable date of founding.

To identify every new firm founded during the decade of the 1960's is probably an impossible task. The firms most likely to have been overlooked are those which were never very visible or successful. Possibly, they existed for only a short time, with the founders never arranging for any publicity or involvement with a trade association. Some data were gathered on a total of 13 "mystery firms" which were known to have existed and which were probably members of the population being studed; however, beyond that, nothing is known about them. They remain "mystery firms." In addition, some firms which were founded in the last few weeks of the 9½ year period under study probably were omitted because they had not yet become "visible" as of July 1, 1969, the cut-off date for the study. It might be added that all of the entrepreneurs contacted did cooperate to a marked degree; only in one company did the entrepreneur refuse to give any information.

CONCLUSION

In many parts of the country, when an engineer or technical manager quits his job, he then goes to work for another established organization. However, in the Palo Alto area during the decade of the 1960's, such a man sometimes founded a new, technologically-based firm. This research focuses upon this phenomenon, and is based upon data gathered in one of the few places where a high rate of technical entrepreneurship could be observed and studied.

Basically, there were three kinds of data-gathering activities. The first involved intensive interviews with individual entrepreneurs and was directed toward understanding how a new firm gets started. These interviews were far-ranging, focused primarily upon qualitative information, and had as one of their results the generation of ideas, propositions or hypotheses about the nature of the entrepreneurial process.

The second kind of activity was directed toward identifying and gathering data about the entire population of new firms, so that conclusions could be drawn about that population. The primary method utilized short, structured telephone interviews. The resulting data, considered in the aggregate, were more quantitative in nature, and could be counted, compared, and analyzed to test various hypotheses.

The third kind of data-gathering activity, less ambitious in scope than the first two, involved intensive interviews with managers of organizations which entrepreneurs had left. This resulted in a mixture of the kinds of information described above, with particular emphasis on the nature of the organizational influence upon the entrepreneur.

In the subsequent discussions and analyses, data from all three sources are drawn upon as they relate to particular aspects of entrepreneurship. Hopefully, the result is deeper understanding, utilizing both quantitative data about the entire population of new firms and qualitative interview data to help to explain the process at work.

CHAPTER III

**A Framework For Analysis And Characteristics
of the Entrepreneur**

What are the events and decisions which lead to the founding of a particular firm? To what extent is the founding of one firm like that of another?

This chapter first presents brief descriptions of how two particular firms were founded. These illustrate how each founding is a unique event, yet also has elements in common with other foundings. Then, an analytical framework is presented for organizing and understanding the factors which influence the entrepreneurial decision. Finally, one of the major factors – the individual entrepreneur and his background – is examined.

COMPANY A

The marketing manager of a rapidly growing electronics firm in Palo Alto had, for several years, considered taking the step of starting his own firm. He had previously worked in engineering for two different firms in the East and then had worked in positions of increasing responsibility in sales for a West Coast firm which grew fifty-fold during his time with it. He then became head of marketing for a Palo Alto firm, and helped that company grow approximately forty-fold during the next few years.

While with the Palo Alto firm, he bagan to disagree with certain important decisions in regard to product development and the selection of key personnel. He said, "I saw myself on a collision path with the president, and knew that I would not stay with the company." In addition to his increasing dissatisfaction with his future in this firm, he had increasingly thought about taking the entrepreneurial step himself. In his own words, "I had finally gotten the bug. I thought I'd like to try it myself . . . to try to create something out of nothing . . . to try to make a company important in its field." In the past, he had considered with certain friends and colleagues a number of product- market opportunities which might be the basis for a new company; however, nothing had quite jelled. Finally, a specific opportunity came into focus, relating to the development of a particular component with technical capabilities exceeding anything then on the market.

In the fall of 1965, he and three other engineers from the same firm left the parent company and started on their own. They estimated that their own savings, including stock ownership, were sufficient to support the company for six to nine months. They believed that they easily could raise additional funds from five different men they knew, all of whom were technical executives who had invested in other new, technologically-based firms in the past. When they started, they had no product developed and had not specifically talked to any customers, yet . . . "We were tremendously confident . . . Even if we had to work 24 hours a day, we were determined to meet our goals."

9

COMPANY B

An engineer with a small electronics firm had previously worked for a large government laboratory and a large aerospace firm. In the government laboratory, he had found the atmosphere relaxed and suitable for a man dedicated to science, but not for a man ambitious economically. At the aerospace firm, there had been little real work for him to do; he participated in developing bids, but none of these bids was accepted during his short tenure with the company. He quit after a few months, and took a pay cut to join a small firm which advertised for an engineer.

Here, he had responsibility for a line of instruments; he either handled personally or supervised the bidding, designing, building, testing, and delivery of the instruments. He worked long hours, and also enrolled in an evening M.B.A. program. During this time he felt increasing frustration about some of the organizational decisions which had been made, the technical help he was able to receive from others on the staff, and his compensation. He prepared a proposal which involved an expansion for his part of the business. The proposal was turned down, and he quit on the spot. He had not planned to quit; he had not planned to become an entrepreneur.

He made the decision to start a company specializing in the same kind of instruments he had been responsible for in his previous job. He tried to raise capital from a number of sources, but was successful only in raising a small amount of money from previous colleagues who planned to join him after the company got going. He bid on and succeeded in getting an order to deliver some technically advanced instruments. Subsequently, he discovered that he had inadequate funds to carry through on the order. Because of financial problems, he changed the strategy of the business and became a sub-contractor, primarily designing and producing particular components for one large local firm. He did not continue with the original conception of developing a line of instruments, but instead directed the company toward considerable growth and prosperity as a specialized sub-contractor.

A FRAMEWORK FOR ANALYSIS

Examination of the sequence of events and decisions described above suggests that the processes leading to the founding of a new firm are complex and that many factors exert an influence. Despite the complexity and diversity, there appear to be common processes at work, such that each founding is influenced by certain factors.

The decision to start a particular business at a particular time and place might be thought of as being influenced by three major factors, each of which has a number of sub-parts:

1.   The entrepreneur himself, including the many aspects of his background which affect his motivations, his perceptions, and his skills and knowledge.

10

2. The established organization for which the entrepreneur had previously been working, which might be termed an "incubator organization." It hires and often brings the potential founder into an area; it trains him and helps him to develop technical, market, and managerial skills and knowledge; it provides the organizational framework which may allow the potential founder to work closely with men of varied skills who might join him in an entrepreneurial team. In addition, the established organization, through the satisfactions and frustrations it provides, helps to influence the motivations of the prospective entrepreneur.

3. Various external factors, many of them regional in nature. These include the availability of capital, accessibility to suppliers, personnel, and markets, and the collective attitudes and perceptions relating to entrepreneurship and the risks and rewards associated with it. Other external influences, more characteristic of the national economy than of a particular region, are the state of the economy and stock market conditions.

This research is concerned primarily with the role of the incubator organization and those external factors which may vary from region to region. The former is considered in Chapters IV and V and the latter in Chapter VI. Certain characteristics of the individual entrepreneur are discussed later in this chapter.

LIMITATIONS ON THE SCOPE OF THE STUDY

Two external factors, primarily national rather than regional in character, are not covered in this research. One is the state of the economy – including the overall demand for the goods or services which might be offered by a new firm. The other is stock market conditions, particularly attitudes toward "new issues" and speculative "glamor stocks." Both of these factors may vary substantially over time and, in fact, often follow cyclical patterns. Their influence may be such that it is much easier to start NTBF's in some years than in other years.

This study covers a limited period and does not permit an examination of the influence of widely differing rates of economic activity upon technical entrepreneurship. It has not involved the gathering of data about growth rates of particular industry sub-segments or measures of the availability of capital, data which could be useful in relating these factors to rates of entrepreneurship. Such extensions of this research are left until another time.

THE INDIVIDUAL ENTREPRENEUR

Under a given set of conditions, some will dream of entrepreneurship, some will find such thoughts to be foreign and unappealing, and a few will actually take the step of starting new firms. What characterize these rare individuals who are attracted or driven to entrepreneurship?

11

Roberts and Wainer have studied more than 200 technical entrepreneurs in the Boston area. They found that an unusually high
percentage of technical entrepreneurs (50%) came from homes in
which the father was self-employed, that the average education
of founders studied was an M.S. degree plus some courses, and
that the average age when starting the new company was 32.[1]

Industrial Research magazine published a study of science entrepreneurs in the Philadelphia area; 35 founders were interviewed.
These entrepreneurs averaged 35 years of age when founding
their firms, and 30 of 35 had college degrees, with nine having
advanced degrees.[2]

Collins and Moore studied the founders of 110 manufacturing
companies in Michigan; these were primarily not high-technology
firms. In their sample, the median educational level was a high
school diploma, two-thirds of the founders came from families
described as "poor," an unusually high percentage (55%) were
either foreign – born or first generation Americans, and a substantial percentage (25%) had fathers who were entrepreneurs. One
of their interesting conclusions was that the typical entrepreneur
finds it difficult to work for others and difficult to function in the
hierarchies of established organizations.[3]

Hoad studied 95 manufacturing businesses started in Michigan
during the year ending June 30, 1960; most of these firms were
not technically oriented. Only 26 of the 95 firms had founders with
bachelors degrees or above.[4]

THE INDIVIDUAL ENTREPRENEUR IN PALO ALTO

In this study, the 30 founders studied intensively in the Palo Alto
area had a variety of backgrounds but the "typical" (median)
founding group can be described as follows:

The firm is started by two founders, both of whom are in the middle
thirties. One usually can be described as the "driving force." He
conceives the idea and enlists the other founder. They come from
the same established organization, and got to know each other
there. One is in engineering development and the other is in marketing. Often, they have achieved significant prior success, with
titles such as section head or director of engineering being common. Their education includes B.S. and M.S. degrees, typically in
electrical engineering. Exhibits III-1 through III-5 give data in
greater detail.

In general, the Palo Alto technical entrepreneurs seem comparable
to those studied in Boston and Philadelphia with respect to those
characteristics on which common data have been gathered: age
and education.

There is a marked contrast with the non-technical entrepreneurs
studied by Collins and Moore and also by Hoad in regard to education; clearly technical entrepreneurs are more highly educated
than the founders of the typical manufacturing firm. This is not
surprising, considering that much of the initial competitive

Exhibit III–I

SIZE OF FOUNDING GROUP AND NUMBER
OF PARENT ORGANIZATIONS REPRESENTED

Size of Founding Group

Number of Parent Organizations	1	2	3	4	5	6 or more	Total
1	9	5	2	3	2	1	22
2		3	3				6
3				1			1
4				1			1
Total	9	8	5	4	3	1	30

mode = 1 founder

median = 2 founders

mean = 2.9 founders

Exhibit III–2

EDUCATION OF FOUNDERS*
HIGHEST DEGREE RECEIVED

No college degree	1
B. S. or B. A.	12
M. S.	6
M. B. A.	2
Ph. D.	8
M. D.	1
	—
Total number of founders	30

13

*For firms with multiple founders, data are for that founder interviewed only. (In most instances, interviewee could be defined as the "driving force.")

Exhibit III-3
NUMBER OF PREVIOUS EMPLOYERS
PRIOR TO FOUNDING COMPANY*

Number of Previous Employers	1	2	3	4	5	6	Total
Number of Founders*	0	9	8	11	2	1	30

mode   = 4 employers
median = 3 employers
mean   = 3.4 employers

*Defined as full-time positions held since getting bachelor's degree and not including military service.

Exhibit III-4

PRIOR LEVEL OF RESPONSIBILITY OF FOUNDERS

	No Subordinates: Bench Engineer, Salesman, or Staff Analyst	Section or Project Leader	Policy-Making Level: Vice-President, Chief Engineer, Marketing Manager, President, etc.	Consultant	Total
Number of Founders	5	9	15	1	30

Exhibit III-5

MAJOR FUNCTIONAL RESPONSIBILITY OF FOUNDERS*

	Prior Position				
	Marketing	R & D	Manufacturing or Development & Manufacturing	General Management	Total
Number of Founders	5	9	6	10	30

*Note: Many of the founders were not easily classified. Those in small organizations or with product responsibility often had broad and shifting responsibilities.

strength of an NTBF is based upon the technical knowledge of its founders, knowledge often based upon advanced education.

There appears to be an interesting contrast with the Collins and Moore study. Based upon psychological tests and depth interviews relating to personal histories and career patterns, they concluded that founders of manufacturing firms had had life-long patterns of relating ineffectively to authority. They often came from homes where the father had died or was not respected. In school, their restlessness, refusal to accept routine, and inability to get along with teachers often led to an early departure. They had not found it easy to work for employers and had rarely stayed long with one firm. They were described as "men who have failed in the traditional and highly structured roles available to them in society."[5]

Founders of NTBF's may differ from the entrepreneurs studied by Collins and Moore in regard to these basic psychological attitudes. Detailed childhood histories and psychological test results are not not available for these technical entrepreneurs.[6] However, data on educational and career backgrounds suggest important contrasts.

Technical entrepreneurs apparently <u>have</u> functioned effectively in the established educational structure. They were willing to go to school for many years, and apparently were successful at it, inasmuch as the typical founder had B.S. and M.S. Degrees.

With respect to career patterns, many of the founders clearly <u>were successful</u> in established organizations. In their previous positions before becoming entrepreneurs, the 30 founders studied included only five (17%) who did not have any subordinates; 50% had advanced to positions of major responsibility, including vice-president, general manager, sales manager, or director of engineering. (See Exhibit III-4)

In that phase of the research involving interviews with senior executives of established firms, they were asked their perceptions of the average level of competence of the entrepreneurs who had left their firms. How did these men compare with the average technical manager or engineer who stayed on with the established organization? Without exception, these senior executives replied that those who had become entrepreneurs were better than the average – more competent, more energetic, more concerned about the progress of the organization. They sometimes added that they considered some spin-offs to be a good sign, an indication that their company was employing the right kinds of people.

These founders did have a history of some job switching, but this may be typical of the West Coast electronics industry (Exhibit III-3). The typical founder was quite frustrated in his current position when he made the decision to strike out on his own. (Data relating to motivations are discussed at length in Chapter IV.) These may be the kinds of men who are not easy to keep contented in established organizations. However, as measured by their positions in the management hierarchy, the Palo Alto founders were men who left successful careers in established organizations to become entrepreneurs.

16

CONCLUSION

The decision to found an NTBF occurs rarely, for most engineers and technical managers never start their own companies. In many parts of the country, including some where substantial numbers of engineers are employed, the event has apparently never occurred. In trying to understand the elements which interact to culminate in this rare event – the birth of an NTBF, we shall use an analytical framework which focuses primarily upon three major influences: the entrepreneur himself, the incubator organization, and various external factors.

The typical technical entrepreneur is in his thirties, has a master's degree, and has achieved considerable professional success in his prior position. In the following chapters, we shall see how certain factors create an environment in which such a man may choose to take the step of starting his own firm.

[1] E. B. Roberts and H. A. Wainer, "New Enterprises on Route 128," Science Journal, December 1968.

[2] _____, "The Science Entrepreneur," Industrial Research, February 1967.

[3] O. E. Collins and D. G. Moore, The Enterprising Man, East Lansing: Bureau of Business and Economic Research, Michigan State University, 1964.

[4] W. M. Hoad, Management Factors Contributing to the Success or Failure of New Small Manufacturers, Ann Arbor: Bureau of Business Research, Graduate School of Business Administration, University of Michigan, 1964.

[5] Collins and Moore, op cit, p. 243.

[6] At this time, Dr. John Komives of the Center for Venture Management is engaged in a research project wherein technical entrepreneurs in the Palo Alto area have been asked to complete certain psychological tests. Findings from this project should provide additional evidence as to whether technical entrepreneurs have the strong resistance to authority found by Collins and Moore in their study on non-technical manufacturing entrepreneurs.

CHAPTER IV

Incubator Organizations

The established organizations in a particular area affect regional entrepreneurship to an important degree. Any established firm is a potential incubator organization, employing and influencing potential entrepreneurs who may "spin off" to establish their own firms.

Regional entrepreneurship is closely related to the established firms or incubator organizations located in that same region. New firms are typically founded by entrepreneurs who are already employed in organizations in the same geographical area. In the Palo Alto area, it was found that 97.5% of the new companies (237 of 243) had one or more founders who were previously working in the area. In 92.2% of the new firms (224 of 243) all of the founders were already located there. One might presume that the Palo Alto area would be particularly attractive to the mobile entrepreneur, both because of its living conditions and the presumed advantages of being located in a "complex" of related firms. Despite these advantages, technical entrepreneurs have not come frequently from other parts of the country to start NTBF's in Palo Alto. Technical entrepreneurs tend to start firms where they are already living and working.

Interviews with founders suggest why they tend to start firms where they are already located. The tremendous number of tasks involved in getting a business started, including securing people and facilities and establishing relationships with suppliers and customers, is made much easier if the founder can rely upon contacts and knowledge already acquired in a particular area. In addition, it becomes possible to get some of these tasks started, to begin laying the groundwork, before abandoning the old job altogether.

The significance of these findings is that technical entrepreneurship in a particular area appears to be related closely to the incubator organizations already there. Unless such incubator organizations exist in a region, it is unlikely that there will be any new, technologically-based firms born there.

NATURE OF PRODUCTS OR SERVICES OFFERED

Established organizations in a given region also affect the kinds of new firms founded there. An entrepreneur typically starts his new firm to exploit that which he knows how to do best. This usually is related to the market and technical knowledge which he learned and helped to develop in the parent firm. In 85.5% of the cases studied in Palo Alto, the new firm served the same general market or utilized the same general technology as the parent company or companies. (See Exhibit IV-1.) For instance, the micro-wave laboratory of one large corporation had two spin-offs, both of which emphasized micro-wave technology. One competed directly with the parent firm; the other utilized similar technology, but emphasized segments of the market which the large firm had ignored. In another case, a semiconductor firm had an equipment division which designed and manufactured equipment for producing semi-

Exhibit IV-1

COMPARISON OF THE TECHNOLOGY AND
MARKET OF THE NEW FIRM TO THOSE OF THE
PARENT FIRM

(n = 220)

Technology

	Similar to Parent	Different from Parent
Market Similar to Parent	139 firms 63.2%	1 firm .5%
Different from Parent	48 firms 21.8%	32 firms 14.5%

Exhibit IV-2

NUMBER OF FIRMS WITH SINGLE FOUNDER AND WITH
MULTIPLE FOUNDERS

	Number of Firms	
Single Founder	88 –	39%
Multiple Founders	136 –	61%
Total Firms	224	100%

Exhibit IV-3

NUMBER OF FIRMS STARTED BY MULTIPLE FOUNDERS FROM
ONE OR MULTIPLE PARENT ORGANIZATIONS

Organizations	Number of Firms	
Single Parent Organization	78 –	57%
Multiple Parent Organizations	58 –	43%
Total Firms with More than One Founder	136 –	100%

21

*Does not include 88 individual founders who started companies by themselves. The principal parent firm is that parent firm accounting for the largest number of members of the founding team. If there are an equal number of founders from two organizations, one is arbitrarily designated as the principal parent.

conductors. There were four spin-offs from this division, all of which concentrated on semiconductor fabrication equipment.

Even though the founder may have worked in other fields in previous jobs, it is in the job which he has just left that he gains the most up-do-date knowledge of markets and technologies. This has implications in helping to explain spin-off rates from established organizations. Potential entrepreneurs within some firms are acquiring technical and market knowledge which cannot easily be applied in a new firm.

Industries vary widely in the extent to which there are attractive economic opportunities which can be exploited by new firms. If an industry is growing rapidly and if there is a high rate of technical change, there may be pockets of opportunity for the fledgling firm; a group of engineers with a product idea may be able to establish a competitive advantage in some segment of the market. Established firms in such an industry are teaching potential entrepreneurs skills which can be applied directly in a small or new firm, and the result may be a high spin-off rate. By contrast, an established firm in an industry which requires heavy capital investment or large organizations to compete is likely to have a low spin-off rate. For instance, many of the employees of an aerospace prime contractor or a large-scale producer of consumer electronic products are acquiring technical and market knowledge which would be difficult to apply on a small scale. On several occasions, the author has talked to engineers in large midwestern firms who hoped to become entrepreneurs. When asked what they could do better than their future competitors, they usually replied that they could produce on a mass basis at slightly lower cost. When asked about the investment required to put them into business, they usually concluded that at least one or two million dollars was required. Their firms usually did not have any spin-offs.

An important consideration in whether an established firm functions as an incubator is the nature of its business, and, in particular, whether the potential entrepreneurs within the organization are developing skills which can easily be exploited by a new firm.

ASSEMBLY OF THE ENTREPRENEURIAL TEAM

The incubator firm provides the organizational environment within which a team of founders can be assembled. It is often the staging area, where prospective co-founders become acquainted, judge each other's skills, and develop plans.

A new firm should have all of the major functional activities – including R & D, production, and marketing – performed reasonably well; there should be no areas of glaring weakness. Since there are few employees in the early days, this means that the founder or founders often must be able to design, produce, and sell the product themselves. Because of these needs, NTBF's are often started by groups of entrepreneurs, whose talents complement each other. In the Palo Alto area, about 61% of the new firms were started by teams of two or more founders. (See Exhibit IV-2.) In addition to the

Exhibit IV-4

NUMBER OF INDIVIDUAL FOUNDERS ON FOUNDING TEAMS
FROM ONE PARENT, "FROM PRINCIPAL PARENT," OR
MINOR PARENT ORGANIZATIONS*

Number of Founders

Single Parent Organization	230	– 54%	⎤ 78%
"Principal Parent Organization"	99	– 24%	⎦
Minor Parent Organization	91	– 22%	22%
Total Entrepreneurs on Founding Teams	420	– 100%	

Exhibit IV-5

MOTIVATION OF ENTREPRENEURS

(n = 30)

Forced to leave previous position	13%
Happy in previous position	17%
Frustrated in previous position:	
Quit without specific plans	30% ⎤ 70%
"Would have quit even if had not become an entrepreneur"	40% ⎦

broader base of talent which a group of founders provides, there are psychological advantages. A typical comment was, "As you take this step, it gives you encouragement to know that others are with you."

How does an entrepreneurial team get together? Typically the team is assembled by one man, who might be termed the "driving force," and who generally becomes the president of the new company. The founders may have gotten to know each other in various ways, including in engineering school, in prior jobs, or through being neighbors. However, in most instances, the incubator organization plays the role of bringing the founders together. For the entrepreneur is already in the incubator organization when he begins to develop specific plans relating to the proposed new firm, and it is in the incubator organization where he has the opportunity to judge closely the compatability and probable contributions of possible co-founders.

Of the firms started by teams of two or more entrepreneurs, 57% of the teams had all of the founders from the same parent firm. (See Exhibit IV-3.) Even when more than one parent firm was represented, it was common to have most of the team from the same organization. Of all of the individual entrepreneurs who were on founding teams of two or more founders, 78% were either from the same parent firm as their co-founders, or were from the "principal parent firm" for that management team.[1] (See Exhibit IV-4.)

One implication of these findings is that the birth of NTBF's is influenced by whether there are conditions under which founding teams can be assembled. Thus, new firms would be more likely to spin off from organizations in which the marketing, development, and manufacturing people have the opportunity of working closely together.

Testing the hypothesis that spin-off rates are related to the way a firm is organized would require data not now available. However, findings presented in Chapter V on spin-off rates from organizations of different size are consistent with these conclusions; in particular, small firms, characterized by close contact among functional areas, have higher spin-off rates.

A functional organization in which engineers talk primarily to engineers and manufacturing men talk primarily to manufacturing men seems relatively unpromising from the standpoint of organizing entrepreneurial teams.[2] Probably the least favorable structure for organizing such teams would involve an installation located in a small, relatively isolated town – away from similar businesses, and organized so that the people there are engaged primarily in only one activity – such as manufacturing. Incidentally, there are many engineers in midwestern towns employed in just such organizations.

---

[1] The principal parent firm is that parent firm accounting for the largest number of founders of the founding team. If there are an equal number of founders from two organizations, one is arbitrarily designated as the principal parent.

[2] One of the founders interviewed had organized his company on a functional basis, rather than a product-decentralized basis, because he thought that this would result in a lower subsequent spin-off rate from his own firm.

MOTIVATION FOR THE DECISION

The established firm also appears to influence to a marked degree the motivation of the individual entrepreneur as he makes this significant personal decision to quit his job and to undertake the risk and effort of getting a company started.

Of course, the motivations are complex and many personal considerations come to bear, including an individual's attitude toward risk-taking and the perceived social-status, risks, and rewards associated with entrepreneurship. In any given environment, some men will become entrepreneurs and some will not. Granting the complexity of these decisions, it was clear that the entrepreneurs studied in Palo Alto were motivated to an important degree by events which they perceived to be happening within the incubator organizations.

In most instances, spin-offs were indications of frustration within the established firm. Of thirty founders studied intensively, 70% could be described as highly frustrated in their previous positions. Of the remaining founders, 17% described themselves as happy in their previous positions and said they would have stayed in the parent organizations if they had not become entrepreneurs. An additional 13% were forced to leave through backruptcy, being "laid off," or the closing out of branch offices or plants with no attractive opportunities elsewhere in the company. (See Exhibit IV-5.)

It might be argued that *post hoc* rationalizations are unreliable, and that, in fact, these entrepreneurs may not have been so highly influenced by conditions within the incubator firms. However, many of these situations were relatively unambiguous with respect to this relationship, e.g. the 13% who were forced to leave by bankruptcy, etc.

Extreme frustration was particularly evident for those founders (30% of the total) who quit their previous jobs without any specific plans for the future. A typical situation involved an engineer in charge of one product line in a small firm. He had grown increasingly disturbed over his relationship with his superior whom he belived to be lacking in competence; he also thought that he was being inadequately paid, considering the long hours he was working. When a proposal he had developed to expand his product line was rejected, he quit. Later that day, he asked himself, "What am I going to do now?"

Forty per-cent of the founders said that, even if they had not started their own businesses, they would have quit their previous positions. They usually went on to add a series of epithets about the extent of their frustration. One man commented, "I had become disillusioned; my immediate supervisor was a 'clod.' By the end of each day, I was so frustrated that it took three or four martinis for me to relax." One group of engineers, disturbed by what they saw as an absentee management unreceptive to new ideas, advertised themselves as a "department available" in the classified section of the newspaper. The major cause of frustration, broadly stated, was a lack of confidence in management, a feeling that poor decisions were being made and that the division or company faced an unpromising future. As these men described their frustration, two areas of concern were mentioned again and again. One centered upon the selection and development of managers and was reflected in comments such as: "I could see the wrong people being placed in key positions;" or, "I couldn't respect my supervisor." The other area of major concern had to do with investment in products and technologies: "Management was investing in the wrong new products;" or, "The president wanted to take the company in a direction in which I had neither interest nor competence."

To what extent were these feelings the reflection of personal disappointment because pet projects were not supported or expected promotions not received? Making such a judgment is not easy, but the detailed comments of the entrepreneurs suggest that an element of personal disappointment was present in only about half of the situations studied. In these instances, there typically was a growing feeling of frustration and lack of confidence in the future of the firm; the turning down of a particular project or the loss of an expected promotion acted to trigger the entrepreneur's decision to leave the firm. The following comment is typical:

> "All of us (who left) had grown increasingly irritated in the prior company. We were expected to work long hours, without any indication this was appreciated. The firm was poorly managed. The key engineers in the firm were on the verge of leaving. Finally, management decided not to produce a product line we had sweated to develop. Two of us quit on the spot."

In about half of the situations, there was no evidence of personal disappointment, but rather a general disillusionment about the firm's prospects. A former manager of a technical group commented:

> "After the acquisition, the parent company left us alone and hoped that profits would come. The local management was inadequate. Although they assured me that I had a bright future with the parent corporation, that would have meant going to corporate headquarters in the east, which I didn't want to do. It appeared the company would continue to disintegrate. It has since withered away."

CONCLUSION

Clearly, regional entrepreneurship depends upon local incubator organizations which hire, train, bring together, and motivate prospective entrepreneurs.

How might one design an organization to have a high or low spin-off rate? A firm with the following characteristics probably would be a very good incubator. It would be in a rapidly growing industry which offered opportunities for the well-managed small firm with good ideas; it would be a small firm or would be organized as a series of "small businesses;" it would be good at recruiting ambitious, capable people; and it would periodically be afflicted with internal crises sufficient to frustrate many of its professional employees and lead them to believe that opportunities were being missed and that *even I could manage the business better."* This, incidentally, is a fairly good definition of many of the firms which have been established in the Palo Alto area in the past ten years.

CHAPTER V

Spin-Off Rates From Established Organizations

In studying technical entrepreneurship, one can observe that some established organizations seem to be prolific incubators. If asked about the chief "product" of some of these firms, one might reply "entrepreneurs." Other established firms seem to have relatively few spin-offs.

There has been little previous investigation of the spin-off relationship. Analysis of spin-off rates from different kinds of organizations should indicate the extent to which, in an area of active entrepreneurship, organizations function differently as incubators. Such analysis should also indicate spin-off rates by type of established organization. This chapter focuses upon analysis of spin-off rates.

Any new, independent, technologically-based firm is defined as a "spin-off" regardless of whether or not it is engaged in the same kind of business as the established organization which the founders left. (Recall that about 85% of the new firms exploited the same general technology or served the same markets as the parent firms.) Although an entrepreneur may have worked for several previous employers, the organization which employed him immediately prior to his starting the new firm is defined as the incubator firm. If the new company is started by a group of entrepreneurs who represent different incubator organizations, (which was the case in about 26% of the new firms), the spin-off calculations are based upon the proportion of the founding group from each firm. Thus, if one founder is from Company A and one from Company B, the new firm is counted as 0.5 spin-offs from each parent company.[1] Only "full-time" founders were counted in determining spin-off rates.

Spin-off "rates" from an established organization are calculated as follows: the numerator consists of the total number of spin-offs from the organization during the period from January 1, 1960, to July 1, 1969; the denominator is the average number of total employees during this period.[2] Thus, a firm which employed an average of 500 employees during the 1960's and which had employed all of the founders of three new firms and half of the founders of another would have a spin-off rate for the decade of 3.5/500.

SPIN-OFF RATES

Based upon data developed in this study, one can calculate the average spin-off rate for the decade of the 1960's for the high-technology companies on the San Francisco Peninsula considered as a group. The average total employment for these companies was about 77,600.[3] There were 243 new firms identified for which incubator firms could be specified. Only six of these new companies (2.5% of the total) were started by founders who were from out of the area; 237 of these firms had one or more founders who had

---

[1] Some founders are more important than others and, ideally, one might wish to weight the spin-off calculations accordingly. However, information as to relative importance of founders is difficult to obtain and evaluate.

[2] Ideally, one might wish to base spin-off calculations on the number of professional employees only, since most technical entrepreneurs are from this group. However, these data were not available.

[3] Estimates of employment were arrived at by first using the survey data collected annually by the Western Electronic Manufacturers Association. These data were supplemented with employment figures for additional organizations known not to have been included in that survey.

been working for companies on the San Francisco Peninsula. The spin-off rate for the high-technology companies as a group was 237/77,600 or 1/306.

Spin-off rates were calculated for 325 firms, including many no longer in operation. The distribution of spin-off rates for these firms is given in Exhibit V-1. There were a number of companies, particularly small ones, which had had no spin-offs.

Among firms that had 3 or more spin-offs, the range in spin-off rates was from 1/3100 to 1/14. Sample spin-off rates, indicating the wide degree of variation, are given in Exhibit V-2. This wide variation is particularly notable when considering that all of these companies were in the same regional environment. Those geographical factors which might encourage entrepreneurship, including the availability of venture capital and the possible advantages of being located in a "complex" of related firms, presumably acted to encourage prospective entrepreneurs in all of the organizations in the area. Despite this, one finds vast variations in the extent to which established firms act as incubators of new firms.

THE EFFECT OF ORGANIZATIONAL SIZE

What kinds of organizations have high spin-off rates and what kinds have low rates? In essence, from what kinds of organizations do entrepreneurs come?

Spin-off rates were calculated for incubator firms in different size classes. Established firms were classified as under 500 employees, over 500 employees, and as subsidiaries of under 500 employees. As can be seen in Exhibit V-3, the spin-off rate for "small" firms was about ten times that for "large" firms. The spin-off rate for "small subsidiaries" was about eight times that for large firms.

These findings appear to be consistent with those reported by Forseth in his analysis of spin-off rates at four M.I.T. laboratories, although differences in definitions used make direct comparison difficult. In his analysis, the size of a laboratory was based upon total funding. He reported that spin-off rates were inversely related to laboratory size, that is, that the smallest laboratory had the highest spin-off rate, etc.[4]

It is common knowledge that certain large firms in the Palo Alto area have been important incubators. Companies such as Fairchild Semiconductor and Ampex have received considerable publicity in this respect. It is thus interesting that the highest spin-off *rates* belong to the classes of small firms and small subsidiaries.

The research suggests several reasons why small firms have higher spin-off rates:

1.   Large firms are often engaged in activities which require heavy capital investment or large organizations to compete; economies of scale are often important. A new firm, established to compete in these same seg-

---

[4]D. Forseth, The Role of Government Sponsored Research Laboratories in the Generation of New Enterprises, S. M. thesis, Sloan School of Management, Massachusetts Institute of Technology. 1966.

Exhibit V-1

FREQUENCY DISTRIBUTIONS OF
ESTIMATED SPIN-OFF RATES

(n = 325)

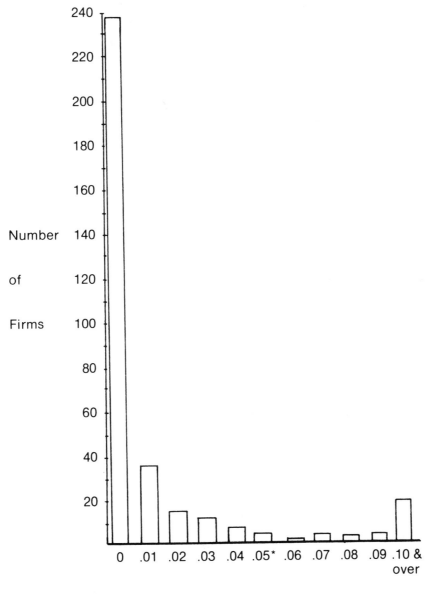

* .04 < Rate ≤ .05
The value at zero is a point reading, not an interval.

Exhibit V-2

SELECTED SPIN-OFF RATES FROM
ESTABLISHED ORGANIZATIONS
DURING DECADE OF THE 1960's

Company	No. of Spin-Offs/Mean Employment	Spin-Off Rate
A	8.3/25,700	1/3,100 = .0003
B	.33/750	1/2,250 = .0004
C	2.8/2400	1/850 = .0012
D	12.75/7,450	1/584 = .0017
E	1.7/600	1/283 = .0028
F	6.05/770	1/127 = .0079
G	3/180	1/60 = .0017
H	3/42	1/14 = .071

Exhibit V-3

SPIN-OFF RATES FROM ESTABLISHED FIRMS
BY SIZE CLASS OF ESTABLISHED FIRM
DURING DECADE OF THE 1960's

Established Firms, Size Class*

	Less than 500 Personnel	More than 500 Personnel	Subsidiary Less than 500 Personnel	All Firms
Spin-Offs/Average Total Employment	96.5/5,800	120.0/70,300	20.5/1,500	237.0/77,600
Average Spin-Off Rate	1/59.2=.017	1/586=.0017	1/73.2=.014	1/306=.0031
Ratio of Rate to Rate of "Large Companies"	9.7:1	1:1	8.0:1	1.8:1

*Does not include spin-offs from universities.

If these spin-off rates were treated as random samples, the probability that all three samples come from the same population, i.e., that the three rates do not differ significantly, is less than .001.

Exhibit V-4

SPIN-OFF DATA
SELECTED NON-PROFIT ORGANIZATIONS

	Number of New[a] Firms Spun-Off	Number of Spin-Offs/ Mean Employment	Spin-Off Rate
Non-Profit Research Institute[b]	3	1.8/1220	1/678 = .0015
Government Research Center	1	1/1950	1/1950 = .0005
University – (engineering faculty and research associates)[c]	2	2/245	1/122 = .0082
(engineering faculty, research associates, and graduate students)[d]	2	2/1040	1/520 = .0019
(engineering, physical[e] sciences, and business)	4	3.75/2760	1/736 = .0014

[a] Number of new firms founded with at least one founder from the organization listed. Because some founders may have been from other organizations, these may count as fractional spin-offs in calculating spin-off rates.

[b] Various non-technologically oriented consulting firms have also spun-off; they are not included. Only those professional and support personnel associated with engineering and the physical sciences are included in the base population which constitutes the denominator.

[c] New firms founded by people from the engineering school divided by average number of engineering faculty and research associates.

[d] New firms founded by people from the engineering school divided by average number of engineering faculty, research associates, and graduate students.

[e] New technologically-based firms founded by people from any part of the university divided by average number of faculty, research associates, and graduate students in engineering, physical sciences, and business school.

ments of industry, may be at a substantial disadvantage. By contrast, the employees of smaller firms are, by definition, learning how to do things which can be exploited by a small firm.

2. Professional employees in small firms develop rather broad backgrounds, often assume substantial responsibilities at early stages of their careers, and learn about the particular problems of managing a small firm. This experience constitutes a valuable education for the prospective entrepreneur. There is close contact among the managers in different functional areas so that it is easier to assemble a team of entrepreneurs with the requisite skills in development, manufacturing, and market.

3. There is probably a self-selection process, whereby those who choose to go to work for small and new firms are the most prone to be entrepreneurially inclined. These attitudes are likely to be reinforced in the small firm environment, as the technical employee learns what is involved in managing a small company and sees before him the living example of a successful entrepreneur – his employer.

4. Large firms probably employ a higher percentage of non-professional employees. These workers are less likely to become technical entrepreneurs than the engineers and managers. Thus, a higher percentage of the total employees in a small firm are potential entrepreneurs.

The extremely high spin-off rate for small subsidiaries is probably due, in part, to the above-mentioned factors. In addition, most of these subsidiaries had, at one time, been independent companies which were subsequently acquired. The management then had to adjust to being no longer independent. Terms of the acquisition often had made them relatively wealthy and liquid; the financing of new ventures was thus more feasible.

NON-PROFIT ORGANIZATIONS

To what extent do technical entrepreneurs come from non-profit organizations? Substantial publicity has been given to the fact that some new firms have been started by professors and students from engineering schools. In fact, it is often believed that the development of a complex of technically-oriented firms requires the proximity of a strong university.[5]

In the Palo Alto area, three major non-profit organizations employing technical personnel are Stanford University, Stanford Research Institute, and the Ames Research Center of the National Aeronautics and Space Administration. Lists of known spin-offs from each organization were developed; as a check on the completeness of these lists, senior personnel from each organization were consulted to determine whether any omissions could be identified. For each of these organizations, spin-off rates were calculated. The findings are listed in Exhibit V-4. The definitions given previously were applied, so that only new, technologically-based firms founded since 1960 were included. Spin-off firms providing consulting of a non-technical nature were excluded.

The spin-off rate for the non-profit research institute (1/678) is about the same as that for large companies as a group. The rate for the government laboratory (1/1950) is very low, in fact one of the lowest rates encountered for any organization studied. The university spin-off rate varies from 1/122 to 1/736, depending upon the base population used. The appropriate population might be defined solely as engineering faculty and research associates; it might also be broadened to include faculty, research associates, and graduate students in engineering, the physical sciences, and business.

In total, these non-profit organizations have served as incubators for slightly less than 3% of the NTBF's founded in the 1960's. The principal incubators have been the industrial firms.

The fact that the Stanford University School of Engineering (one of the most prestigious in the country) has had relatively few spin-offs was surprising. There appears to be a marked contrast with the experience at the Massachusetts Institute of Technology; M.I.T. and its laboratories appear to have had much higher spin-off rates.[6] It is difficult to make direct comparisons of data, because of differences in definitions used; for instance, in this study of Palo Alto spin-offs, part-time businesses, as well as management consulting and computer software firms, were not included. Situations in

---

[5]For instance, see: E. Deutermann, "Seeding Science-Based Industry," New England Business Review, December, 1966, and "More Professors Put Campus Lab Theories to Work in Own Firms," Wall Street Journal, March 13, 1967.

[6]Roberts and Wainer, op cit, pp. 78-79.

which professors served as part-time consultants were not counted as university spin-offs. Further research, focusing upon differences in the Stanford and M.I.T. experience would be illuminating. One factor which may account for some differences is that Stanford, unlike M.I.T., does not employ large numbers of full-time researchers in semi-independent laboratories.

In response to queries about the low spin-off rate from the government laboratory, two reasons were suggested most often by those who knew the laboratory. One was that much of the work being done there did not appear to have great commercial applicability. In addition, the typical professional employee was described as more scientifically oriented and less commercially and entrepreneurially oriented than his industrial counterpart.

VARIATIONS WITHIN LARGE ORGANIZATIONS

For some of the large, prolific incubator firms in the area, spin-off data were available for individual parts of the organization. The data are illustrated by the following examples.

a. One rapidly growing firm had eight spin-offs during the decade of the 1960's. Eighty percent of the firm's employees were in one division whose activities were concerned mainly with one large government contract and the associated follow-on contracts. Only one of the firm's spin-offs was from this division, while the remaining spin-offs were from the other 20% of the company's business.

b. One semiconductor manufacturer had about 85% of its personnel working on the development and production of semiconductor devices, with the remainder in the equipment division which developed production equipment for manufacturing semiconductors. Of the firm's six spin-offs, four were from the small equipment division.

c. One large firm had had no spin-offs from the major division which accounted for 50% of its sales. All seven of its Palo Alto spin-offs came from smaller departments which offered a variety of products and which made up the other 50% of the business.

Such evidence suggests that in large firms the spin-off rate is likely to be highest in those departments which constitute the "small businesses" of the firm. This hypothesis is entirely consistent with the finding that small firms as a class have higher spin-off rates. The reasons advanced for explaining the high spin-off rate for small firms probably also apply here. In addition, small divisions of larger firms may, on the average, be more poorly managed than the large divisions and may have more frustrated managers. This may be because of their low visibility, the fact that top management often comes from "backbone divisions," and because the small divisions lack internal bargaining power to obtain discretionary resources such as investments in new products.

CONCLUSION

The founding of new, technologically-based firms seems to be closely related to the characteristics of established "incubator organizations." In this initial attempt to examine the phenomenon of rate. The non-profit organizations have served as incubators for less than 3% of the new, technologically-based firms in the 1960's.

4. Limited evidence suggests that in large firms the largest divisions have the lowest spin-off rates.

Clearly, spin-off rates vary widely among established firms, and some kinds of organizations appear to function as incubators to a greater extent than others. This research suggests the importance of the organizational setting as a variable influencing the entrepreneurial decision.

CHAPTER VI

Regional Differences in Technical Entrepreneurship

Why does technical entrepreneurship seem to take root in some areas and not in others? In 1967, the "Panel on Invention and Innovation" took note of these regional differences:

> "Cities and regions appear to vary markedly with respect to successful generation of new technologically based enterprises. Unfortunately, there are no statistical data to show this. But our personal experiences – and we claim no more proof than that – tell us that cities and regions do vary widely in their propensity to exploit their innovative potential. We surmise that important factors exist which go beyond such indexes as the total number of scientists in the area, or the total R & D expenditures, or the availability of capital."[1]

Previous observers have pinpointed several factors which may be important in creating a favorable climate for entrepreneurship. One researcher concluded that the significant differences between the Boston and Philadelphia experiences were due primarily to two factors: the attitudes of the banks and the presence of strong graduate engineering schools.[2] The observation that the leading complexes to date have grown around strong universities has led to the conclusion that this is a critical factor, with university policies which permit and encourage consulting and close relationships with industry being additional requirements.[3] Since highly-trained technical people are mobile and often can choose where they want to live, sunshine and cultural attractions are believed to be highly desirable.[4] Local sources of venture capital, sympathetic to technical ventures, is another factor sometimes mentioned.[5]

Despite the above references, previous research into causes of regional differences in entrepreneurship has not been extensive. It is obvious that the processes influencing entrepreneurship are complex and that a number of factors act and interact. Clearly, no single factor is sufficient to create a climate favorable for entrepreneurship. One can point to regions which have strong engineering colleges, or delightful climates, or the presence of thousands of engineers, but which do not have significant technical entrepreneurship. One can also note that some regions change over time, Palo Alto had relatively little technical entrepreneurship before World War II, and most of the NTBF's founded in Minneapolis-St. Paul were started since 1950. Apparently, the regional climate for entrepreneurship can change over time, with various casual factors at work.

One approach to understanding the environmental influences upon entrepreneurship is to study how individual firms get started in an area of active entrepreneurship and to determine those regional factors which seem to exert influence. Ideally, one might wish to study such a region over time, as the rate of entrepreneurship

36

[1]Technival Innovation: Its Environment and Management, p. 13.

[2]Deutermann, op cit.

[3]D. Allison, "The University and Regional Prosperity," International Science And Technology, April 1965.

[4]J. F. Mahar and D. C. Coddington, "The Scientific Complex - Proceed With Caution," Harvard Business Review, Jan. - Feb. 1965.

[5]A. Shapero, R. Howell, and K. Draheim, The Structure and Dynamics of the Defense R & D Industry, Menlo Park, Calif.: Stanford Research Institute, 1965.

changes. One might also gain insights from explicitly studying and comparing different regions with contrasting rates of entrepreneurship.

This study, with its focus upon new firms founded in the Palo Alto region during the 1960's, does not have some of the dimensions of the "ideal study" described above. However, it does permit us to identify a number of regional factors which seem to be important, and to develop a theory of how these factors interrelate in creating a climate favorable to technical entrepreneurship.

MAJOR INFLUENCES

In "A Framework for Understanding Entrepreneurship," presented in Chapter III, three major influences upon entrepreneurship were discussed. They were the individual, the incubator organization, and "various external factors, many of them regional in nature." Although all of these may influence regional entrepreneurship, the evidence in this study relates particularly to the role of the incubator organization and those external factors which differ from region to region.

The decision to found a new firm is an intensely personal decision, and those past experiences which affect an individual's inclination to take this step are clearly important. One can speculate as to whether engineers in different parts of the country have differing inclinations toward entrepreneurship. Unquestionably, on a national scale, there is a migration of engineers to the West.[6] Possibly, those who migrate are more inclined to be risk-takers, resulting in an accumulation of engineers on the West Coast who are more likely to undertake high-risk activities such as becoming entrepreneurs. We do not have evidence relating to these interesting speculations at this time. Future research may show whether there are regional differences in these personal traits.

The nature of established incubator organizations clearly does vary substantially from region to region. As discussed in Chapter IV, the Palo Alto experience suggests that established firms influence entrepreneurship in several ways, including the location of the new firms, the nature of products or services offered, the assembly of founding teams, and the motivations of the founders. We further note that, even within an area of active entrepreneurship, established organizations vary widely in the extent to which they function as incubators.

The implications of these findings for understanding regional differences in technical entrepreneurship are the following:

1. Within a given region, unless there are established organizations employing potential technical entrepreneurs, there are unlikely to be any NTBF's founded.

2. Whether spin-offs occur depends, in part, upon the nature of the established organizations. Their size, the way they are organized, their success in recruiting capable, ambitious people, and the extent to which they

[6]Ibid, pp. 27-39.

provide satisfactions or frustrations for their professional employees are determinants of whether founders will
spin off. It is also important whether potential entrepreneurs are acquiring technical and market knowledge
which relates to areas of expanding opportunity which
can be exploited on a small scale by a new firm.

Regional differences in technical entrepreneurship reflect, in
part, regional differences in the presence and nature of established,
potential incubator organizations.

Another influence which appears to vary from region to region consists of a network of external factors, many of which appear to
depend upon past entrepreneurship. Some of these appear to be
much more important than others. They include: 1. an "entrepreneurial environment;" 2. the existence of new, small incubator firms
and a "pool" of experienced entrepreneurs; 3. the presence of
specialized sources of venture capital; 4. the role of universities;
5. the presence of a "complex" of related firms; and 6. the presence
of attractive living conditions.

ENTREPRENEURIAL ENVIRONMENT

The decision to start a new firm obviously involves considerable
risk. The prospective founder must weigh the risks and rewards of
entrepreneurship as he perceives them, and then decide whether
this step, with all of its sacrifices and uncertainties, should be undertaken by him and his family.

The environment in which a p   pective entrepreneur finds himself
can significantly affect his perceptions of the risks and rewards
involved in entrepreneurship. The San Francisco Peninsula area
has developed what might be termed an "entrepreneurial environment," and this has probably been an important factor in the high
birth rate of NTBF's in that area.

An entrepreneurial environment might be defined as a situation in
which prospective founders of new firms have a high awareness of
past entrepreneurial action, of sources of venture capital, and of
individuals and institutions which might provide help and advice.
In such an environment, surrounded by examples of success and
information about entrepreneurship, the prospective founder may
perceive the risks associated with entrepreneurship to be relatively
low and the rewards to be relatively high.

Most of the founders of the 30 companies studied intensively knew
of many examples of the action which they were considering.
Many had observed prior spin-offs from the firms they were leaving.
At the time they made the decision, 93% of the founders knew of
other founders of NTBF's; many were known personally. (Interestingly, they tended to know of successful NTBF's, but rarely of unsuccessful ones.) In thinking about the decision which they had
made, most thought that their decision had been made easier because they were located in an area in which technical entrepreneurship abounded. A typical comment was, "Men whom I had gone to

school with had already taken this step and were doing well. If they could do it, I thought I could too."

As they made the decision to start a firm, most of the entrepreneurs later described themselves as very confident. Seventy-seven percent said they admitted almost no chance of failure, and were sure they could make the new business succeed; only 13% admitted to serious concern or saw themselves as undertaking a very risky venture.

Contrast the experience of these thirty founders with that of some engineers in the Middle West recently interviewed by the author. These men were trying to become the first spin-off from a very large technically-oriented business located in a small Midwestern town. This business operates in an industry which has had many spin-offs in the Palo Alto area. These men did not know of any prior spin-offs from their company; in fact, they did not know personally any technical entrepreneurs. They did not know of any regional sources of venture capital. If they surrendered the security of their monthly paychecks and risked their life savings, they could not reassure themselves or their wives that this was a step which other men, like themselves, had taken and succeeded at. Eventually, they gave up their plans and went to work individually for other employers.

Study of the Palo Alto area during the 1960's does not answer the question of how an entrepreneurial environment gets started. Presumably, the first instances of entrepreneurship in a region take place without this influence. Each successful new firm then provides an example for others who may follow. In time, an environment may develop such that the prospective founder is exposed to many successful examples of entrepreneurship and finds it relatively easy to learn about what is involved in starting and financing a company.

THE EXISTENCE OF NEW, SMALL INCUBATOR FIRMS AND EXPERIENCED ENTREPRENEURS

An executive who is considering the major step of founding a new firm must ask himself, "What is involved in getting a company started and do I know how to do these things?" He must also consider whether managing an established small firm will present problems similar to those he has dealt with in the past.

The fact that substantial entrepreneurship has already occurred in the Palo Alto area means that many new and small firms are now located there; in many ways these small firms are almost ideal incubators. The employees in these firms are, by definition, acquiring market and technical knowledge which can be exploited by a small firm. They are also learning what is involved in managing a new, technologically-based firm. Recall that study of spin-off rates in the Palo Alto area indicated that the class of firms with less than 500 employees had a spin-off rate 10 times as high as firms with more than 500 employees.(See Chapter V.) Thus, past entrepreneurshjp generates new and small firms which seem uniquely suited to function as incubators.

Past entrepreneurship also generates experienced entrepreneurs. Some of these men stay with their firms as they grow. However, many of the firms are acquired and many of the founding teams break up. After the merger or after the fight with the co-founder, what does the former entrepreneur do? Often he turns to entrepreneurship agian. Eight of the 30 companies studied intensively in the Palo Alto area were founded by men who had been in the founding groups of other companies previously. One man was starting his fourth new business. Without exception, these men indicated that it was easier to start a company the second time, both in regard to making the decision psychologically and in regard to knowing what was involved in launching a firm.

In the Palo Alto area in the year 1968 alone, there were 44 NTBF's founded, involving some 118 individual entrepreneurs. There are probably almost 1000 experienced technical entrepreneurs in the Palo Alto area. The presence of these men makes future entrepreneurship more likely.

SOURCES OF VENTURE CAPITAL

The birth of new firms depends upon the availability of venture capital. In the Palo Alto area, a number of sources of venture capital specialize in investing in and assisting NTBF's. The presence of some of these sources is clearly related to the high level of entrepreneurship which has existed there in the past. During the 1960's, a major source of venture capital was the successful entrepreneur of the 1950's.

A typical situation involves the entrepreneur who has founded a successful firm and then later sold out; he may be wealthy and still relatively young. Often, there are many investors who previously have made money through backing his judgment; he may feel that the one thing which he knows best is how to help an NTBF get started. What does the successful entrepreneur do? In the Palo Alto area, he sometimes has become a venture capitalist, investing in and advising the next generation of entrepreneurs. His influence often extends beyond his own fortune, for there are investors willing to back his judgment again.

There are also a substantial number of experienced entrepreneurs, still managing their firms, who play a key role in advising investors and prospective entrepreneurs. One company president estimated that, on the average, he judged one new company proposal per week. If the venture looked promising he helped the prospective founder get together with what he termed his "stable of investors." This is typical of the well-developed communication networks which permit the prospective founder to make contact with sources of capital.

The success of many of the firms in the Palo Alto area has created substantial stock values, not only for the founders but also for key employees. An important source of initial capital in 43% of the

Exhibit VI-1

PRIMARY SOURCE OF CAPITAL

(n = 30)

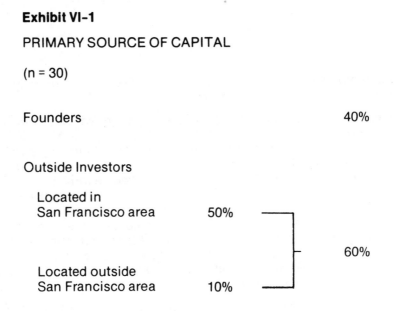

Founders   40%

Outside Investors

    Located in
    San Francisco area   50%

                                     60%

    Located outside
    San Francisco area   10%

firms studied intensively was stock held by the founders in the firms for which they had previously worked. Some of these men had been founders previously; others had been able to exercise stock options. Since stock ownership is often seen as a way of tying an executive to a firm, it is interesting to note that this ownership has often made if financially possible for key men to leave and start their own firms!

In the Palo Alto area, there are also a number of venture capital firms which specialize in investing in and advising NTBF's. A continuing flow of entrepreneurs seeking capital has provided the opportunity for such firms to develop there. Although there has been some venture capital imported from other parts of the country, most new firms have been financed locally. Of 30 firms studied intensively, 18 raised outside capital, and 15 of these raised all or a substantial part of their capital in the San Francisco Bay region. (See Exhibit VI-1.) Many of these founders believed it would have been much more difficult to sell stock in other parts of the country. (Some had, in fact, tried to do just that, with little success.) Several reasons for this belief were advanced: 1. they lacked ways of learning about and making contact with the "right" potential investors in other areas; 2. investors in the San Francisco Bay area were more likely to understand and be sympathetic to technologically-oriented businesses; 3. potential local investors could easily check into the background of the aspiring entrepreneur — they often knew him already — and they could keep in close touch with the new firms; presentations and proposals to such local investors did not have to be so elaborate.

In Palo Alto, past entrepreneurship and the wealth created by these successful firms have made possible the growth of a local venture capital industry. Future entrepreneurs are by no means assured of venture capital; however, it is relatively easy for them to make contact with institutions experienced in helping NTBF's.

Certain other regional factors, sometimes presumed to be important, appear to have played a secondary role in the Palo Alto area in the 1960's. These are discussed below.

THE ROLE OF UNIVERSITIES

There is a general feeling that a first-rate university is important in the overall process of creating a complex of technically-oriented firms.[7]

However, this study indicates that the universities have not played an important role as incubators of NTBF's. Only 6 of 243 firms studied had one or more full-time founders who came directly from any of the universities in the area or their laboratories. (See Chapter V.) In the 30 firms studied intensively, the founders did not appear to give any weight to the presence of the universities in making the decisions to start their companies.

In the early days of the development of the Palo Alto complex, many of the new firms apparently did have close relationships with Stanford, in some instances spinning off directly from the university. Some of these firms, such as Hewlett-Packard, subsequently had substantial economic impact. It might be argued that the universities played an important role in seeding and nurturing the early development of this complex.

During the 1960's, the local universities appear to have contributed to technical entrepreneurship in a less direct manner than through being major incubators. They have educated many of the entrepreneurs; in some instances, entrepreneurs first came to the Bay area to pursue a degree and then chose to stay on. (Of the 30 entrepreneurs studied intensively, 29 had university degrees; 17 of these received their last degree in the San Francisco Bay area, and 9 of these received their last degree from Stanford.) In the continuing struggle to keep abreast of current scientific knowledge, the local universities provide consulting assistance, as well as opportunities for continuing education for professional employees. They have apparently helped to attract the branch plants and laboratories which have, in turn, spun off new firms. According to the entrepreneurs interviewed, the universities have also added to the overall attractiveness of the area and have given the new firms advantages in recruiting technical personnel. However, during the 1960's in the Palo Alto area, it has been the industrial firms, not the universities, which have served as the principal incubator organizations.

A COMPLEX OF RELATED FIRMS

The many technologically-based companies in the Palo Alto area, and particularly the electronics firms, create a complex of inter-related businesses, some of which buy from and sell to each other. One might presume that an NTBF, starting in such a complex, would enjoy a competitive advantage, because of close proximity to customers and suppliers, and because of access to trained personnel. Thus, one might predict that NTBF's would be established primarily in existing complexes.

The experience of the 30 firms studied intensively indicates that location in a complex is very important for some new firms, but is not a significant competitve advantage for most of them.

Five of the 30 firms were primarily suppliers to other Palo Alto area electronic firms. These companies, emphasizing custom

---

[7]For instance, see: Deutermann, op cit; "More Professors Put Campus Lab Theories to Work in Own Firms", Wall Street Journal, March 13, 1967; Allison, op cit; Roberts and Wainer, op cit.

fabrication, relied heavily upon face-to-face contact with the technical personnel of the customer companies. For these satellite firms, initial location outside an existing complex would have been difficult if not inconceivable.

However, the rest of the founders either saw no significant marketing advantages to being located in the Palo Alto area, or noted that their primary markets were in other parts of the country. Often, these latter executives would say that, from a marketing standpoint, they would be better off to be located in the Middle West or on the East Coast.

In regard to specialized suppliers, 9 of the 30 founders saw marked or slight advantages associated with being located in the Palo Alto complex. However, the other founders thought they could have been serviced as well in almost any major city, and 4 of the founders thought that certain other locations offered advantages in regard to supplier relationships.

The ability to attract and keep good technical personnel is important for rapidly growing firms which exploit new technology to achieve a competitive advantage. Most of the founders believed that location in Palo Alto gave them an advantage in this respect. One founder commented, "In our technology the best-trained technicians in the world are located in this valley, and we're in a position to hire them."

One particular advantage of the established complex is its ability to support consultants. Almost one-third of the founders left their former jobs without specific plans for the future. In many instances, consulting provided a way for the founder to support himself while plans were crystallizing and capital was being raised.

In certain other respects, this location was considered to be relatively unattractive by the entrepreneurs. Wages for non-professional personnel, taxes, and manufacturing space are all considered to be relatively expensive in the Palo Alto area. As one founder commented, "This is not a low cost area in which to do business."

Location in an established complex offers competitive advantages for some NTBF's. However, it would be a mistake to assume that all or most of these NTBF's require location in the Palo Alto complex to be successful. On the whole, most of these firms did not appear to be located in this complex because of careful economic analyses of the implications of location. Rather, they were located there because founders tend to start new companies where they are already working, and these founders were already there.

ATTRACTIVE LIVING CONDITIONS

Potential technical entrepreneurs are usually highly trained people who could choose from many job opportunities. They are also the kind of people who are concerned about living conditions, including the quality of schools, recreational opportunities, and cultural attractions. Most observers would consider the Palo Alto area superior in regard to all of these factors. To what extent have desirable living conditions directly influenced the high rate of technical entrepreneurship on the San Francisco Peninsula?

One cannot argue with the proposition that attractive living conditions can play an important role in attracting technically-trained people to an area. For this reason, established firms often choose to locate branch plants and laboratories in such regions, where they expect to enjoy a competitive advantage in recruiting. In fact, of the 30 founders studied intensively, 14 came from elsewhere to take jobs in the Palo Alto area; in addition, other founders came to the San Francisco Bay area to get university degrees and then stayed on.

However, recall that most of the entrepreneurs were already living and working in the Palo Alto area when they founded their firms; despite attractive living conditions, very few founders were attracted from elsewhere at the time they started their companies.

For those founders who were already there, the decision to start a new firm did not seem to be influenced directly by living conditions. Exceptions were two instances in which the established organizations were to be moved to other parts of the country and the engineers or their wives did not want to go. Most of the entrepreneurs did express a liking for the region, and this may have been one factor causing them to be willing to make a permanent commitment. However, as entrepreneurs described those factors which they perceived to have influenced their decisions, opportunities and frustrations were often mentioned, but living conditions were not. The "sunshine and surf" may be a primary factor in attracting potential technical entrepreneurs to a region; however, it does not appear to play a prominent role in subsequent decisions to found new firms.

CONCLUSION

Based upon the previously discussed findings, how can we explain regional differences in technical entrepreneurship? Ideally, one would like to be able to study a region through time as the rate of entrepreneurship changes. However, based upon this intensive study of the Palo Alto area, it is possible to construct a theory about how entrepreneurially active areas get that way.

If an area is to develop technical entrepreneurship, organizations which can serve as incubators must be present or be attracted or created. Since founders tend to start firms where they are already living and working, there must be organizations which will hire, bring into the area, and train the engineers, scientists, and technical managers who may someday become technical entrepreneurs.

However, the nature of these organizations is critical in determining whether spin-offs actually occur. It is certainly not difficult to point to cities where thousands of engineers are employed, but where there is little entrepreneurship. If the established firms serve markets which are stable or declining, there is little incentive for the prospective entrepreneur to enter the field. If the established firms are in industries which require large capital investments or substantial organizations to compete, it will be difficult to assemble the critical mass needed to get a new firm started. If the potential incubator firms hire relatively undynamic people, train them narrowly, and organize so that engineers talk only to engineers, etc., then it will be difficult to assemble a founding team with the needed knowledge and skills in marketing, engineering, and manufacturing. If the established firms are well-managed and avoid periodic crises, there may be little incentive for potential founders to leave comfortable positions.

In an environment in which the established firms are as described above, there probably has been little past entrepreneurship. Under such conditions, a would-be founder will find the going difficult. If he seeks to bolster his confidence or to gain advice, he will find few successful founders who have preceded him. If he seeks to support himself as a consultant while formulating his plans and raising capital, he may find this difficult if he is in a "one company" town. Sources of venture capital experienced in investing in NTBF's may not be available locally, and making contact with possible investors may be laborious and time-consuming. In such an environment, the prospective founder's personal experience is likely to have been in large, established firms; he is likely to know little about what is involved in starting and managing an NTBF.

If there are new firms started in such an environment, the founders are likely to come from promising new ventures or particular "small businesses" within the established firms. Possibly, they involve those rare instances in which the founder comes from another geographical location or starts a new company not related to the business of the parent firm which he has left.

If the first new companies are successful, then their success begins to change the environment. These new firms are likely to be better incubators, that is to have higher spin-off rates, than the older firms which their founders left. Their success many begin to convince others that entrepreneurship is feasible and rewarding. Potential investors may be encouraged or created by the success of the new firms; financial consultants and venture capital firms may then develop. Future founders then find a more promising environment than those who went before.

The rate of entrepreneurial activity may be accelerated or diminished by a number of factors. One of the most important is the development of the markets and technologies on which the area's industry is based. If the rates of market growth and technological change decline, then technical entrepreneurship will lessen, for potential founders will find fewer areas of opportunity. Public attitudes relating to the "new issue market" are also Important, for they affect substantially the availability of venture capital.

However, if these factors are favorable, a self-reinforcing process takes place, in that past entrepreneurship makes future entrepreneurship more likely, and, in time, a high rate of entrepreneurial activity may develop.

CHAPTER VII

The Birth And Death Of Firms Over Time

How has the birth of NTBF's in the Palo Alto area changed over time? During the nine full years for which data are available, the number of new firms started annually varied from 16 in 1965 to 44 in 1968. (See Exhibit VII-1.) (During the first half of 1969, 18 foundings were identified; this number is undoubtedly understated because new firms often do not become "visible" until several months after founding, and the cut-off date for the study was July 1, 1969.)

Spin-off rates were calculated for each year, based upon estimated total regional employment in technological enterprises for each year. The spin-off rate per year varied from 1/4656 or .00021 in 1965 to 1/2170 or .00046 in 1968.[1] (See Exhibit VII-2.)

The discussion of regional factors affecting technical entrepreneurship in Chapter VI suggested that feedback mechanisms operate such that past entrepreneurship makes future entrepreneurship more likely. This leads to the conclusion that, other things being equal, the birth-rate of new firms should increase over time.

The average number of firms founded in the later years of the decade was somewhat higher than in the earlier years. (During 1960-1963, the mean number of firms founded annually was 20.2, and during 1965-1968, the mean number was 31.2.)

However, examination of birth *rates* in the scatter diagrams in Exhibit VII-2 shows a decline from a peak in 1961 to a lower level in the middle 1960's and then an increase toward the end of the decade. Evidence from this limited period does not indicate a marked increase over time in the annual birth-rate of NTBF's. Possibly, examination of a longer period of time, including the early days of the development of the Palo Alto complex, would disclose whether the birth-rate of new firms has increased over time.

VOLATILITY OF THE FIRMS

What happens to the new firms after they are founded? In studying these new companies, one is immediately impressed by their volatility. The firms seem always to be changing — their management, their ownership, even their names. After a firm is founded, the passing of each additional year increases the probability that it will have been acquired or that one or more of the founders will have left. (See Exhibit VII-3.) After five years, only slightly more than half of the NTBF's were still operated as independent firms with the original founding team intact. The actual frequency of change is undoubtedly greater, inasmuch as it is often difficult to learn about these changes.

Known instances of outright failure appear to be quite rare.[2] This contrasts sharply with an earlier study which showed the discontinuance rate for manufacturing firms as a whole to be much

---

[1] These spin-off rates are annual rates. Those calculated in Chapter V are rates for the decade, in which the numerator in the calculations is the number of firms founded during the 9½ year period studied.

[2] The failure rate may have been higher had the period of study been extended beyond mid-1969, so as to include the recession months which followed.

Exhibit VII–1
NEW ENTERPRISE FORMATION
IN PALO ALTO AREA
BY YEAR

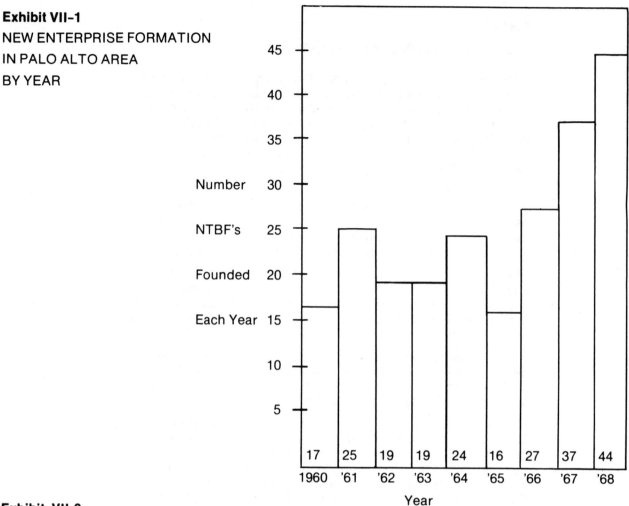

Exhibit VII-2
ANNUAL RATIO PALO ALTO NTBF BIRTHS
RELATIVE TO EMPLOYMENT BASE
NTBF's Founded / Regional Annual Employment*

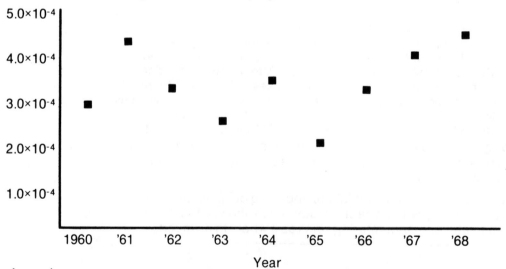

Annual

*Annual employment in technologically-oriented organizations in Palo Alto Area. Employment estimates are based upon the annual surveys of the Western Electronic Manufacturers Association, adjusted for organizations known not to be included.

Exhibit VII–3

VOLATILITY OF FIRMS

Percentage of Firms Founded Each Year Which Subsequently Failed,
Were Acquired, Or Had At Least One Founder Depart by July 1, 1969

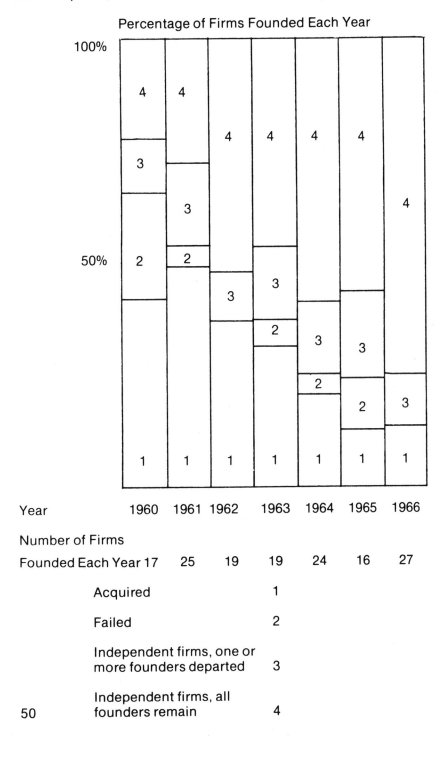

Year	1960	1961	1962	1963	1964	1965	1966
Number of Firms Founded Each Year	17	25	19	19	24	16	27

Acquired	1
Failed	2
Independent firms, one or more founders departed	3
Independent firms, all founders remain	4

50

higher than that found here. Of newly established or acquired manufacturing firms, about 40% did not survive the first 1½ years and 67% the first 4½ years. Non-survival included sale or liquidation. About 40% of the non-surviving firms were liquidated and the remainder were sold.[3]

In a study of NTBF's in the Boston area, Roberts and Wainer found "a total failure rate of only 20% over the full average four to five years period of existence of our new enterprises."[4]

It may be that the failure rate in the Palo Alto area is understated. The firms most likely to have been overlooked in the study are those which failed before they ever acquired much visibility.

However, there is another reason why the failure rate seems low. The end result for both successful and unsuccessful NTBF's is often the same — acquisition. Even a group of founders who have been unable to develop a viable business are usually worth something to an acquiring firm because of their know-how. Thus it is that one will learn that the "X Electronics Company," which had two employees, has been acquired, with the president of "X" slated to become a department head in the acquiring firm. The general feeling in the industry may be that "X" failed, yet the former founder will be quick to point out that they did not fail, but were only acquired.

The departure of founders occurs with surprising frequency, even from successful businesses. About 61% of these companies were started by two or more full-time founders. Focusing only upon these multiple-founder firms which are still in existence as independent firms after 4 or more years, one finds that only 52% still have their full founding teams intact. (See Exhibit VII-4.) As the new firm struggles for survival, the relationships in the founding group often come under intense pressure. Struggles for power are not uncommon. Some founders prove to be incompatible, lacking in the necessary skills, or unwilling to continue the fight.

Interestingly enough, even name changes are common among these new firms, particularly during the early months when things are most fluid. Of 243 firms founded during the 1960's, at least 36 had changed their names by mid-1969. Several had had more than two names. Often the change was slight, such as from Smith Development to Smith Optronics; in other instances, the successive names seemed to be completely unrelated. When the new firm had had limited success, the new name seemed to be a way to tell the world that things had changed, that with new capital, new key people, and a new name, there was to be a fresh start. It might be added that these name changes complicate the task of studying all of the NTBF's that have been founded in an area.

The high degree of change associated with these firms perhaps reached the ultimate in regard to the following company, which experienced these changes during a period of somewhat over 10 years:

[3] B. C. Churchill, "Age and Life Expectancy of Business Firms," Survey of Current Business, Vol. 35, No. 12, December 1955.
[4] Roberts and Wainer, op cit, p. 80.

Exhibit VII–4

DEPARTURE OF FOUNDERS FROM INDEPENDENT FIRMS

Year of Founding	1960	1961	1962	1963	1964	1965	1966	Total
Number of Firms Founded by Multiple Founders	9	14	11	9	9	5	13	70
Number of Multiple Founder Firms Still in Existence And Independent	3	7	7	6	7	4	12	46
Number of Independent Multiple-Founder Firms With Founding Group Intact	1	2	5	3	3	1	9	24
Percentage of Independent Multiple-Founder Firms With Founding Group Intact	33%	29%	71%	50%	42%	25%	75%	52%

"Smith Electronics" was acquired by an eastern company which renamed it and operated it as an independent subsidiary. Subsequently, this subsidiary was sold to another firm and renamed again. One of the divisions of the firm was then sold to a midwestern company and set up as an independent subsidiary with another name. When the midwestern company was itself acquired, this subsidiary was unwanted. A new corporation was set up, in part by a man who had been a key executive of the firm, and this new corporation bought the subsidiary and renamed it again.

CONCLUSION

The average number of firms founded annually was somewhat higher in the later years of the decade than in the earlier years. However, the birth-rate of such firms, taking into account the growth in regional employment, showed no marked increase.

Once established, the NTBF's appeared to have a low failure rate, in the sense of outright liquidation. However, in other ways they were quite volatile, often being acquired or enduring the break-up of founding teams.

CHAPTER VIII

Conclusions And Implications

Based upon this study of new firms founded in Palo Alto, can we explain how a particular individual founds a firm at a particular time and place?

Clearly, the individual is the starting point. New firms are started not by impersonal processes, but by men who choose to take this step. But, why do some individuals become entrepreneurs, and not others?

The processes influencing the individual entrepreneur are many and complex, yet certain events and influences appear to be important. To start at the beginning, of all those born at a given time, some may be more qualified than others for genetic reasons, inasmuch as technical entrepreneurship seems to require above average intelligence and energy levels. Childhood experiences undoubtedly exert an influence. For instance, it appears that those who have a childhood model – a father in business for himself – are more likely later to become founders. Children who have an orientation toward science and mathematics clearly are more likely to become *technical* entrepreneurs.

The population of potential technical entrepreneurs narrows substantially as educational decisions are made. Unless a person chooses to go to college and unless he chooses to study engineering or the physical sciences, he is unlikely to have the technical background necessary. Even among all engineering or science students, some are more likely to have the psychological characteristics, energy level, technical mastery, and personal goals which may later culminate in entrepreneurship.

All of the engineers and science students with a possible orientation toward entrepreneurship do not become founders. Career decisions to join particular firms are important. The organization which any given engineer joins initially and other organizations which he may move to later on become successive educational institutions. His professional experiences may or may not enable him to develop the technical, managerial, and market knowledge which could later be capitalized upon in a new firm. Some possible entrepreneurs follow career paths in which their personal experience is narrow, or in which they do not have the opportunity to have close contact with colleagues in other functional areas with whom they might form founding teams. An important factor is motivation, including the extent to which potential founders achieve satisfaction, or endure frustration in their work for established organizations. For most men, it is difficult to leave the "warm bed" of a secure and satisfying position; events must occur within the incubator firm which make them determined to make a change, despite the risks and effort involved.

Many potential technical entrepreneurs work in geographical regions where there has been little past entrepreneurship. Even if they have the motivation and the capabilities, it is difficult for entrepreneurship to take root in such an environment. In such a community, the prospective founder sees few models for the kind of behavior he is considering; there are no experienced and successful entrepreneurs from whom to seek advice and reassurance; contact with experienced sources of venture capital may be elusive and frustrating. Some possible entrepreneurs quit jobs with no specific plans for the future, but are located in communities where it is not easy to achieve self-support through consulting, while deciding what to do next. Under such conditions, the possible founder faced with supporting a family must take a job and make a commitment to another organization, with the consequence that the half-formed idea about founding a new company rarely develops in competition with the duties and loyalties associated with the new position.

Many potential technical entrepreneurs, if they ever take the step of starting their own businesses, do so when they are in their thirties. It is in this age and experience range that most men have significant experience to draw upon, as well as the youthful vigor and willingness to take risks which are necessary. Thus, for many potential entrepreneurs, the conditions which exist when they are in this period of their careers are critical. The conditions within the established organizations for which they *then* work and the regional influences where they are *then* located may determine whether they take this step at all.

Overall conditions relating to the nature of the economy and the availability of venture capital may favor some generations of potential entrepreneurs more than others. Those men in the prime entrepreneurial age who find themselves in an industry with declining fortunes or with a stock market which has just "gone sour" on new issues by NTBF's may miss their chance. By contrast, others may find themselves in the right place at the right time, with mastery of technical and market knowledge about some exploding new technology and with sources of capital literally thrusting money upon them.

The various influences upon the entrepreneurial decision are summarized in Exhibit VIII-1.

IMPLICATIONS FOR ESTABLISHED FIRMS

Although this study is primarily about the starting of new firms, there are important implications for executives of the established firms from which the entrepreneurs come.

Many spin-off firms are highly successful and, to the dismay of management, draw off the very kinds of dynamic, entrepreneurial people which the established firms would like to keep.

Some executives may be inclined to bemoan the loss of good people, but to believe that conditions beyond their control are largely responsible. For instance, they may believe that if you are in the seimconductor industry in Palo Alto during the 1960's, you are going to have some spin-offs. To some extent this may be true. However, the findings reported in Chapter V demonstrate that, even in a region of active entrepreneurship such as Palo Alto, there are wide variations in spin-off rates. Within a given industry, some firms function as incubators to a much greater extent than others.

Exhibit VIII-1

INFLUENCES UPON THE ENTREPRENEURIAL DECISION

Antecedent Influences
Upon Entrepreneur

1. Genetic factors

2. Family influences

3. Educational choices

4. Previous career experiences

Incubator Organization

1. Geographic location

2. Nature of skills and knowledge
   acquired

3. Contact with possible fellow
   founders

4. Motivation to stay with or to
   leave organization

5. Experience in a "small business"
   setting

Environmental Factors

1. Economic conditions

2. Accessibility and availability
   of venture capital

3. Examples of entrepreneurial
   action

4. Opportunities for interim consulting

5. Availability of personnel and
   supporting services;
   accessibility of customers.

Entrepreneur's
decision

Interviews with founders suggest that, if a firm has a flurry of spin-offs, there is usually something wrong. It is often an indication of considerable frustration, at least among those who have departed.

What might an established firm do to decrease its spin-off rate? This objective may be elusive for two reasons. One is that certain organizational characteristics which seem to have an influence are not easily changed. The second is that some of the actions which give promise of decreasing spin-offs might, in some circumstances, make the organization less dynamic and less profitable. Organizational attributes which may be associated with a high or low spin-off rate are summarized in Exhibit VIII-2. Some specific proposals which seem likely to decrease spin-off rates are examined below.

1. Change the hiring policies. Spin-offs appear to be a reflection, in part, of the kinds of people being hired. Screening methods could probably be developed to lessen reliance upon people who are likely to leave and become entrepreneurs. The problem is that entrepreneurially oriented people may be very valuable to an organization. The man who might start his won firm some day might be highly suited to starting a new department or to making it grow. Some of the executives interviewed commented that they see some spin-offs as a good thing: an indication that their firms are hiring the right kind of people.

2. Change the organizational structure and the typical pattern of career development. Spin-off rates appear to be highest in small firms and in departments organized as "small businesses" within large firms. Broad experience seems valuable to the entrepreneur. A functional form of organization, rather than a product-decentralized form of organization, seems likely to give fewer technical managers the broad experience of working in a small management group responsible for a product line.[1] Although such an organization might lessen executive satisfaction and thus increase the urge to spin off, it would probably lessen the capability of doing so. However, the problem with this recommendation is that decisions about organizational structure and the breadth of experience which executives acquire must be based upon many considerations. It may be desirable to organize on a product-decentralized basis to provide for greater flexibility, greater innovation, and better executive development. Narrowly trained managers may be less likely to become entrepreneurs, but they may also be less able to produce profits for their organization.

3. Concentrate upon products and markets which cannot easily be exploited by new firms. Many of the firms studied which had high spin-off rates were in industries which were attractive to new firms. Their employees were acquiring knowledge and skills which could be applied directly in new enterprises. Company strategies

---

[1]One entrepreneur had chosen to organize his own firm on a functional basis because he thought it would lessen spin-offs.

Exhibit VIII-2

INDUSTRY AND ORGANIZATIONAL ATTRIBUTES
RELATED TO THE BIRTH-RATE OF NEW FIRMS

Characteristics of Industry

Low Birth-Rate	High Birth-Rate
slow industry growth	rapid industry growth
slow technological change	rapid technological change
heavy capital investment required	low capital investment required
substantial economies of scale	minor economies of scale

Characteristics of Established Incubator Organizations

Low Birth-Rate	High Birth-Rate
large number of employees	small number of employees
functional organization	product-decentralized organization
recruit average technical people	recruit very capable, ambitious people
relatively well-managed	afflicted with periodic crises
located in isolated area of little entrepreneurship	located in area of high entrepreneurship

There is no suggestion that all of the attributes in a given column are necessarily found together or are required to bring about a given spin-off rate. Various combinations may exist.

involving commitment to fields requiring large investment, large organizations and involving substantial economies of scale seem likely to result in fewer spin-offs.

The problem, of course, is that company strategy decisions cannot be influenced solely or even primarily by spin-off considerations. Fields of rapid growth and change are attractive to established firms, yet, in many instances, are the very fields in which new firms can compete most effectively. A firm making steam radiators may avoid spin-offs, but may also also find profits to be elusive.

4. Locate in a geographical area which has had little technical entrepreneurship. There appear to be feed-back processes, such that past entrepreneurship makes future entrepreneurship more likely. Other factors being equal, a facility located where here has been little past entrepreneurship is likely to have fewer spin-offs. A firm's headquarters or principal facilities may not be moved easily, regardless of spin-off considerations. However, new facilities might be located with this as one factor in mind.

5. Seek to reduce causes of frustration among technical personnel. Since most founders seem driven from their previous positions by frustration, identification of specific causes of frustration and action to remedy these seems a promising area for management concentration.

In Palo Alto organizations, major causes of frustration centered upon decisions about investment in products and technologies and decisions about placing people in positions of responsibility. In rapidly growing, technologically-oriented firms, these decisions occur frequently, and are of great importance. If they are made poorly, the organization may appear to have a dismal future.

The answer cannot be to support all proposals or to promote all aspiring managers. In fact, many of the entrepreneurs frustrations were rooted not in personal disappointments, but in a feeling that projects were being supported and individuals being promoted who did not deserve this support. Improvement in management decision-making in these key areas may lead to a substantial pay-off in lower spin-off rates.

6. Under some circumstances, management of the established organization might consider the radical proposal of supporting spin-offs, rather than trying to prevent them.

Some technical managers may be determined to start their own firms. Some possible applications of the parent firm's technology lie outside its fields of major interest. Some product-market opportunities might better be exploited by a small firm.

In such situations, if the parent firm were to assist the entrepreneurs, possibly even serving as a source of venture capital, the new firm might be brought smoothly into being and the parent firm might benefit as an investor and through an association with a dynamic new firm.

Of course, it can be argued that too many employees would wish to become entrepreneurs and that this sponsorship might lead to the creation of potential competitors (even though the new firms presumably would not be directly competitive initially). In fact, several firms in the Palo Alto area have provided varying degrees of assistance to entrepreneurs who have spun off from them.

IMPLICATIONS FOR PROSPECTIVE ENTREPRENEURS

What are the implications of the Palo Alto experience for the man who hopes to participate in the founding of an NTBF some day? In approaching this question, it must be recognized that most founders do not seem to undertake a planned series of jobs and experiences which will bring them systematically to the threshold of entrepreneurship. One might suppose that the would-be-founder with a determination to be well-prepared would say something like the following:

> *"I plan to start my own business in the semiconductor field in about ten years. However, first I'll work for five years for the "X" firm in product development, and then I'll work for about five years in manufacturing, possibly for the "Y" firm."*

It does not seem to be that systematic or preplanned. Most jobs appear to be taken with some expectation of permanence, or at least a "we'll wait and see what develops" attitude. Specific opportunities which a new firm might exploit are rarely perceived much in advance. Later, as opportunities develop and are perceived, and as frustrations in a particular organization increase, the founder moves to act — typically with specific plans being developed in a period of months, rather than years.

We can take note of these typical career patterns while, at the same time, pointing out that the man with a long-term goal of becoming a technical entrepreneur might make intermediate career decisions which increase the probability of his eventually being able to start his own firm.

1. Established organizations serve as schools, possibly training for entrepreneurship. The would-be-entrepreneur should take a position with an organization which promises to be a good incubator. Some of the characteristics of such an organization are described in Exhibit VIII-2. Within established firms, the aspiring founder might systematically seek broad personal experience and involvement in promising newer technologies.

2. The aspiring entrepreneur should locate in an area of active entrepreneurship. He will find it easier to start a company in an entrepreneurial environment.

3.   The prospective founder might begin to acquire knowledge systematically about sources of capital, marketing practices, possible suppliers, etc. The starting of a new firm is, to a great extent, the establishing of relationships with various parties — including co-founders, investors, customers, and suppliers. Detailed knowledge and a network of relationships can be useful in the appraisal of specific opportunities, as well as in getting the new firm started.

IMPLICATIONS FOR REGIONAL ECONOMIC DEVELOPMENT

Many communities would like their own versions of Boston's Route #128. Although this goal may be unfeasible for many regions, the Palo Alto experience suggests a number of factors essential for developing and nurturing regional technical entrepreneurship:

1.   The nature of the established organizations already in a region may well be the most important single factor influencing entrepreneurship. Unless a region posesses promising incubators, or can attract or develop them, other goals for regional economic development should be sought.

It is interesting to speculate about whether a region could develop, possibly under university auspices, a self-supporting incubator organization, which would have as one of its objectives the nurturing of technical entrepreneurs. Such an organization would have to be involved in developing technologies which give promise of having commercial application. It would have to be successful in attracting very good professional people. It would be desirable if the organization could be involved in some marketing and possibly even manufacturing activities, so that skills and knowledge in these areas might be developed. There might be two kinds of people within the organization. One would be full-time employees, possibly having joined the organization without any clear expectation of becoming entrepreneurs. A second would be aspiring entrepreneurs, who had perhaps quit previous jobs, but had not yet developed specific plans relating to the founding of a firm. The latter group might be employed on a part-time basis, while devoting the rest of their time to the investigation and development of plans relating to their entrepreneurial ideas. There might be some founders just getting started, not employed at all by the organization, who utilized certain facilities and drew upon certain services while paying fees for this support.

Clearly, one can foresee difficulties with these proposals, most notably in trying to make the organization self-supporting. There also would be questions relating to conflict of interest and competition with established firms. The author sees no easy answers to these problems, but believes that entrepreneurship is most likely to be nurtured by the presence of incubator organizations with particular characteristics. In the past, some organizations have proved to be good incubators, more by accident than by design. Is it possible to develop a self-supporting organization, which would be judged to be successful if it has a high spin-off rate of successful new firms?

2. As previously discussed, past entrepreneurship develops an environment which makes future foundings more likely. What can be done in a region to create some of the features of an entrepreneurial environment?

In an area where there has been little past entrepreneurship,, potential founders often do not know of others who have done this; they have no models for this kind of behavior, and the idea of starting a firm may seem foreign to them and to their associates. An additional problem is that, under such conditions, their experience is likely to be in established, often large, firms. They lack knowledge of what is involved in managing small firms and they do not have access to experienced technical entrepreneurs who can give them advice.

Courses (or possibly short conferences) on entrepreneurship, offered at night or on weekends and aimed at the prospective technical entrepreneur, might alleviate some of these problems. The author believes, based upon personal experience as a teacher, that such courses can serve to teach skills and knowledge relating not only to administration in general, but also to the special problems associated with starting and managing a new firm. Such courses also can influence attitudes and perceptions relating to the fluence attitudes and perceptions relating to the feasibility of entrepreneurship. Outside speakers who are successful entrepreneurs, as well as cases about the founding of new, technologically-based firms, can provide a background of experience, such that entrepreneurship seems less foreign and more realizable.

The entrepreneurial environment appears to offer a number of advantages to the prospective founder wanting to raise funds. These include well-developed communication networks to bring founders and investors together, local sources experienced in appraising NTBF's and investing in them, and local wealth created by past investment or stock option participation in successful NTBF's.

The creation of local venture capital firms, with the particular goal of assisting NTBF's, might be feasible in some areas; they might participate in the Small Business Investment Company program. There are difficulties in such a proposal. It can be pointed out that most SBIC's have not been very active, and most have not invested in NTBF's. There must be qualified personnel with competence in appraising and assisting NTBF's. In many regions, such qualified personnel are not to be found or are not available for this purpose. In other instances, the amount of entrepreneurship seems insufficient to justify supporting a staff.

Possibly, a more modest and realistic proposal is to create communication networks whereby local technical entrepreneurs might find it easier to make contact with experienced investors in NTBF's located in other areas. Perhaps, particular individuals in universities or financial institutions might train themselves for this role, including the acquisition of a good understanding of the investment goals and preference of particular venture capital sources. There are obvious problems with this proposal, including the difficulty of acquiring such skills and knowledge, particularly in a region where few entrepreneurs come forth. However, methods of facilitating contact between prospective founders and those experienced in investing in and assisting NTBF's may pay large dividends.

The Entrepreneur's Quiz

Alfred North Whitehead once said, "The greatest invention of all is the invention of inventing inventions." If that is the case, the person who introduces an invention to the world — the entrepreneur — must share that greatness. An entrepreneur is a person who creates an on-going business enterprise from nothing.

Much has been written about the Entrepreneur — his desires, his motivations, and his characteristics — but most of this literature has been the result of deep scientific investigation that has neglected the "human" side of the issue.

Actually, it is very difficult to study the entrepreneur. Many, if not most, are absorbed into the business world and eventually cannot be separated from the whole. This is especially true of the majority of entrepreneurs whose ventures fail. Therefore, most previous studies have been made only of successful entrepreneurs.

During the past several years, Joe Mancuso has worked directly with more than 250 entrepreneurs in a variety of businesses and industries. He has been their confidante and sounding board. He has worked with winners and losers alike.

What makes an entrepreneur run?

Why is he more at home in his swivel chair than his living room? What makes him willing to lose his wife, his wits, and even his wad — not once, but three or four times? Why can't he be happy working for someone else? Why does he always have to go it alone? What's with him anyway?

When the other kids were out playing ball, why was he busy hustling lemonade? When his friends were dating cheerleaders, why was he organizing rock concerts? Or marketing grandmother's pickle recipe? Or inventing a better fly swatter? Is he really smarter than the rest of us? Or just crazy?

What Joe Mancuso found out was that, strangely enough, entrepreneurs do share many traits. Too many to be purely coincidental. And, when he started to dig deeper, he hit on all kinds of weird phenomena.

The questionnaire is the result of this investigation. While it lacks hard statistical back-up, it does offer insight into the entrepreneurial philosophy. Why not try it yourself to see if you've got what it takes to be an entrepreneur. You can even score it in the privacy of your home or office. No one needs to know the real truth but you.

1) An entrepreneur is most commonly the _____ child in the family.

a. oldest   c. youngest
b. middle   d. doesn't matter

There is no doubt about this answer. All the independently conducted studies agree that entrepreneurs are high achievers. Dr. David McClelland at Harvard and Dr. Stanley Schacter at Columbia have written about achievement motivation. Along with others they conclude the first born (or oldest) child in a family normally is the high achiever or in my words — an entrepreneur. In my work, this single finding was almost infallible. Especially when one considers the reality that two thirds of all people are not first born.

In fact, George Washington, Abraham Lincoln, Thomas Jefferson, Woodrow Wilson, Franklin D. Roosevelt, all were first children. Of the first 23 astronauts to go on U.S. space missions, 21 were first born. In a recent analysis of merit scholarship winners, 60% were also first born children. Well over 60% of the entrepreneurs I have worked with were first children.

A small point of interpretation here may be helpful. A high need achiever is normally the oldest child in the family but not always. Of late, families have had children in clusters. Let's say, for instance, a family has children age 12, 10, 8 and then has a new addition to the family. This new addition can also be considered a first child. An only child is also a first child, naturally.

So, if you missed this one — watch out you may be bucking some severe odds.

2) An entrepreneur is most commonly:

a. married   c. widowed
b. single   d. divorced

Here's a touchy topic. The data is fluid and interpretations vary widely. In my research with over 300 entrepreneurs primarily based in the Northeast and the West Coast, I concluded the vast majority were married. Most men in their 30's are married so this alone is not a significant finding. However, I did find the successful entrepreneur had an exceptionally supportive wife. She provided love and stability to balance the insecurity and stress of the job.

Marriages without an extremely supportive

wife ended in divorce. No doubt, divorce among entrepreneurs is higher than competing but similar professions. In addition, unsuccessful entrepreneurs had the largest divorce rate of all.

So, I guess my message is simple. A supportive (non-women liberation type) wife significantly increases the entrepreneur's chances of success. Otherwise, a successful, divorced entrepreneur is the next logical step. A strained love life is just too much to add to a strained business life.

This question was offered as an easy one to help improve your score. But it also might start you thinking.

3) An entrepreneur is most typically a
a. man   c. either
b. woman

Almost everyone gets this question right. Everybody knows only a handful of women have started an on-going business enterprise from nothing. Entrepreneurship is one of the last male strongholds. While women are making headway into business and even in sophisticated segments of business, such as management consulting, to date they haven't penetrated the entrepreneurial ranks except in a few isolated but small industries (cosmetics, fashion).

So, chalk up another correct answer.

4) An individual begins his first entrepreneurial company at which age?
a. teens   c. thirties   e. fifties
b. twenties   d. forties

The data on this topic has shifted over the past twenty years. In earlier studies by Profs. Collins & Moore (Univ. of Michigan, The Enterprising Man, 1958) found the answer to this question between 38-42 years old. Prof. Ed. Roberts at MIT found the average age in the early and mid-sixties was between 35-40 years old. My work, conducted around the late sixties and early seventies, indicates the average age to be between 30-35 years. Hence a downward shift in age has been the trend during the past 20 years. I have noticed a number of individuals who began their first entrepreneurial venture while in their twenties.

Most people answer this question correctly but the added knowledge of this shifting pattern may make this answer of "thirties" incorrect in the 1980's.

5) An individual's entrepreneurial tendency first appears evident at which of these stages?
a. teens   c. thirties   e. fifties
b. twenties   d. forties

Entrepreneurial traits show up very early in life. The enterprising boy becomes the enterprising man. I found many entrepreneurs had begun little businesses before their teens. But somewhere during high school or college these characteristics almost always blossom. This finding applies to well over 3/4 of the entrepreneurs I have surveyed. Coin and stamp collecting, rock concerts and dances, selling clothes and appliances, lawn and snow services, and a paper route are common examples.

Hence this leads me to conclude these entrepreneurial traits are obvious early.

6) An entrepreneur has typically made the following educational progress:
a. grammar school   c. bachelor's degree
b. high school diploma   d. master's degree
                         e. doctor's degree

This question is controversial. Few other writers agree with this finding. The work done in the 50's concludes most entrepreneurs neglected to complete high school, never mind college. Ed Land at Polaroid is a popular example of the self made man who dropped out of MIT to begin his entrepreneurial venture.

My data concludes the master's degree is the most common degree. It can be in either business management or a technical discipline. Contrast this finding with the obvious fact that most businessmen have at least a bachelor's degree today. Entrepreneurs are showing more respect for education (being high achievers) and obtain the master's degree. Few carry this respect to the extreme of going for the doctorate. This takes too much time and is seldom worth the extra effort, in their view.

This finding contradicts earlier research but it appears to be extremely accurate. Most of you probably got this question wrong, but don't worry easier questions are coming.

7) An entrepreneur's primary motivation for starting his own business is:
a. to make money
b. because they can't work for anyone else
c. to be famous
d. as an outlet for unused energy

The answer here is pretty well agreed upon by everyone. Entrepreneurs seldom leave a secure environment and a steady job for the primary purpose of making money. Their view, in my opinion, is that the attainment of wealth is a by-product of a more noble goal — to be famous is almost never the reason for starting a business.

An energy outlet is equally irrelevant to a would be entrepreneur. He is usually more concerned about his use of time than just to start a business to have something to do.

The last reason, he can't work for anyone else, is more to the point. He is an independent free spirit. He has great difficulty following other's directions. He seeks to do his own thing. This is central to all entrepreneurs. They have to be boss.

8) The primary motivation for the entrepreneur's high ego and need for achievement is based upon his relationship with:

a. his wife
c. his father
b. his mother
d. his children

This is also an obvious question. Most everyone guesses "father" as the answer and, from my research, they are right. His children and his wife enter his life too late to do more than modestly alter his basic characteristics. The mother and father are more predominant in the entrepreneur's personality development.

The real question is the varying impact of the roles of mother and father. The mother has the greatest exposure to a growing child, but the father-son relationship is central to the entrepreneur's motivation. The entrepreneur either seeks to show his old man who is best or, in the case where the father has left the family, the oldest boy often has to assume immense responsibility early in life.

So, in my experience, the father provided the motivation and drive for the entrepreneur. Even when he is in his thirties, and his dad is retired, the approval and praise of his father still provides a basis for his drive.

9) An entrepreneur brings which of these items from business to business:

a. desk
c. all office furniture
b. chair
d. none of these items

The answer is a chair. Most guess this answer correctly. However, this phenomenon has not been discussed by any other researcher. Most others have chosen to ignore it even when they discovered it.

I discovered entrepreneurs fall in love with a good chair. Vaguely equivalent to Archie Bunker's favorite chair. It's his and no one dares sit in it for fear of offending him. It's not really as dramatic as that example, but most do have a strong preference for a certain chair.

For reasons of comfort and convenience, entrepreneurs prefer a chair over any other piece of office furniture — so much so, in fact, that they strive to carry the same chair from business to business.

10) To be successful in an entrepreneurial

venture you need an overabundance of:

a. money
c. hard work
b. luck
d. a good idea

While this may cause concern for you, and most get this question wrong, as I see it the answers should be obvious.

We all know money alone is not enough to make an entrepreneurial venture successful. The classic story of Viatron where about $50 million was invested before bankruptcy indicates the ineffectiveness of money alone.

Hard work and a good idea are helpful in starting and succeeding in a small business. But mere hard work seldom can make a troublesome situation into a success. A good idea offers a greater chance of success as well, but also a good many good ideas end up in the garbage heaps.

Now luck is a different matter. More and more luck, significantly compensates for other weaknesses. Of the successful entrepreneurs I lived with in the past 8 years, all agreed that they were damn lucky. A few key breaks early, according to them, were what made the difference. Sorry you answered this question incorrectly — you just weren't lucky.

11) Entrepreneurs and venture capitalists:

a. get along well
b. are best of friends
c. are cordial friends
d. are in secret conflict

The answer to this question always causes great difficulty, especially for money men. These folks universally prefer to believe they are best of friends with their entrepreneurs, and, in a few cases, it's true.

In the great success stories, entrepreneur and venture capitalist are pictured walking along hand in hand. My research strongly indicates this is the exception, not the rule. Most small businesses fail (some say about 9 out of 10). Every business, save a handful, needs second and third rounds of financing. At these stages the entrepreneur — venture capitalist relationship shifts from cordialities to stress. Many times this causes a permanent split or, in other words, a divorce. The marriage needs more money and this issue divides them and puts them in conflict.

For the few success stories, such as Digital Equipment Corporation and American Research and Development and Data General Corporation and Mr. Fred Adler, there are hundreds of failures. Sorry again.

12) A successful entrepreneur relies on which of these groups for critical manage-

ment advice:

a. internal management team
b. external management professionals
c. financial sources
d. no one

The overwhelming answer to this question is external management professionals. In fact, of the successful companies involved in my research, every single one had used a consultant of one sort or another at one time or another. Not so for the unsuccessful companies. This is a fascinating finding.

Entrepreneurs seldom rely on internal people for major policy decisions because they conclude early that employees' view have an axe to grind. They seldom offer serious conflicts on big decisions and, in the end, the entrepreneur is dominant in every decision. Outside financial sources are even less common sounding boards for entrepreneurs. Not only do banks and accountants lack a feeling for the real stresses of managing an entrepreneurial venture — they are too conservative. They say "no" most of the time. This goes against the optimistic, fun-loving nature of entrepreneurs. So, he prefers outside professionals including other entrepreneurs, consultants, college professors, or other successful businessmen.

13) Entrepreneurs are best as:

a. managers   c. planners
b. venture capitalists   d. doers

While they are not poor managers because they eventually succeed at accomplishing tasks through other people, they all have difficulty delegating responsibility. The basic reason for this is their outstanding ability as a doer. They do everything faster and always better than anyone else, hence they are reluctant to delegate because they could do it both better and faster.

Hence they are best as doers, not planners or managers.

They are seldom effective as venture capitalists even after they accumulate wealth. They are more at home with products, markets and technologies. The skills of a successful venture capitalist are at a much higher level of abstraction. Entrepreneurs do best not by maximizing capital but by maximizing their own doing talent. Managing money and making financial bets is not as much to their liking as finding market niches or exploiting new technologies.

14) Entrepreneurs are:

a. high risk takers (big gamblers)
b. moderate risk takers (realistic gamblers)
c. small risk takers (take few chances)
d. doesn't matter

Contrary to popular belief, entrepreneurs are not high risk takers. I'll bet most of you answered this question incorrectly. The correct answer is moderate risk takers. They set realistic and achievable goals.

They do take risks, but they are more calculated risks. They are extremely aware of the consequences of failure. They are reluctant to bite off more than they can chew.

Most previous research into entrepreneurs, especially by Dr. David McClelland of Harvard, agree with this finding. It's especially true for successful entrepreneurs but it is true of unsuccessful entrepreneurs as well.

15) The first step in starting a business should be:

a. find a product
b. get some money
c. select a partner
d. consult a lawyer

While it may be nice to already have a product, or some money or a partner, the first step should be to see a lawyer. He'll set the business in motion. Once he has decided upon the appropriate legal set-up, you in fact have a business.

Neither a product, money or a partner alone is sufficient to classify as a business. Once the lawyer has completed his work — you are in business. So he should be the first visit.

ANSWERS

1) oldest
2) married
3) man
4) thirties
5) teens
6) master's degree
7) can't work for anyone else
8) father
9) chair
10) luck
11) are in secret conflict
12) external management professionals
13) doers
14) moderate risk takers
15) consult a lawyer

NUMBER OF QUESTIONS ANSWERED CORRECTLY	SCORE
11 or More	Successful Entrepreneur . . .
10-11	Entrepreneur
9-10	Latent Entrepreneur
8-9	Potential Entrepreneur
7-8	Borderline Entrepreneur
7 or Less	Hired Hand